Making an Entrance

Making an Entrance is the first practical introduction to the teaching of dance with disabled and non-disabled students as equal contributors. This clearly written, thought provoking, and hugely enjoyable manual is essential reading for all those addressing difference through the art of dance.

Benjamin takes Improvisation as his central focus and asks what it has to offer as an art form and how it can be better used to meet the changing needs within dance education and professional performance. He considers the history and place of integration in dance, and its role in an all too disintegrated society.

The book includes over fifty exercises and improvisations designed to stimulate and challenge students at all levels of dance. It also highlights the practicalities of setting up workshops, covering issues as diverse as class size, the safety aspects of wheelchairs and the accessibility of dance spaces.

Adam Benjamin is one of the leading practitioners in his field. He is founder and former Artistic Director of CandoCo Dance Company and has pioneered work in South Africa, Ethiopia, Israel, Japan and throughout Europe.

Making an Entrance

Theory and practice for disabled and
non-disabled dancers

Adam Benjamin

London and New York

First published 2002
by Routledge
2 Park Square, Milton Park, Abingdon, Oxon, OX14 4RN

Simultaneously published in the USA and Canada
by Routledge
270 Madison Ave, New York NY 10016

Routledge is an imprint of the Taylor & Francis Group

Transferred to Digital Printing 2007

Typeset in Sabon by
Keystroke, Jacaranda Lodge, Wolverhampton

British Library Cataloguing in Publication Data
A catalogue record for this book is available
from the British Library

Library of Congress Cataloging in Publication Data
Benjamin, Adam, 1958–
Making an entrance: theory and practice for disabled and
non-disabled dancers/Adam Benjamin.
     p. cm.
Includes bibliographical references and index.
ISBN 0–415–25143–5 (alk. paper)–ISBN 0–415–25144–3
(pbk.: alk. paper)
1. Dance. 2. Handicapped dancers. 3. Dance–Social aspects.
I. Title.

GV1799.2 .B47 2001
793.3′087–dc21   2001041226

ISBN 0–415–25144–3 (pbk)
     0–415–25143–5 (hbk)

In memory of Lea Parkinson

'The only inexplicable thing about life is that it is inexplicable.'

(After Albert Einstein)

Contents

Figures

Foreword

This book represents a radical and seminal contribution to the field of dance and the arts. The author is a distinguished practitioner who writes with clarity, insight and humanity and this ensures that potentially difficult and emotive issues are dealt with directly, and through language that is designed to communicate, not alienate.

Dance is perceived as an empowering vehicle which should be accessible to all, and this work sets out a vision of how this might be achieved. It is provocative and original, demonstrating a boldness of vision in charting a new path through issues of disability and participation; potentially one of the most important and controversial areas for dance, the performing arts and for society in general.

This work stems from wide experience and deep reflection, and has been informed by a breadth of understanding of both issues and people, which cuts through received dogma and opinion. It is provocative, and will challenge or reaffirm the views and practices of the reader; it will, however, not leave the reader impassive, as it addresses fundamental issues in the practice and understanding of the arts.

The book also contains some very practical strategies for implementing inclusive dance practice. These are framed within a distinctive historical and artistic context which makes clear that the central issue is the democratisation of dance practice and, by implication, society as well. Its scope, therefore, exceeds any narrow understandings of either (dis)ability or dance. The author makes clear that the path he charts does not exclude other routes and he acknowledges that some suggested strategies are not definitive, but rather should be seen as ways of questioning accepted practices. The diversity that has informed his journey is seen as central to an art form which can, and should, celebrate both the individual and the community.

This is, therefore, a substantial contribution to the understanding of, and debate about, the arts, as well as a very practical guide to ways in which dance practice can be made more inclusive. The foundations of a new dance practice have been investigated and set out clearly; the future will reveal the extent to which the proffered vision is realised.

Professor Christopher Bannerman
April 2001

Preface

Making an Entrance reflects a still relatively new approach to dance, one that draws on the experimentation and exploration of disabled and non-disabled people. Its aim is to create an opening through which people can venture into one another's worlds, not so much an attempt to make the current dance educational model work for a new group of students, but rather, an attempt to change the model, and some of the ways we think about dance and dance education. Although it will undoubtedly be of help to those wishing to teach dance to disabled people, this is not a book specifically about disability, or disabled people; it is not another book about 'them', it is a book about all of us, and about what happens when we dance together.

Most dance books start with a disclaimer, to paraphrase Isadora Duncan – if it were possible to put it in words, there would be no point dancing it – or to quote from a more recent source 'To write about dance is to fix and make secure the thing that reveals itself as it disappears.' (Corporealities 1996, vix) Certainly in the earliest drafts I repeatedly found myself describing what the book was not about, which seemed a far easier task, than trying to pin down a subject that risked becoming lifeless and prescriptive on the page. Yet the demand for written material had been repeatedly voiced at dance conferences across Europe and further afield, and reiterated by isolated teachers struggling to work in inclusive settings with insufficient resources or experience.

Teaching in the UK in the early 1990s I realised that, while non-disabled students were progressing on to university or dance school, their disabled contemporaries were too often left at the end of a project asking 'When will you be coming back? When is the next workshop?'. Although in the intervening years there has been an increasing number of community-based dance projects springing up in the UK, with a few notable exceptions, the doors to further and higher education in dance and the performing arts have remained firmly shut to disabled students. It was in response to these demands and as an aid to those pioneering new dance courses and projects that I began to set ideas to paper. In 1998, with the aid of a Wingate Scholarship I began to translate that body of work into a book. In the following pages I have tried as much as possible to seek out the terrain in which dance remains the property of us all, and to write a book that is as relevant to non-disabled as it is to disabled dancers and dance students. Not being disabled myself, I will doubtless be asked the same question I have been asked as a choreographer and director. 'Why are you choreographing? Shouldn't disabled people be making (and writing about) their own work?' Although essentially my answer to the question is an unequivocal 'yes' I also believe that it would be irresponsible to hand over directorship, either of a workshop programme, or a professional production to anyone without having first set in place the training opportunities and resources that were available to me as a student, and through which I was able to learn my craft as a teacher and director. Just as the workshops and performances have been an unofficial training ground for many disabled and non-disabled people who now dance and teach together professionally, I hope that *Making an Entrance* will provide another tool for those wishing to develop or expand their practice.

The book is divided into two halves, Part I is theoretical and Part II mainly practical with some discussion and examples. In Chapter 1 I describe my meeting with Celeste Dandeker, the subsequent formation of *CandoCo Dance Company* and the development of a personal vision of what I believe dance has to offer as part of current educational practice. Chapter 2 introduces Improvisation as the central approach to dance used in the book. Chapter 3 is an attempt to define some terms in a field in which they are constantly changing and further explores the meaning of 'integration'. Chapter 4 describes the development of The *Simpson Board*; and eye indicator board and choreographic tool for profoundly disabled students who have very restricted movement and are without speech. Chapter 5 is a very personalised re-interpretation of dance history form Ancient Greece to the present day, which considers current prejudices about time, place and the dancing body in the light of some ancient myths and cultural dislocations. Chapter 6 is an attempt to tease out some of the ethical considerations behind inclusive dance practice, and seeks to determine whether this might provide insight into the discipline of the improviser. Chapter 7 *The Great Mistake* looks at the role of accident and its implications in teaching. Chapters 8 and 9 look at the idea of 'Tension' as a way of understanding dance, and offer suggestions for developing a more critical approach to viewing improv (and choreography) and providing feed-back. Chapter 10 considers the difficulties and blocks to creativity that arise in improvising and ways to deal with them. Over the last decade, disabled and non-disabled dancers working together have sought to distance themselves from the world of therapy and to establish a place within mainstream dance and dance education. Chapter 11 considers this position in the light of New Dance concerns with health and self expression, and considers the difference between the creative process and the choreographic process. Chapters 12 and 13 considers the place of those with learning difficulties within integrated dance practice and the difficulties dancers emerging from contemporary dance training may encounter when working with these groups. Chapter 14, *Access and Excellence* looks at the different aims and objectives of inclusive groups and considers implications of group size and composition.

Part II includes, but does not exclusively represent, ideas I first developed while directing the education programme for CandoCo Dance Company in the early 1990s. It also incorporates many ideas and approaches that I have developed since that time through working with other companies and dancers around the world, and so represents a personal and eclectic approach to dance and improvisation (improv). It is offered as a contribution to a constantly growing and evolving dance practice shared among a diverse, international, community of artists and is intended, less as a manual, more part of an ongoing dialogue about dance, the performing arts and education. I hope that the book will be approached not just as a series of exercises, but as stimulus for debate, discussion and exploration. The exercises are aimed at developing body awareness and physical/kinetic skills or techniques, usually within an improvisatory/playful frame (rather than through a formal technical frame). The improvisations are fields of exploration in which these skills might be put to the test, used creatively, and expanded or modified in the response to personal experience. There is considerable overlap between the exercises and improvisations and the boundary between them is intentionally porous.

The methodology behind the teaching has evolved from trying to apply the basic agreements set out in the section on ground rules, and has arisen as much from my mistakes as a teacher, dancer and director as from my 'successes'. It rests on the basic agreement to respect oneself, to respect individual differences, to encourage individual freedom of choice and to refrain from the use of force. Just about everything in this book is based on the pursuit of these simple but elusive principles. In the same way that I teach, the book follows the logic of dance, taking unexpected turns and making unusual connections. This is reflection of how I see art and dance; both should retain the capacity to make us jump from time to time! For every solution I have found to the problems I have encountered, there have been countless other dancers who have found different and equally satisfying ones, so this is therefore only one of many ways of looking at dance.

Acknowledgements

In addition to my experience as joint artistic director and co-founder of CandoCo Dance Company (1990–98), the book draws on work with HandiCapace Tanz Kompanie in Germany. With Danny Scheinmann and the dancers and musicians of the Stare Cases Project, The Besht Tellers, Tardis Dance Company, and A and BC Theatre company, with Adam Benjamin and Dancers in Belgium, Holland and the UK, Vertigo Dance Company, Israel, Tshwaragano in South Africa, the Adugna Community Dance Project in Ethiopia, and with Kim Itoh in Japan. It is a practice that has been enriched by encounters with dancers, artists and musicians across Europe and as far afield as Africa, Asia, Israel and the Americas.

In addition to those mentioned above I am particularly grateful to all the extraordinary dancers and administrators past and present of CandoCo Dance Company (too many to mention by name) and to the many assistants and trainees who have accompanied me on my travels, but most of all, to Celeste Dandeker, without whom CandoCo and all that followed would never have happened.

The essential principles of 'listening and dialogue' contained in this book are drawn from many sources and many teachers. I am indebted to Franklyn Sills who taught me to listen with my hands. To Ken Waight who taught me to open them. To Don Strickland and David Walker-Barker for leading me to see in different ways; to Peter Borsos and Miss Li for Tai Chi and Ba-kua and to Dr Jay Dunbar and Kathleen Cuisick for Tai-Chi partnering and San-Shou. To Lesley Main for Humphrey technique and for putting breath and body together; Judy Sharpe and the wonderful improvisation class at Middlesex University (1987–90), Bob Carlisle, Linda Hartley, Claire Hayes and Wendy Cook who gave me the confidence to dance when I decided that that was what I wanted to do with my life. Most of what is good and useful I have learned from these and other teachers, friends and colleagues, the remaining irreverence and aberrations contained in this book are, I confess, my own.

I would like to thank, in no particular order, those people who have helped me directly and indirectly to write this book. Shannie Ross and Mark Scantlebury for first sending me in the right direction, Val Bourne who supported my application and Jane Reid and The Wingate Foundation who funded the early research, Rosie Waters and Talia Rodgers at Routledge for having faith in the idea and making me do the work to turn it into a reality. Lea Parkinson, Louise Katerega and Jonothan Thrift for endless support and reading the early drafts, Francis de Cornick, Cylla Dyke for always encouraging me to write, Mark Benjamin for history lessons, Carol Brown for running and reading, Leila Monaghan for rowing, reading and advice, Rachel Duncombe-Anderson for tying up all the loose ends and Isabelle Maury whose love and support got me through the hardest moments.

Lisa Simpson, Louise Katerega, Bill Robbins, Scott Clark, Jonothan Thrift and the Roehampton students for work on the Simpson Board, Theresa Beattie, Nicole Richter, Simon Benjamin, Steve Munn, Pascal Notolli, Sue Holiday, Margaret Taylor, Peter Stanford and the charity ASPIRE for their support over the years, Biff Crabbe for clarity and hilarity, Brigitte Jagg, Steve Paxton, Alitto Alessi, Riccardo Morrison and Emery Blackwell for precious time in Austria, Russell Maliphant for endless dancing and merriment, Alysoun Tompkins for always challenging me, Trisha Glynn who helped me make difficult decisions, Rina and Nimrod Koren for letting me take over their kitchen table, Keith and Gail Critchlow and family for timeless inspiration. Yuko Ijichi for supporting the work in Japan, Sunsaku Fukuda, and the Hotaka Yojoen for giving me space to work. Jill Waterman in Johannesburg for lessons in life. All the photographers whose pictures say more than I can ever say in words, in particular John Hogg in South Africa and Claus Langer in Germany who have been so generous and supportive of my work, Toshinao Nakazawa for his remarkable snow picture, Yuko Ijichi for supporting the work in Japan, Sunsaku Fukuda and the Hotaka Yojoen for giving me space to work, and Thale, Noelle and Christiane who long ago both encouraged me to dance. Finally, my wife Tamami Fukuda-Benjamin for helping me finish the job and renew my vision.

And in fond memory of my three parents. My father Joe Benjamin, whose pioneering work on the adventure playground informed much of my thinking about dance. My mother, the artist Rivka Black who filled my earliest years with paints and brushes, and my step-mother Pauline Crabbe who taught me some of the most important lessons of integration.

Part I
Introduction

1   Introduction: life after *Stages*

Beauty is the breadth of human experience – the struggle can also be beautiful. And so much of dance is to deny the struggle.

(Lloyd Newson, 1998)

Philosophy is an activity not a theory.

(Wittgenstein, 1922)

I did not come into dance via the usual channels but was a late starter having spent my own teenage years on the sports field. I was 20 before I became interested in other approaches to movement having seen the Pilobolus dance company in the USA in 1976. In 1980 I was introduced to the Chinese art of Tai Chi Chuan and a new world of possibilities opened up that eventually led me to study dance and fine art at Middlesex University. Tai Chi Chaun is an 'internal' or 'soft' martial art that relies on sensitivity, awareness and timing rather than force. I had been teaching Tai Chi for some years when Celeste Dandeker joined one of my classes at an integrated recreation centre run by the charity ASPIRE.[1] Celeste had been a professional dancer with London Contemporary Dance Theatre (LCDT), but an on-stage accident had left her with virtually no movement in her legs and severely restricted movement in her arms. Tai Chi's partnering exercises, commonly called Pushing Hands, now provided an ideal means to explore differences in physicality, in strength and range that existed between us.

The accident that had ended Celeste's career with LCDT was an event that in many ways would set the agenda for the coming involvement of disabled people in dance. The accident occurred in an acrobatic piece called *Stages*.[2] By a strange twist of fate, our word stage comes from the Latin *stare* meaning 'to stand' and Celeste's fall devastating both its impact on her and her colleagues, excluded her seemingly from both the standing world and the dancing world. It would be another sixteen years before she would return as anything other than a spectator to The Place – the home of London Contemporary Dance.

When we met in 1990, Celeste possessed a precise and articulate movement style and an undiminished presence, qualities that had been recognised and celebrated one year earlier, when the choreographer and dancer Darshan Singh-Bhuller made a film for television loosely based on her life.[3]

Despite the success of the film, Celeste had had no intention of taking her dance activities any further, and it was only after some persistent bullying on my part that she eventually agreed to return to the dance studio, not such an easy move for someone who had once danced professionally.

I often had my doubts coming from a fairly rigid background of ballet and Graham Technique which is so physical and at times it has been very hard dancing with non disabled dancers knowing that once I could move like them.[4]

Despite Celeste's reservations, we began working together as equals exploring our very different experiences and knowledge of the body.[5] In particular we wanted to understand how Celeste's refined articulate movement could lead and shape the movement of a non-disabled dancer. Our early work (much of which is covered in Part Two) convinced us that we could produce vital and engaging dance work. I wrote at the time

> The chair which initially separated us as dancers began to be involved as an extra element which we could choose to use or leave behind as we wished. Much of the early work pointed uncompromisingly toward choreography . . . the act of a woman physically supporting a man is always an eloquent dance statement and one that cuts across the conventional male/female roles; how much more so when that woman is in a wheelchair. And so we started playing with social stereotypes not the least that which assumes that the person who is being looked after is necessarily the one seated in the chair.
>
> (*DICE*, no. 15, April 1991)

1.1 Celeste Dandeker, Lea Parkinson and Adam Benjamin in *Christy Don't Leave So Soon*. CandoCo, 1992. Choreography by the dancers. (Photographer Helen Baggett)

1.2 Flying in the face of CandoCo. Choreographed by Adam Benjamin, assisted by L. Parkinson 1992. (Photographer Eleni Leoussi)

We soon began teaching and within the space of two short years our once-a-week class transformed itself into the first professional touring company of physically disabled and non-disabled dancers in Europe, for which Celeste chose the name CandoCo – (the can do company – see Figures 1.1 and 1.2). We accompanied the tours with a full-time workshop programme that introduced students to the improvisations and choreographic devices we employed in devising work.

CandoCo's first professional residency was in Leeds, where Celeste, Lea Parkinson and I had been invited by Emilyn Claid (then artistic director of the Yorkshire Dance Centre) to create and perform new work.[6] The workshop participants included many who had never danced before, some with cerebral palsy, others using wheelchairs for a variety of different reasons. There were people with visual impairments, and others with learning difficulties together with undergraduates from the nearby Northern School of Contemporary Dance, a bastion of Graham-based technique. The group consisted of humanity in all its glorious shapes and sizes.[7] By one of those delightful quirks of fate the studio below was being used to house the regional junior ballet trials, so there was this extraordinary juxtaposition of different approaches to dance going on in the same building at the same time. On the third floor, our students, some of whom couldn't see, some of whom couldn't walk, and one of whom had no legs,[8] were increasingly believing in their individual ability to express themselves through movement, each realising that they and their bodies were full of possibilities, each trying on that daunting title of 'dancer', while beneath us on the second floor, children whose every dream was to become a ballet dancer, were having their bones measured simply to gain access to the auditions. Their future depended not on talent or creativity but on how they measured up to someone else's idealised 'standard'. For the girls, that meant the short, slim ballerina capable of being effortlessly lifted by their male partner. The majority of these children were being told quite openly and matter of factly that their body was not the right shape, and this fact, this object (and not them) was going to make it impossible for them to get into ballet school. Anyone who has passed through dance training will testify to the psychological repercussions of this objectifying of the body, and the subsequent attempts of young impressionable students to achieve and maintain this 'idealised', balletic figure, not to mention the effects of trying to cram young, still growing, feet into pointe shoes. It is not usually until much later in life that ballet dancers begin to question exactly where this highly praised, elevated and emaciated model of beauty arose (see Chapter 5 of this volume; Nunez, 1995).

The process of teaching dance proposed here is not about providing 'moves' behind which we can hide, it is in fact quite the opposite. It is about learning to be present in our bodies without artifice; it is about understanding how we use our weight and our breath; how we balance movement and stillness, tension and relaxation. But it is about more than just what we do with our bodies; it is about how we negotiate decisions in time and space, how we empathise with others, while having the courage to develop our own ideas. It is about creativity and criticism. In short, it is about how we make best use of our physical and mental resources. This is dance used as a true physical education; an education about the body and mind through the use of body and mind.

It is an approach that I hope can both complement current practice, and offer something of value to the huge number of disabled and non-disabled students failed by our current emphasis on competition as the sole means of educating (or controlling) the body. Those children who are made to sit in the changing room or walk endless circuits round the playing field while others play, because they won't or can't take part in sports. Children already at odds with their bodies, who are reinforced as physical failures at every so-called 'physical education' class.

The aim of this book might be summarised thus: **to know how our bodies work, to understand and be comfortable with how they may differ, and to seek in everybody, the fullest possible expression of what it means to be human.**

Notes

1 The Association for Spinal Injury Research Rehabilitation and Reintegration. Celeste was a board member of the charity.
2 Choreographed by Bob Cohan (1971).
3 *The Fall*. Dance for Camera 1989. BBC Arts Council.
4 From conversations with the author
5 We would soon be joined by a third dancer, James Hewison, who went on to dance with VTOL Dance Company.
6 This was where *Christy Don't Leave So Soon* was choreographed.
7 See Christy Adair's article in *Dance Theatre Journal*, 10(1), autumn 1992.
8 This was David Toole's first dance workshop. A dancer who was to radically alter the meaning of virtuosic performance.

2 Improvisation – access – training – touching on a definition

Improvisation calls for reflection and a great deal of scratching at one's chin and hairline. It calls for sitting down and smoking cigars while awaiting inspiration; it calls for copas in the whorehouse, and it requires fixing one's eyes on the middle distance and visualising pulleys and gantries. Now and then it required departing with a team of bulls to fetch more telegraph poles, or trunks of mahogany to saw into planks.

(Louis de Bernières, 1998)

You can deny, if you like, nearly all abstractions: justice, beauty, truth, goodness, mind, God. You can deny seriousness, but not play.

(J. Huizinga, 1970)

Whenever we join a new group, just like those who entered the first residency in Leeds, we are each in some small way brought face to face with our own uncertainties: will we be accepted? Will people be open? Will we be able to give a good account of ourselves? When disabled and non-disabled people meet in the dance studio, especially for the first time, such feelings may be magnified. Each of us may be confronted with situations that are unique, unfamiliar, unsettling. Faced with creating something out of our meeting, and without yet knowing how our physical differences might lead to a dance experience, we must explore the unknown territory together and, rather like children, our research takes the form of play; we have to make it up as we go along, in other words we have to improvise: **composing as one goes along** from Latin *improvisus*, 'unforeseen', from IM- (not) + *provisus*, from *providere* to foresee.

The capacity of dance improvisation to accommodate different bodies and its freedom from preordained steps makes it highly accessible, yet despite this, there is still a marked resistance in many schools to incorporate it as part of formal dance training. As more time and resources are devoted to teaching technique (to attract students and produce dancers 'for the profession') there is growing concern among teachers about how choreographic talent is developed, in other words, how the need for discipline and technique is balanced with the ideal of fostering creativity and free thinking. When disabled and non-disabled students dance together, this dilemma is brought into sharp focus, and at the same time offers up a solution; in sharp contrast to segregated groups, inclusive groups require us to look at and think about bodies and movement in new ways, to be both physically and verbally articulate and to recognise problems and devise solutions, in short, they train us to think like choreographers.

As Robin Howard, patron of the London Contemporary Dance Theatre realised in the 1970s, the arts are reliant on environments in which experimentation can be encouraged alongside the development of technique (in the way that experimentation with paint is accompanied by the discipline of life drawing). When technique alone becomes overvalued, the arts become disconnected from their creative source, and we begin to see forms that are merely imitative. This is particularly true of dance, where so much training requires such single-minded discipline. Dance in England in the 1970s was arguably far more open to innovation than it is today; the fact that more disabled people did not get involved at the time was not due to the inaccessibility of the art form itself, but to the inaccessibility of the idea of disabled people as dancers. Attitudes began to change gradually in the 1980s and 1990s; the Disability Rights Movement and Disability Arts did much to shift public awareness, but although theatre companies like Graeae were producing professional work, the age-old obstacles to training remained firmly in place. Faced with a disabled applicant, even the most willing of school administrators would find him or herself saying 'Sorry, we'd love to have you, but you won't be able to manage the steps.' Today, with more and more schools and public buildings being made accessible, the future debate in dance is no longer going to centre on the concrete steps that lead up to the studio, but on the technical ones that confront the disabled student when he or she gains access. How dance is taught, and what role it is considered to play in education now determines whether or not disabled and non-disabled students will be encouraged to study and dance together, or whether they will be viewed as impediments to one another's progress and channelled into separate institutions or courses (see Figure 2.1). The earliest attempts to route disabled dancers through conventional dance training programmes either in the USA or the UK have not been particularly successful and it is clear that different approaches will need to be explored if we are going to realise the potential inherent in our different bodies.[9]

Perhaps one day we will see training programmes in the mainstream that respond to physical difference in the way that a music school responds to the different requirements of those studying string, wind or percussion; where every student is given time to understand the unique requirements and possibilities of his or her own instrument as well as being expected to participate as part of the orchestra or ensemble.[10]

The entrance of disabled people into dance studies creates vital openings for new experience, for confusion, for connection and, most importantly, for dialogue about what the art of dance can signify. Each new student to our class should encourage us to re-evaluate the body and the body of knowledge that we have come to take for granted. Assessment procedures in schools may need to be revised when we recognise that each student is playing a different instrument, and although this appears to create insurmountable objections for some dance schools, the assessment of difference is a requirement central to those who teach in the arts, and dance cannot hide from this issue if it wishes to attain the status of a mature art form alongside visual art and music.

Possible areas of assessment for disabled and non-disabled students on inclusive dance courses might revolve around:

- the achievement of set and agreed physical goals in dance technique;
- demonstrated levels of understanding of dance terminology;
- interpretation and adaption of set material;
- individual performance skills;

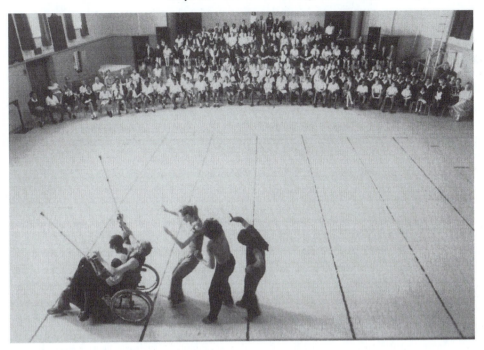

2.1 Tshwaragano workshop demonstration, National School of the Arts, Johannesburg, 2001. (Photographer John Hogg)

- partnering skills;
- communication/teaching skills;
- choreographic skills;
- mixed media – dance and film, dance installations, etc.;
- improvisational skills;
- dance history;
- history of the body in art and culture;
- aesthetics – and the articulation of beauty;
- disability arts;
- the body politic: the body in history and literature.

Not all disabled students will benefit from formal technique classes. Finding what is appropriate, what can be adapted and what is inappropriate is an important part of the learning process. In some areas of dance studies, people with comparable physical disabilities or sensory impairment have begun to generate specific techniques and shared training programmes, and have succeeded in accelerating their learning by focusing on their specific requirements and communication needs in a way that may not be possible or feasible in classes that attempt to include everyone.

Perhaps the most important issue for new courses to bear in mind is that integrated practice is about problem-solving, and that rather than trying to fit new students into pre-existing structures, the course itself should be geared to address and deal with problems as they arise, and should therefore be resourced and structured flexibly in order to do so. It is hoped that every new intake of students (on any course) will identify shortcomings with course content and delivery, and disabled students in particular will highlight inaccessible features of a course, raising issues simply by their presence. How well they and their non-disabled classmates (and teachers) deal with these problems is a measure of how successful they will be as dancers, choreographers, administrators or activists on graduating. It is a nonsense to expect integrated practice to begin once a student graduates from a course, it must begin the moment they enter the building, with the construction of the first ramp and accessing of previously inaccessible libraries. Integrated practice is linked to the environment in a very direct sense. It is an approach which demands that any theorising be linked with a commitment to effect change. Such an approach is clearly at odds with much of current dance teaching, which is more commonly about following instructions rather than asking questions.

This chapter began by looking at improvisation and we have now come via inclusive dance courses to the need to develop a problem-solving ethos in students. One of the few areas in education that positively promotes this kind of mental and physical activity (when properly taught) is dance improvisation, but it remains one of the least-valued areas of dance training even, surprisingly, within courses that are aiming to produce teachers for the community. This issue is taken up in more detail in Chapter 4.

In criticising ballet early in the twentieth century, Isadora Duncan talked of movement 'that dies as it is made' and it is just this feeling that still characterises the tentative offerings of many ballet and contemporary trained dancers when asked to improvise. Eager to create the right shape or position, they glance continually at the teacher, or the mirror, anxious to measure up to someone else's expectations of what they should and shouldn't do. Of course, many ballet teachers have a more enlightened approach to their students and ballet can provide an exact and exacting training for those wishing to dance professionally. Dance, however, cannot exist in a vacuum and though I am a great admirer of technique and a believer in the importance of proper training, we might bear in mind that only a tiny percentage of those who study dance ever become professionals. Those of us who teach dance have a responsibility not only to make our subject accessible to all our students, but also, like the dance pioneers who went before us, to make it relevant to the world as it is today. Perhaps I can put this into context through the experience of two members of the German dance company HandiCapace who, in 1998, were accosted on the street in Stuttgart by a young man who suggested that they would have been better off going to the gas chambers; or the disabled conference participant in Bregenz, Austria, two years later, who was told by a group of youngsters that he belonged in the zoo; or the young Ethiopian boy who had grown up hidden from sight and then, when he finally got help, was denied access to education by his parents on the grounds that they were not receiving payment.

People who react to difference in this way appear to have missed out on what physical education should or could be about. Damaged by whatever sort of moral and physical training they have received, they grow up fearful of those who may be different and, as adults, propagate ideologies that continue to damage those around them, even those they love.

The political environment and school environment in which new dance exists today is a less volatile, perhaps less questioning one than the 1960s when postmodern dance first emerged. The issues facing us today may not be as clear as they seemed at that time, but they still relate strikingly to difference and to conformity, to the acceptance of other and to the idealisation of the self. Today, we still need to think just as deeply about the world we live in, to seek to understand and value differences rather than eradicate them, to celebrate our (bio)diversity and uniqueness; in short, we need to be educating people whose concerns are both aesthetic **and** ethical and, dare I say it, the need for this kind of person currently far outweighs the global demand for ballet dancers. Perhaps, who knows, there is room for both.

Dance may yet help students make sense of their actions and the consequences of their actions in a way that our education system and formal physical education have so far failed to achieve. These lessons, however, can't be learned if we make the mistake of imposing egalitarian values on dance, of insisting for example that we all hold hands and dance to the same tune, or split into groups of stronger and weaker, faster and slower. Such imposed structures deprive students of the difficulties they need to address and resolve in order to grow and learn. If such an approach seems daunting, it is because the pursuit of integration and the study of improvisation straddle a tantalising paradox: condemning and at the same time delighting in inequality.

Notes

9 From conversations with David Toole (in the UK) and Alex Spitzer (in the USA).
10 This 'orchestra' model in fact takes us back to the origins of western dance. 'Orchestra' comes from *orkhiestha* – a word which refers to the level dancing ground of the Ancient Greeks before the advent of the raised stage and the orchestra pit (see Chapter 3 of this volume).

3   A little on language, disability, integration and inclusivity

A spastic must be taught to make the best use of the hands which he has and to develop an aggressive cheerfulness in overcoming some of his handicaps.

(Zaidee Lindsay, 1966)

Our knowledge about bodies is shaped by and shapes the discourse and knowledge of an era.

(Petra Kuppers, 2000)

The quote from Zaidee Lindsay above, so jarring today, appeared in a book on art education in the 1960s. No courses or colleges were mentioned under the 'Useful addresses' heading at the back of the book, for there was simply no expectation that 'spastic children' would be capable of attending further education. Today, those of us involved with disability in some way will know that it is language rather than anything else that most frequently threatens our equilibrium and continues to limit expectations. This leads to no small amount of anxiety among newcomers when it comes to talking about the body of work and the working body. A difficulty that, if anything, is exacerbated by international differences.

In the UK, current thinking among disability activists and scholars favours the term 'disabled people'. A term which comes from viewing disability as a social, rather than a medical, construct. The 'medical model' has viewed disability through a doctor's lens and historically placed disabled people in the role of recipient or patient. Someone who, when 'treated' or 'better' would be reintegrated into society. This 'ablist' society is one that sees no obvious reason to change in either its attitudes or in the design of its buildings in order to accommodate those who are different.

In the social model, disability is apparent in the interaction between the impaired person and the social environment. A disabled person has an impairment, such as short arms, blindness or an inability to read. It is only when this particular form of embodiment encounters a society in which long arms, visual communication, and the written word are favoured, that the impairment becomes a disability. For a woman using a wheelchair, it is not her body or the wheelchair, but the stairs that disable her.

(Kuppers, 2000: 125)

On the whole, it is the organisation of society, its material construction and the attitudes of individuals within it, that result in certain people being *dis*-abled.

(Brisenden, 1998: 23)

In this book I use the term 'disabled people' acknowledging those colleagues with whom I work in the UK who firmly identify the social, attitudinal, economic and architectural features of our society as being the principle disabling features affecting their lives. In the USA the term 'handicapped' is still widely used, while having been rejected in the UK in favour of 'disabled' and 'non-disabled' people. In France the terms '*handicapé*' and '*valide*' are still widely used. The linguistic implication here being that if you are handicapped, you are not valid. In South Africa the term 'people with disabilities' is preferred over 'disabled people'. Signs to the toilet in Cape Town read 'Physically Challenged' which to the British makes going to the toilet sound like attempting an assault course; also, to the British, a 'disabled toilet' suggests one that doesn't work! Perhaps one day signs everywhere will just read 'accessible'.

Does it make sense to talk about a disabled dancer, a dancer with a disability or impairment, or a person with a disability who dances? A professional dancer (who is disabled) or a professional disabled dancer? The words we use will continue to evolve with the changing discourse on the body and disability. In a radio interview in Johannesburg, the announcer tumbling over himself in hopeless pursuit of the correct terminology referred to me as 'Adam Benjamin: a phys . . . a non . . . a physically capacitated dancer'. In the end we can only be guided by what people want to be called and respect international, regional and personal differences. Christian Panouillot, a disabled colleague/colleague with a disability/handicapped colleague in France, has suggested that when talking about a disabled person who dances, we might refer to the '*danseur singulier*' which roughly translates as a 'singular' or 'remarkable dancer'. In contrast, he talks of '*danseurs habituels*' or 'habitual dancers', that is, those who dance as a usual part of their daily life.[11]

Of course there are an increasing number of disabled people who are now 'regular' or 'habitual' dancers, but his suggestion is at least more acceptable than the current French valid/not valid interpretation, and delineates dancers whose body marks them as noticeably different or unique.

This discourse on language also affects how we talk about the dance of disabled and non-disabled people. In Britain, the 'special needs' work and work with special communities of the 1970s and 1980s gave way to 'integrated' work in the 1990s, which in some areas is now being replaced by the term 'inclusive'. This latest change is due to the association 'integration' has had with the medical model of disability.

For the purposes of this book, I use the term 'inclusive' to distinguish a group that has moved away from segregated dance structures and that is open to disabled and non-disabled participants. I have retained the term 'integration' or 'integrative' in its wider sense when talking about what takes place within the dance process or the making of a dance piece, a decision I will explain below. Perhaps all of these terms will appear dated in years to come, but will, I hope, be helpful now in order to clarify my approach and to distinguish it from others in the field. Looking at the *Oxford English Dictionary* (OED)[12] we find the following definition:

> 1a The making up or composition of a whole by adding together or combining the separate parts or elements; combination into an integral whole: a making whole or entire.

Its Latin root *tangere*, meaning 'to touch' gives it an immediate affinity to the physical art form of dance. Integration is about putting the divided parts (of a society or ourselves) back in touch with each other. Integration has no natural or linguistic association with 'disability' and we should resist any tendency to use and think of these terms as if they were in some way symbiotic. Integration has implications for us all, it asks 'What is our unique contribution? How do we find our place with others? Whom do we exclude by our actions and our prejudices?' In that sense it is closely related to the word integrity – the quality of having no part missing or left out. The *OED* entry continues:

> 1b The combining of diverse parts into a complex whole; a complex state the parts of which are distinguishable; the harmonious combination of the different elements in a personality.

Integrity might be regarded as the goal of integration, it implies that every individual has an essential and unique contribution to make. When I use the word integration, it is an acknowledgement that the existing 'exclusive' vision of dance is incomplete and in need of reform. If we are bringing together the 'diverse parts of a complex whole', then what we are accustomed to thinking of as 'normal' is by definition incomplete, and each of us will be somehow touched and changed by any new arrival. As a young Swiss student said to me during a particularly difficult project '*L'intégration, c'est une lutte*' ('Integration is a struggle'). Integration invariably implies a certain amount of questioning, no small amount of friction and last, but not least, it commits us to change. The third *OED* definition gives:

> 1c The bringing into equal membership of a common society those groups or persons previously discriminated against on racial or cultural grounds.

Unravelling problems and making new connections is not only central to integration, it is also central to improvisation; the former presents us with the problem of how different parts of a whole fit together, the latter insists that if we come across a difficulty or an obstacle when we are dancing, then we should consider ourselves not only part of that problem, but also, in some way as yet unknown to us, part of the solution.

Since 1990 I have danced, taught and choreographed extensively both with professional and community-based groups consisting of disabled and non-disabled dancers. It is a field widely referred to as 'integrated dance', rather as if it were one of the range of dance styles, like jazz, tap, contact improvisation or Graham. Looking at just some of the numerous companies[13] now referred to as 'integrated', it is evident that few of them work in the same way, either physically, artistically or philosophically. CandoCo, for example, was influenced by contact improvisation and Graham-based technique. Originally making its own work, the company went on to commission pieces from a diverse range of international choreographers among them Siobhan Davies, Emilyn Claid, Guilherme Botelho, Javier de Frutos and Doug Elkins. Each choreographer brought radically different approaches to the company.

In contrast Amici, founded by Wolfgang Stange in 1980, continues to show the influence of central European expressionism and of Stange's teacher Hilde Holger. In the USA, Dancing Wheels (previously known as Cleveland Dancing Wheels) work within the balletic genre, Taihan in Japan is influenced by Butoh, while the Israeli soloist, Tamar Borer, has synthesised her own dance style from Butoh and western influences; Touch Compass in New Zealand have excelled in aerial work, whereas Joint Forces again from the USA have a movement basis firmly located within contact improvisation.

3.1 CandoCo in *Back to Front with Side Shows,* choreography Emilyn Claid, 1993. Dancers: Sue Smith, David Toole, Helen Baggett, Kuldip Singh-Barmi and Jon French. (Photographer Anthony Crickmay)

Axis, again from the East Coast of America, created much of its early work, but in the late 1990s began to commission work from 'high-profile' choreographers such as Bill T. Jones and Stephen Petronio. In the year 2000, David Toole, ex-CandoCo, danced in DV8's piece *Can We Afford This?* along with a cast of disabled and non-disabled dancers. Does this this make DV8 an integrated company or *Can We Afford This?* an integrated piece? The term 'integrated' or 'inclusive' actually tells us very little about the work. Instead, it functions a bit like a road sign warning the unwary theatre-goer of possible encounters with wheelchairs – it tells us that we can expect to see a disabled person on stage, which can only leave us asking, 'Is that really necessary? Who is it that needs to be warned?'

Occasionally, dance emerges that manages to tear down the barriers between audience and performers without recourse to any label. *Les Ballets C. de la B.* Ensemble Explorations. lets op Bach (1998) by Belgium choreographer Alain Platel is a piece that does just that. Within its deceptive informality it accommodates street performers, musicians, dancers, children (and a woman in a leg cast). It crosses lines and taboos, revealing bodies in all their many states. Framing and reframing the activity on stage in a way that repeatedly made me question what I considered dance to be, and what I placed 'outside'. This was achieved through the varied skills of the performers and the extraordinary vision of the choreographer. It is the most integrated piece of work

I have seen in years, yet contained no disabled performers. Integrated dance is dance that works. It needs no more introduction than that. A piece that includes a disabled performer can still fail to integrate sound, light and music, worse still it can fail to integrate movement and ideas. In South Africa I have seen groups that include disabled students but clearly maintain racial distinctions that should have been discarded with the overthrow of apartheid. Should such groups still be described as doing integrated work?

I have seen professional work in which disabled people have been given no opportunity to explore their physicality or make a significant contribution. Where no matter how well intentioned their inclusion, their presence evokes only a sense of tokenism. In one piece I watched, a physically disabled composer sat immobile in her wheelchair while a non-disabled company danced to her music. The composer's presence on stage had clearly not been integrated into the performance, and so not only disrupted the dance, but served to diminish her achievement by patronisingly putting her 'on show' when we, the audience, should have been paying attention to the music she had written, not the fact that she was a wheelchair user. She would clearly have been far better advised to join the dancers for a curtain call at the end of the piece.

'Integration' may currently be falling out of favour, but the word itself, and its relationship to touch, encourages a radical dance ideology, one that I believe to be more demanding than the new term 'inclusive'. It is easy to 'include' someone without asking how they find their place, or doing the necessary work to discover their particular and unique contribution.

In pursuing an integrated vision, my concern is not solely with physical access to the stage or the art form, though clearly access is essential; nor is it solely with the needs of disabled dancers, though these have to be addressed. My overriding concern is how the group's aims and objectives serve everyone involved, disabled and non-disabled. In terms of teaching methodology, an integrated workshop or class can function perfectly well without the presence of a disabled student; it simply doesn't miss a beat when a disabled person joins it. Its ongoing interest is how things are put together, how they connect. Integration is as much about stretching the mind as it is about stretching the muscles. If this dual activity is absent, then you can be certain that what you're involved in may be many things, but integrated practice (read good practice) isn't one of them. Integration is not, as I understand it, a dance form, organisation or style. It may, unless we are very careful, end up as one. My intention here is not to ensure the future of either 'integrated' or 'inclusive' groups as little islands of practice, but rather, to encourage those who recognise such labels to be no more than temporary signs that we can discard once we know each other and the territory a little better.

Perhaps one of the most encouraging signs of the success of new-dance practice in British dance is the degree of interaction between community companies and their professional counterparts, a situation that has arisen from the dance animateur movement of the 1970s and the subsequent growth of the regional dance agencies. There is no other country outside of America where disabled and non-disabled community dancers are able to talk to, debate and socialise with, their professional counterparts. In the UK in particular there is a constant exchange of professional dancers working alongside people from the community so that serious choreographic concerns and skills are expected as part of community productions. Some of the most interesting work around seems to grow from this synthesis, and is often far more satisfying on many levels than 'purely' professional pieces presented in the mainstream.

3.2 CandoCo in *I Hastened Through my Death Scene to Catch Your Last Act*. Choreography by Javier de Frutos, 2001. Dancers: Welly O'Brien, Stine Nilsen, Katie Marsh and Jürg Koch. (Photographer Anthony Crickmay)

Today it is increasingly possible, despite the obstacles that exist, for a disabled student to say: 'I want to be a professional dancer' and be taken seriously. This is a sign that the initiatives of disabled and non-disabled dancers in the 1970s, 1980s and 1990s, and the many different approaches that have been pioneered, are bearing fruit.

There will always be a need for companies like Axis and CandoCo in breaking new ground, particularly in areas where there is little awareness. These companies have, over the last ten years, provided benchmarks for what might be achieved by disabled performers. The need for the label 'integrated company' will, I hope, pass. Phoenix Dance Company, founded in 1981 in England, is a marvellous black contemporary dance company, but it would be another matter if it had remained the sole company to employ black dancers in Britain: it would be an indictment not a triumph. It is likely that the first mainstream established companies to work with disabled performers will make many mistakes. They may not have the long-term understanding that evolves in the established 'integrated' companies and which allows for more vital and organic connections to be made between performers. They may even be accused of jumping on the bandwagon, to which I can only say 'Jump!' We may then, however, rightfully enquire how the company is considering and addressing training and access opportunities for minority groups. Jumping does, after all, have its consequences.

3.3   Vertigo Dance Company (Israel) in *The Power of Balance*. Choreography Adam
      Benjamin, 2001. (Photographers Dorit Talpaz and Michal Chitayat)

Notes

11 In correspondence with the author. 'Puisque le danseur singulier "stigmatisé" dans son
    corps est considéré comme danseur au même titre que les danseurs non handicapés, nous
    pouvons, pour désigner le premier parler de "danseur singulier" et pour les autres de
    "danseurs habituels soit commun".'
12 *OED* (1989) 2nd edn, Oxford: Oxford University Press: 1,065.
13 Many companies of disabled and non-disabled dancers refuse or resist the use of this label
    to describe their work.

4 Disability-specific groups and the Simpson Board

It is a simple enough system. You read the alphabet . . . until, with a blink of my eye, I stop you at the letter to be noted.

(Jean-Dominique Bauby, 1997)

In the early 1990s Steve Paxton and Anne Kilcoyne pioneered a training programme for blind and visually impaired dancers. At the time they wrote 'the teaching of Contact Improvisation to a mixed disability group compounds communication problems, and we prefer to work with specific disability along with the able-bodies within each workshop' (*Dance Research*, 1993 XI(1)). (It is interesting to see how language has changed within the last decade.) Anyone who has struggled to teach groups in which too many needs begin to compete with rather than complement each other, will appreciate the clarity that can come from such a decision. It was just such a realisation that led to the development of what was to become known as the Simpson Board.

When I first met her, Lisa, a young woman with cerebral palsy, was a student at Hereward College, one of the few institutions in England where disabled and non-disabled students study alongside one another. She had attended several dance workshops at the college and had shown a real passion for the subject. Despite her interest, the spasticity of her muscles and the restrictions imposed by the arduous task of communicating without words repeatedly frustrated her in her efforts to communicate even the simplest of movement ideas, let alone those of a complex nature regularly used in the world of dance. (The same problem that is faced by many profoundly disabled people and those who work with them on a daily basis.) Lisa's primary means of communication was through her eyes.

It was in recognition of the different ways in which students, like Lisa, communicated, which first encouraged me to question the usual structure of dance residencies where, all too often, the pressure would be to create a finished piece for performance. So it was with a sense of curiosity and relief that we finally set out to address the issue of communication with this, and not improvisation or performance, as a final goal.

The research that led to the Simpson Board took place during a five-day residency at the college, which I led with Lea Parkinson in 1995. Our aim was to explore how profoundly disabled students could be more fully involved in thinking about, understanding and creating dances (performance, choreography and appreciation), rather than simply 'taking part' in dance improvisations or performances. The project included students from Hereward's expressive arts course who were joined by undergraduates from Coventry University for the Performing Arts (CUPA) plus two professional dancers based in Wales.[14] During the week, various methods of communication were tried and tested, a process which led to the development of the prototype Simpson Board.

Margaret Taylor, the Head of Expressive Arts, had prepared the ground for us before our arrival; students with profound physical disabilities and who were without speech had been selecting and placing found objects on different surfaces.[15] The resulting works generated some strikingly beautiful images. Lisa's work was of simple starfish and circular patterns of gravel dotted with pebbles; other students had made arrangements of sun-bleached twigs or coloured paper. When we finally got into the dance studio, we projected slides of the students' work onto the wall and these served as the starting point for our exploration of movement. First, we looked at how we might use the visual designs as scores and/or stimulus for dance improvisations.

All of the students (disabled and non-disabled) selected the slides they wanted to work with and while some began to improvise and then set movement, Lisa was given a diagram of her favourite design on a large sheet of paper and we explained how the diagram could be used to represent the studio floor. Lisa then orientated the 'floor plan' so that she had a front and back. We then superimposed a grid on the diagram so that we could locate areas more easily when Lisa looked at them. In this way Lisa's design became a map of pathways and locations that she could now use as guidelines for ordering dancers in space (see Figure 4.1).

The borders of the sheet gradually became filled first with useful and frequently used words and then with 'option boxes', offering choices such as 'Touch', 'Don't Touch' and 'Improvise'. Lisa, using her spelling board, added words such as 'Relax' and 'Stretch'. As the week progressed, these option boxes and extra diagrams were extended

4.1 Lisa Simpson (left) and students from Bretton Hall, University of Leeds, with an early version of the board. (Photographer Adam Benjamin)

and then grouped to deal specifically with space, time and action. These were later expanded, rationalised and made more easily identifiable through the use of colour. Lisa watched the movement phrases that the other students were producing from the slide images and then, using her eyes, began to select and order them in time and space. Using her floor plan as a guide, she placed some of her dancers at the edge of the studio, while carefully positioning others in the space, on spots identified by her 'pebbles'. By indicating the lines of her original image, Lisa was able to dictate the pathways along which the dancers were to travel. She started some couples together, while others she separated, introducing them from opposite sides of the studio. She then began ordering these events in time. This process was full of invention and surprise, for example, after having selected when she wanted her third duet to begin, Lisa refused to accept any of the choices offered for her fourth. While the dancers working with her tore their hair, Lisa simply waited until it became clear that an alternative option was possible; that she wanted the fourth and fifth duets to begin simultaneously. Moments such as these made it clear that we should always offer more than a simple either–or choice; the conditional 'Or neither of these' attached to any simple binary, 'this or that' question served to loosen what might otherwise have been a hidden choreographic strait jacket. This led to a game in which 'leading questions' were identified and outlawed.

Lisa's delight in what she was doing was matched by the growing realisation among the other dancers that they were uniquely placed to serve as translators for this woman's vision. Lisa demonstrated speed, sophistication and an almost tangible appetite for the art of making dances, for the freedom to select, organise and craft the movement of bodies in space. As the board became increasingly comprehensive, Lisa was able to take greater control of the choreographic process, but as the residency neared its end it became clear that a more ordered and detailed chart would give her the opportunity to determine the movement and position of individual dancers with greater precision. She was already far beyond the delineations of her earlier designs. It was at this point that we approached Jonathan Thrift at the Roehampton Institute, London, whose particular area of expertise was dance analysis and notation.

Jonathan teamed up with another disabled student, Bill Robbins. Bill had a very similar level of cerebral palsy to Lisa and had already had extensive performance experience with Wolfgang Stange's company, AMICI. Together with the assistance of a number of enthusiastic dance students from Roehampton they began to fine-tune the board. Lisa and the dancer/teacher Louise Katerega had already formed a teaching partnership in the Midlands and were soon followed by Jonathan and Bill in the South. The Board as it now exists owes a great deal to these two teams, who have pioneered its use and helped to refine and improve it.

Apart from those with visual impairment, eye movement/coordination is frequently one aspect of movement over which most people have control. For those with profound physical disabilities, this eloquent use of the eyes often becomes the principal channel of communication. The Simpson Board as it now exists is designed to use and extend this ability: eye direction or focus is used to select words and symbols laid out on an A3 laminated sheet. The information on the Board is dance-specific, consisting of body-and-movement concepts and illustrations. The simplicity of design means that the board is affordable, is not reliant on expensive or complicated technology, and is easily carried, or stored in the back of a wheelchair. It is a tool that can be used to develop precision as well as to foster creativity and, unlike cumbersome, expensive and, as yet, painfully slow, voice simulators, does not trap the user behind unwieldy machinery.

The Board allows access not just to dance but to the experience and the expression of that most basic of human rights: freedom of movement. No one is better equipped to realise the ideas of those who cannot move, and have no voice, than contemporary dancers: a community of artists dedicated to the language of movement whose most urgent – and some might say rarely satisfied – need is to find a choreographer who has something important to say. It is no small irony that a project designed to give voice to those who cannot speak has also provided a means of teaching choreographic skills to those who can speak but often fail to communicate with clarity or precision; the Board has proved to be an extremely useful tool to help students to focus on the accuracy and detail of the information that they convey to one another when they work in the studio.

While it is clear that very real benefits can come from disability-specific groups, particularly when they arise in response to the demands of disabled performers them-selves, I am wary when similar attempts to classify people by body type extend into performance or wider community workshop setting. Regimenting people into visually impaired or paraplegic-only dance companies as though dance were a branch of the Paralympics[16] can, if we are not careful, lead us towards a competitive (quasi-medical) model where people are segregated or separated on the grounds of their differences, rather than an arts model in which difference is used as the basis for exploration and the starting place for new dialogue. In the end, regardless of how many body-specific training programmes a dancer attends in order to develop as a performer, I would hope that they will want to dance together with people with whom they share more than just a particular physical attribute/impairment, or pair of wheels, and whoever teaches that group or class will still have to solve problems that arise from difference.

It is also hoped that more will be written on the experiences and discoveries of disability-specific training programmes in the future. This book, however, deals with the more chaotic world of dance that most of us are likely to encounter when working in the community today; its subject is difference and is addressed through the art of improvisation and an approach that sets out to meet and deal creatively with problems as they arise.

The Simpson Board can be obtained from the Language of Dance Center. See Appendix 1.

Notes

14 Francis Newman and Gem Treays.
15 A process facilitated by 'study support' who respond to eye movements of the students.
16 Wheelchair dancing was accepted as a Paralympic sport for the Winter Paralympics to be held in Salt Lake City in 2002.

5   A serious dislocation

How like thought. How like the mind it is.

(Helen Keller)

Disability is not a 'brave struggle' or 'courage in the face of adversity' . . . disability is an art. It's an ingenious way to live.

(Neil Marcus, *Storm Readings*)

What follows is more of a leap and a bound through history, an improviser's tale rather than a historian's. It is an attempt to connect some of the disparate threads of a fractured and fractious past. For its omissions I can only apologise, plead 'artistic licence' and hope that its shortcomings will stimulate those with a more historical bent to read, research and write in more depth. More than any other part of this book, it was for me a venture into the unknown, one that took me on a journey to look at the origins of western art and the complex and unpredictable dance that ensued. It is decidedly not a history of disability, which as Simon Brisenden has argued should be charted and written by disabled people themselves, but a history of fracture. The fracture and division of the elements that constitute dance. The fracture of time, place and movement.

My experiences of working with dancers in Africa was what first convinced me that western dance as I knew it had suffered a serious dislocation both from its connection to the ground and from its role as a vital part of community life. It made me curious to trace how this separation had come about. My enquiry took me back to the Ancient Greeks and the beginnings of the professionalisation of dance, a development that would see dance dissociated from its place on the earth and placed up on a stage, beyond both the physical and aesthetic reach of most ordinary people. I have chosen to illustrate this story of dislocations through the stories of three gods worshipped by the Ancient Greeks, the brothers Apollo, Dionysus and Hephaestus. It is clearly a male-centred view, not because I wish to refute feminist interpretations of the past, but because I have chosen to view this dislocation as an essentially male problem.

The god, the bad and the ugly: three approaches to dance in one mythical family

Dionysus was revered as the god of mystic revelry (read improvisation, sexuality and alcohol) of spring earth rites (cycles of destruction, creativity and recreation), the inspirational force behind the dances of the Ancients.[17] The rites of Dionysus were originally performed exclusively by women in wild celebratory dances long before his worship was transferred and transformed into the early formal festivals of the civil theatres (the *dithyramb*). It perhaps needs stating that the sexual, ebullient nature of some of his festivities would have made DV8 and Wim Vandekeybus appear tame in comparison! This wayward, unpredictable and at times threatening deity gradually fell from favour as first Greece and then Rome sought to promote art, and through art, ideals, that would serve to reinforce the order and stability of their increasingly patriarchal civilisations.

The god Apollo, half-brother to Dionysus, came to lend a less threatening, more predictable face to the arts. Associated with the sun, he was to provide a better fit for Roman politicians seeking to sell the idea of a centralist, top-down bureaucracy. As Rome itself was increasingly threatened by foreign armies and cultures, uniformity became exalted and exhibited as an example to Roman citizens, and dance was harnessed to promote this ideal of an ordered and orderly populace – an ideology and art form that people could look up to, and which those at the top could shape and direct. Improvising and cavorting was no longer to be considered a virtue. Discipline was what was needed.

The myths of the Ancient Greeks shed light not only on the origins of our current attitudes to dance but also on attitudes, both past and present, to disability. Apollo and Dionysus regularly feature in dance-history books, but their brother Hephaestus has for the most part failed to gain a mention. Born weak and possibly disabled, Hephaestus was hurled from Mount Olympus by his own mother, Hera, who considered him unfit to live, and certainly unfit to be a god.[18] This was a fate shared by many disabled children at that time, at the hands of their own parents. According to myth, however, Hephaestus landed in the sea and, thanks to the ministrations of the goddesses Tethys and Eurynome, survived, growing up to become the muscular, virile god of smithies. Unable to walk, he crafted leg-supports from gold and made three-wheeled, flying tables to deliver his creations to the gods. Hephaestus's story epitomised the surmounting of limitations through ingenuity and invention. But Hephaestus was not only a problem-solver and inventor, he was also in his time a famed dancer. His hobbling 'partridge dance' has accompanied the storytelling traditions associated with the art of metal work and is still found today as far afield as West Africa and Scandinavia.[19] Hephaestus' displacement from the history of dance would wait many centuries to be readdressed.

Like those disabled children hidden from sight in Ethiopia today, children born disabled in Ancient Greece may have been looked on as a punishment wrought on the family by the gods; their concealment spared the family embarrassment in the eyes of the community. Yet this was also a time when impairment of one sort or another must have been commonplace, either from natural causes or from wars, and there is actually no reason to suppose that those who managed to make their way through life may not, on occasion, have danced within their communities, at least in the days before Apollo's classical influence overshadowed both Dionysian improvisation and the careening steps of Hephaestus's dance.

Apollo's mission: the elevation and inaccessibility of dance

The *orkhiestha* or dance space of the Ancient Greeks was a level, dusty arena which, had you been in a wheelchair, you could have entered without difficulty. The dance festivals themselves, however, became increasingly competitive so ruling out those outside of the classically proportioned mould. It was the beginning of the division of dancers and spectators. Those fit to dance, and those fit only to watch. As Apollo's star ascended, Dionysus's statues were gradually removed from the *dithyramb*, and the age-old connection between dance and a reverence for the earth was severed. In the centuries that followed, dancers, who had once acknowledged the fecundity of the earth through every Dionysian rite, would find themselves drifting upwards towards the light, like balloons that had lost their moorings, until they stood, unnaturally, on the very tips of their toes. In the twentieth century, the full-rounded female form of the Ancients became more and more emaciated, and dancers became ever thinner, their limbs elongated and their hips narrowed, their breasts shrunken. The Dionysian connection to procreation (with its lineage to far older female deities) and to the earth as the source of creativity was lost and replaced by an illusion of femininity, controlled, sanitised and ordered to fit the philosophies that had been generated by men like Plato and Aristotle who expounded the perfect proportions with which beauty and truth must equate.

In time, the most accomplished dancers would be further elevated, placed on a raised stage for all to see, as the very embodiment of a clean, symmetrical and increasingly boyish Apollonian virtue, devoid of feminine threat or earthy mess. Deserted, the *orkhiestha* was colonised by musicians, who could be any shape or size, and who in any case were only required to be heard, not seen. These players would disappear into the orchestra (*orkhiestha*) pit. And so the dancing ground was swallowed up, leaving no more than an airy chimera of its previous self.

The popularity of Apollo as a single 'heavenly' deity eased the transition from the pagan gods to Christianity, and although the radical teachings of Jesus Christ seemed to promise a new equality for the dispossessed, for women and for the disabled, Christian theologians would eventually re-emphasise the division between heavenly, masculine, ideals (above) and the sin of the feminine, human body and its earthy and earthly functions (below). Dionysus's association with the earth meant he had nowhere to go but 'down' in the popularity stakes. Disinherited, disdained and eventually dismissed from godly duties, the horned, horny, drink-loving Dionysus would eventually be subsumed into the camp of the devil. Interestingly, today's street usage of the word 'dis' ('to put something down'), harks back to the Latin interpretation of Ha*dis*, the underworld of the Greeks. Life indeed continued to be hell for many *dis*abled people in the centuries of the Holy Roman Empire that followed.

Louis XIV: the king who stole space to make steps

Space and time proved to be major casualties in the historical *dis*integration of dance and society and it is their splintered remnants over which we trip as soon as we try to reunite in the dance studio. Why should faster be better? Why can't we take our time? Why do we place people on pedestals? Why do so many steps forward deny access?[20] The West has inherited a very particular interpretation of space, time and body and it is an interpretation that has been shaped and sculpted by history.

In the epoch following the Greek and Roman empires, the rulers of Christendom would refer back to classical ideals particularly when they needed to reinforce a political message (from on high). No one did this more effectively than Louis XIV of France (1638–1715; reigned 1643–1715), the widely acknowledged patron/founder of modern ballet. In his political policies as in his dance, Louis sought obedience, adulation and absolute control. His patronage created a wondrous court theatre; a fictional world of strictly ordered physicality, where the people of France appeared to pay grateful homage to their wise and omniscient lord – a part that was danced by Louis himself in the role of Apollo. Ballet as we know it today, emerged from the courtly dances of the royal houses of Europe, the dance of those attempting to display the distance between themselves and common people who lived on and from the earth. Dis *stance*, quite literally – a different standing. The purpose of courtly dance was specifically to establish and physically mark as different those who lived closer to the gods – or, if you were a royal like Louis, thought you were one.

Drawing on the philosophies of Plato and Aristotle, beauty, symmetry and order represented the new truth, these essentially masculine-oriented philosophies that had already established that free men stood at the top of the worldly hierarchy, above women, the disabled and the slave. Louis now elevated the relationship between beauty (state-sponsored art) and truth (State decision-making) to new heights. In an accolade to his own taste he founded the Académie de Danse Royale, and the Académie d'Opéra, institutions that underpinned much of the future development of the classical arts in the West, but Louis's 'high art' concealed an ugly secret. His fund-raising strategies were indeed state of the art; for the cost of this beatific dream was borne, neither by himself, nor his court, but by those who could least afford it, and who could offer up least resistance. Louis systematically brutalised, starved, evicted and falsely taxed his own subjects, the peasantry of France, in order to fund his self-delusional fantasies.

So as western dance continued its upwardly mobile trajectory, the poor got poorer and the disabled and disadvantaged again found themselves outcast; the object of ridicule, curiosity or abuse, a spectacle sometimes to be viewed in sideshows, prisons or circuses. The legalised theft of space (communal land) instigated by Louis XIV, proved so effective as a fund-raising strategy that it was implemented by neighbouring countries across Europe. Borrowing on the French model, Charles II of England, another great patron of dance and theatre, similarly taxed millions into poverty, 'enclosing' their land and dance spaces to create larger properties and larger profits for the ruling classes. Perhaps of all possible human dislocations, this forced separation of people from their place in and on the earth has proved to be the most damaging, and in many parts of the world today, continues to be one of the most painful.[21][22]

Thanks to Louis's patronage and the development of élite dance companies, the abilities of professional dancers soon outstripped the capabilities of their former patrons and ballet evolved into a highly specialised art form to be watched, admired and owned rather than danced; a signifier of the wealth, taste and elevation of its patrons rather than an activity shared by a community, other than, that is, that new, exclusive community of professional dancers. By 1836 Charles Dickens comments 'Many years ago we began to be a steady and matter-of-fact sort of people, and dancing in spring being beneath our dignity, we gave it up' (*Scenes of London Life*).

Darwin, eugenics and state control

> If I had my way, I would build a lethal chamber as big as the Crystal Palace with a military band playing softly, and a cinematograph working brightly; then I'd go out in the back streets and main streets and bring them in, all the sick, the halt, the maimed; I

would lead them gently, and they would smile a weary thanks; and the band would softly bubble out the 'Hallelujah Chorus'.

(D.H. Lawrence, 1908)[23]

Where once Dionysus, and before him countless other gods and spirits had dwelt in and on the earth, ensuring a measure of respect and care in farming and hunting, the land was increasingly being lorded over by a religion which sought to establish a single, uncontested, heavenly authority. By the nineteenth century, with the gods of the earth effectively banished, Charles Darwin's theory of evolution by natural selection finally erased the notion of a shaping or spiritual presence from the earth altogether. Science and commerce were now effectively given sanction to carve up what remained of the world's resources. Viewing the world simply as matter without spirit or soul was an attitude which would eventually be extended to the dispossessed – those displaced individuals unable to resist the tide of materialism and unable to contribute to 'production'. The number of people thrown on the mercy of the state would multiply dramatically through the upheaval of the Industrial Revolution and the depopulation of the countryside. Without the protection of local communities, vulnerable people would find both their bodies and minds increasingly the subject of state-controlled social and medical intervention. In an age which sought scientific solutions to the world's problems, a 'solution' was sought to the growing number of dispossessed (those who had only time and no space). The 'solution' when found was grafted disingenuously onto the back of Darwin's theory of evolution, or 'the survival of the fittest'.

Eugenics was a theory of its time. Coming to prominence at the turn of the twentieth century, it proposed that the human race should further its own evolutionary process by selective breeding and the enforced sterilisation of those deemed either mentally or physically unfit. Garnering support not just among scientists, but from white intellectuals and academics on both sides of the Atlantic, it conveniently ignored the question of who defined how such selections were to be made, or on what basis. It was later proved to be racist, sexist and disablist, but while the classically featured Apollo continued to serve as an ideal template for what a perfect human being should look like, and while white ballet companies continued to represent and reinforce this figure, the scientific community did not appear to be too bothered.

In England the Mental Deficiency Act (1913) legitimised the forcible detention of, among others, unmarried mothers, so-called 'difficult' children, people with cerebral palsy as well as those with mental illness and learning difficulties. In America, sterilisation was to become the favoured 'treatment' of the disabled, a practice that continued quietly in some countries well into the 1970s.

Ballet had continued to evolve as a high-art form throughout the eighteenth and nineteenth centuries, but it was not until the artistic and social stirrings of the twentieth that a new dance form began to emerge in the West. Pioneers in the early 1900s like Rudolph Laban and Isadora Duncan sought an alternative to the élite and conservative world of ballet; both were concerned with the natural unforced movement of the human body, of freeing the foot from the confines and distortions of the ballet shoe, in reconnecting dance with the earth and in giving dance and dancers a voice of their own. Laban in particular with his *choric dance* was concerned with issues of community and belonging (though not with disability). His early pioneering work in Europe was soon accompanied by the developments of a new dance form in America, that would match the mood of a young and developing nation.

Modern dance emerged in the 1930s as Martha Graham sought to ground dance powerfully in the earth and the breath, while her contemporary Doris Humphrey sought to reunify Apollonian (rising, aspiring) and Dionysian (falling, earthed) principles in a dance form that might address the fractures of a world rapidly descending into the chaos of the Second World War.

The1930s also saw new ideas being explored in Japan by artists like Kazuo Ohno. Ohno initially looked to western dance, then Turning his back on tradition, they sought a dance form that reflected the real world he experienced. Ohno and dancers like Tatsumi Hijicata drew their inspiration from the weather-worn bodies of peasant farmers, blind street singers or the lurching gait of a village drunk. They wanted to make dance that could represent these real bodies, which they felt carried so much power and beauty. As a consequence, Butoh though still essentially imitative or *mimetic* was to emphasise 'being' rather than 'moving'.

> If Isadora Duncan danced 'leaves on the tree' she would have tried to capture it in the movement of leaves blown by the wind. But Butoh dancers' aim is to become the leaf itself. So in Butoh, even when trying to express a spiritual or invisible thing, it has to be shown by the presence of the body, not by the action or motion.
>
> (Keisuke Sakurai, 1999)

Butoh, radical in its own way, recognised the significance of different bodies and the beauty contained within non-classical pedestrian movement. Like traditional Japanese performing arts, emphasis was placed not on 'how much' a performer moved but more simply how and when they moved, ideas that would gain currency in western dance practice in the 1970s.

'Some of the people' v. 'All of the people'; Hitler v. F. D. Roosevelt

> There will always be movements which are the perfect expression of that individual body and that individual soul; so we must not force it to make movements which are not natural to it but which belong to a school.
>
> (Isadora Duncan, 1928)

> The first condition of my collaboration is, that you must grant me the privilege to try, and err, because trial and error is the basis of all healthy development.
>
> (Rudolf Laban, quoted in Preston-Dunlop, 1998)

While the seeds of Butoh were being planted in Japan, America was sliding into catastrophic economic decline. In 1933, as the Great Depression worsened, Franklin D. Roosevelt was elected president. With support from his energetic and determined wife Eleanor, he set about radically improving the social welfare system, pushing through the Social Security Act which would ensure financial security for thousands of disabled people, not as an act of charity but as a right. Roosevelt was himself disabled with polio which he had contracted in 1920. Helen Keller (1880–1968), the famous disability rights campaigner (who was both deaf and blind) was to say of Roosevelt: 'more than any other president, I believe since Lincoln has he stressed the need to find in Government a means to promote the economic security and well being of all the people'. Five weeks after Roosevelt's first inauguration, Hitler came to power in Germany. He too would address the social deprivation of his country but unlike

Roosevelt his welfare reforms would only be extended to 'some of the people'. Like Louis XIV, and the Roman emperors before him, Hitler would harness the use of spectacular show and dance to represent his new order and symbolise his resurgent nation. For the first time in Germany since the First World War, dancers were in demand and were being paid for their services (so long as they were of Aryan origin). Goebbels, Hitler's propaganda minister, enlisted Rudolph Laban, the great German dance pioneer, to work as a choreographer and as director of *Deutsche Tanzbühne*. In 1936 Martha Graham in America was sufficiently informed about Germany's racist policies to publicly spurn Laban's invitation to dance at Hitler's Olympic games (Preston-Dunlop, 1998: 191).

Though he had never been a member of the Nazi Party, Laban's failure to see or respond to what was taking place all around him remains an unexplained episode in his remarkable story. Doubtless, Hitler's seemingly paradoxical belief in, and massive support for, the healing arts and natural food, his reintroduction of midwifery and his promotion of a health-conscious lifestyle all appealed to Laban's holistic and spiritual bent.[24] Laban's fascination with the geometry of Platonic solids may also have inclined him towards an ideology which placed a dangerous importance on the purity and perfection of the human form. Whatever his motivation, Laban's decision to continue making dances while students and colleagues were being persecuted remains a chilling reminder of the dangers implicit in the blinkered pursuit of perfection. Laban was neither the first nor the last artist who considered himself and his aesthetic choices to be spiritually or artistically absolute and thus above politics.

In the event, neither Graham nor Laban's work was seen at Hitler's Olympics. At the last moment Goebbels rejected Laban's choreography as being insufficiently imbued with Nazi zeal, Laban eventually woke up to the dangerous game he had been playing and, in 1937, under investigation by the Gestapo, fled to find sanctuary in Dartington in England. America too was rudely awakened when in 1941 the Japanese attacked Pearl Harbour, an act that finally spurred Roosevelt to join the war against Fascism. It would be Roosevelt, who would prove to be Hitler's nemesis.[25] As the war spread across Europe, economic pressures continued to favour the eugenicists' arguments and in Germany, Nazi ambition to create a pure-blooded, god-like nation, translated into a new and terrible policy. A quarter of a million of Germany's own disabled (referred to as the 'useless eaters') were murdered at the hands of the Nazi doctors. Soon the methods used on Germany's disabled would be extended to Jews, Poles, Gypsies and Germany's own artistic, dissident and gay community until there was, quite simply, no one left to protest.

The Nazis' attempts to eradicate those who differed either physically, mentally or ideologically from the Aryan ideal caused an exodus of German dance artists to Britain and the USA, bringing with them improvisational, educational and choreographic concerns that had been blossoming in the early German expressionist movement. The door that had slammed shut in Germany would open again in Britain after the war in a more tolerant and optimistic age, and Laban's work in particular would help to prepare the ground upon which community dance would develop.[26]

Natura non facit saltum: leaps of the imagination – Cunningham and Keller

The Eugenics movement that had served Nazi ideology so well, rested on a flawed assumption that had been inherited from Darwin himself. In dismantling the ancient creation myths, Darwin insisted Nature was merely a random mix of atoms that was shaped through the eliminative process of natural selection. Nature he argued *non facit saltum* ('Nature does not make leaps'). Without knowing it, Darwin was also arguing that nature does not dance; *saltum* was the original word used to describe dance before the French term 'danse' came into favour in the thirteenth century. Darwin and most of science that followed believed that evolution was a piece-by-piece adjustment of successive genes fitting themselves to new conditions (a process that could therefore be imitated and manipulated by scientific genetic manipulation). According to Darwin and those who followed him, there was no ordering principle, no guiding hand other than competition and necessity.

It would take someone not so blinded by logic, to realise the error of this argument and to propose that nature not only leaps, but dances into pattern and order. It was with typical clarity that Helen Keller, in a chance meeting, reiterated the belief that a leap (or dance) is the mind's way of moving forward into new order and insight, and that the mind is not something separable from either body or nature.

> Merce jumped in the air in first position while Helen's hands stayed on his body. Everyone in the studio was focused on this event, this movement. Her hands rose and fell as Merce did. Her expression changed from curiosity to one of joy. You could see the enthusiasm rise in her face as she threw her arms up in the air and exclaimed, 'How like thought. How like the mind it is'.
>
> (Graham, 1992: 149)

The young dancer whose movement so touched Keller's imagination was Merce Cunningham, at that time still dancing in Graham's company, before he made his own particular imaginative leap, one that would launch the postmodern dance movement and change the face of dance in the West forever. Confined by the theatrical and emotional themes of Graham's work, and aware of radical departures that were taking place in music, art and society as a whole, Cunningham, with his collaborator John Cage set about reinventing dance (and music) for the post-war generation. Drawing on Zen Buddhism and Taoism,[27] Cunningham began creating dances through random selection of material and random positioning. He turned his back on the age-old *mimetic* or imitational nature of dance, and set about creating a dance form that might exist in its own right, that simply 'was', rather than attempting to represent something. In so doing, Cunningham introduced two radical ideas that would begin to liberate dance from the long despotic shadow of Louis XIV. In his choreographed work, Cunningham insisted that all of his dancers were equally important, that there was no need for a star performer (Apollo shocked). Second, he believed that chance, rather than the ideas of a single director, might be allowed to play a 'creative' part in the shaping of dance works, and that nature, left to its own devices, might create patterns far more intricate and beautiful than any single person could achieve (Apollo outraged).

Natura facit saltum: nature dances, and so do disabled people; contact improvisation and developments in America

Satisfyin Lover was the apotheosis of walking.

(Banes, 1977)

To understand the route by which disabled people in the West first found their way into professional dance, we need to return to the civil rights and anti-war movements of the 1960s. It was a period when the whole of western youth seemed to be in protest. In 1964 Nelson Mandela was imprisoned in South Africa; in 1968 students and workers fought the police in the streets of Paris; in Britain there were the CND marches and in the face of growing racial unrest, the passing of the Race Relations Act, which inspired many disabled people to begin campaigning for their own rights. In the USA wounded ex-servicemen returned from the war in Vietnam and the number of disabled people soared. The veterans found a country in transformation. A new 'youth culture' questioned the ethics of a society that had emerged from the Second World War and seemed hell-bent on starting the third (and possibly final) one.

The dancers of this generation inherited Cunningham's egalitarian use of space, of chance procedures, and the assertion that 'walking' was the starting point for dance. But whereas Cunningham continued to favour virtuosic dancers and highly technical steps, the new generation sought a dance language that did away with the need for the classical dancerly body. Yvonne Rainer looked to the ordinary movement of people on the street and what she termed 'found' or 'pedestrian' movement, while Steve Paxton, a dancer who had performed in Cunningham's company, demonstrated an early recognition and commitment to dance that would work for 'people', regardless of their size, shape or form. He made works like *Satisfyin Lover* (1967) in which large groups walked, sat or gathered together following simple choreographic directives. Like Cunningham, Paxton had initially returned to what he considered the simplest of human movements; walking.

> In retrospect, Paxton realised (the) walking was crucial. It opened up a range of non dance movement, a variety of non-hierarchical structures, a performance presence that could be simultaneously relaxed and authoritative. It became the currency of Paxton's populist stance. Walking is something that everyone does, even dancers when they are not 'on' . . . there is no single correct way of walking. Anyone's method is appropriate for that person.
>
> (Banes, 1987: 60)

Sally Banes's statement 'Walking is something that everyone does' raised few eyebrows when it was written in 1977. Paxton's work was to be a definitive, if, at the time, unknowing step towards those who would never have considered themselves 'soloist' or even dancers, indeed towards those who could not 'begin with walking'. For the time being, however, the dance of disabled people remained 'unfound'. In the 1960s, disabled people were still a relative rarity among the pedestrian population, something that was to change as they made their thoughts and their bodies visible through the disability arts movement and the campaigning of the disability rights organisations.

During the 1960s and 1970s a growing number of individuals and groups began to push for reforms in government legislation both in the USA and Britain.[28] Writers like R.D. Laing (1927–89) and the influential French philosopher Michel Paul Foucault (1926–84) began to turn the perception of institutions and institutionalisation on their head. Like Ken Kesey in *One Flew Over the Cuckoo's Nest*, they attacked the medical model of disability arguing that the underprivileged, the disabled and the deviant were oppressed by the accepted knowledge and ideologies of the period in which they lived. Serious questions were being asked about the authority of educational, social and medical institutions to control peoples' lives and there was a concurrent shift towards self-advocacy and civil rights among disabled people.

A dance whose time had come: disabled people make an entrance

The dancers of the Judson Church Group[29] in America, who were at the forefront of postmodernism in dance, absorbed movement traditions from East and West and imbibed the heady mix of influences that made the 1960s revolutionary in so many ways. In an era that had seen the world's politicians take the planet to the brink of nuclear catastrophe, these young dance pioneers were seeking alternatives to hierarchical, dictatorial and male-dominated structures. In dance, this meant doing away with the time-honoured role of the choreographer and creating dance forms in which spontaneity and chance would play a central role. The postmodern dancers not only questioned the dance techniques of the previous generation but, in a climate of radical, social experimentation, they felt able to identify and, to some extent, dismantle the physical barriers that prevented dancers interacting with the real world. Like figures leaping from a canvas, they abandoned the raised stages of the theatres in search of a more vital connection between dance and the volatile world they were living in.

Paxton, Lisa Nelson and others like them sought a dance form capable not only of usurping the choreographer's control but one that would leave a doorway open to the unexpected and unforeseen. It was a form that celebrated partnerships above soloist, that encouraged support and dialogue without doing away with virtuosity and, in open celebration of the earth and the earth's attraction, accepted falling as part of the dance. Contact improvisation (CI), as the dance was named, developed primarily as a duet form in which movements arose through a sensitive sharing and readjusting of a partner's body weight while in physical contact. The resulting dance could be delicate and balanced, or dynamic, energetic and off balance. Its radicalism lay in its accessibility to all, regardless of background or experience, and in that advanced or professional dancers could dance with beginners and 'non-dancers'.[30] In the gyms and church halls where they performed, and in radical opposition to the raised stages and rigid seating of the arrangements of the theatres they had vacated, the dancers once again began to share common ground with those who watched. In many ways, these dance gatherings had more in common with many 'native' and ancient dance traditions where audience and performers inhabited the same space and in which anyone could be called forward or inspired to join the dance. Organisationally, CI rejected the hierarchies of most dance styles and schools relying instead on grass-roots support rather than on an institution and director. It was a dance form less concerned with control and leadership from above and more concerned with communal ownership and shared responsibility from below. As CI was taking its earliest faltering steps in America, a young disability rights activist named Bruce Curtis was beginning to think about dance and dancing.[31]

> I was in Washington D.C. at a party of disabled people socialising after a conference. There was some music on and we had to push our way onto a small dance floor. There were no models or examples about how disabled people in wheelchairs danced at that time, or that many examples of people willing to do it and so this is what people would do, they would kind of bounce around in their chairs or link arms and kind of go around in circles. In many ways it doesn't matter what people

do when they're having fun, it's how people have fun. But I looked at it with a critical eye and felt a little bit awkward about joining in because it didn't satisfy my sense of what dancing could be like, or should be like or might be like and I have a problem in seeing disabled people trying to do what non disabled people do and it always seems to me to fall short of what is considered beautiful, acceptable, exemplary.

(From correspondence with the author)

A few years later having made some experimental forays into theatre and dance, Curtis met and began experimenting with a non-disabled dancer who was involved in contact improvisation.

This person started moving with me in a way and interacting with me in a way that I had never been interacted with physically before in dance. Their knowledge and ability to relate to my movements and my patterns and anticipate it and work with me in a non-awkward way was impressive. I was totally fascinated but immediately I realised that the potential of what this dance form meant in terms of the quality of the relationship between a disabled and a non-disabled person, to truly feel equal in a dance relationship was an amazing concept, not just from an art position, but from a social position.

(From correspondence with the author)

In 1986 Curtis was joined by Alan Ptashek, a dancer already well versed in CI. The two formed the Exposed to Gravity Project. In 1990, Curtis and Ptashek took their dance ideas and teaching methods to the University of California at Berkeley, and taught a course called 'The Moving Body'; it was the first attempt to provide an accessible model for the inclusion of disabled students in an American dance department.

While Curtis was making his way into dance, another story was unfolding further up the west coast in Eugene, Oregon. Alitto Alessi was a dancer who had grown up dancing hip-hop on the streets and, following a serious injury, had trained in body work and Tai Chi Chuan. In 1972 he was one of the organisers of the Eugene Dance Collective and it was in this environment that he was drawn into the professional dance world, 'learning by osmosis'. In 1973 he began exploring ideas with Rob Faust (who had danced with Pilobolus) and they were soon exchanging ideas with dancers like Karen Nelson, Nancy Stark Smith, Andrew Harward and Riccardo Morrison who had all trained in CI. Joint Forces emerged as a professional company from the Eugene collective in 1979. Alessi and Nelson's explorations and their desire to extend their movement vocabulary led them to connect with Mobility International and to facilitate a dance exchange programme for disabled people from Germany, thereby completing a circuit of improvisational dance ideas back and forth across the Atlantic that had begun in the early 1900s. Alessi had an intimate knowledge of disability within his own family and was already working with disabled youngsters in schools, but the professional company originally had no disabled members.[32]

Alessi met Emery Blackwell quite by chance. Seeing Blackwell (who has CP) riding a customised bike on the street in Eugene, Alessi thrust a dance programme into his hand and invited him to come to the studio (see Figure 5.2). Despite initially dismissing the invitation as absurd, and Alessi as some kind of lunatic, Blackwell was eventually persuaded by a friend to go and see, and he soon became hooked.[33] Alessi and Blackwell

5.1 Bruce Curtis and Alan Ptashek. (Photographer Danielle Haim)

began showing work in the mid-to-late 1980s as part of Joint Forces. They felt no need to redefine what they were doing as dancers, Blackwell's presence merely confirming Banes's statement; if Paxton's *Satisfyin Lover* had been the apotheosis of walking (Banes, 1977: 60), then a new perspective had to be in the offing. In 1987 Alessi and Karen Nelson invited Bruce Curtis and Alan Ptashek from Berkeley (Paradox Dance), and Kevin Finnan and Louise Richards (Motion House) from the UK to share teaching and practice at what was called the 'Dance With Different Needs' workshop, part of the 1987 New Dance Festival. It was to be the first major gathering in a growing field of dance events that sought to place access at the top of the agenda. The following year Alessi became Director of the DanceAbility Project which, since 1990, has been in residency at the University of Oregon. (And where inclusive movement classes are now a part of the dance curriculum.)

Around this time a number of companies (not all of them CI-based) began to emerge across America; AXIS in Oakland; Paradox Dance in Berkeley, California; Dancing Wheels in Cleveland; Mobility Junction in New York City; and Light Motion in Seattle, all of which consisted of disabled and non-disabled performers. Contact improvisation had already given rise to a rapidly growing network of professional and non-professional dancers. The emergence of DanceAbility and later Diverse Dance directed by Karen Nelson provided a channel through which increasing numbers of disabled people began to link up with this network and make connections with the dancing community. Independent of any institution CI provided a network in which

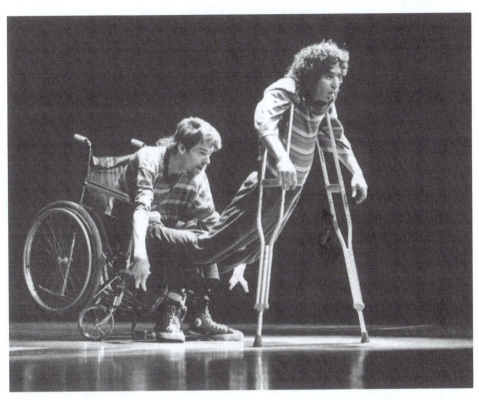

5.2 Emery Blackwell and Alito Alessi in *Wheels of Fortune*. (Photographer Edis Jurcys)

discoveries were being made and shared in a way that outstripped anything that was happening within formal dance or physical education programmes.

The extraordinary physicality made possible by CI also influenced dance in the main-stream throughout the 1980s. Its techniques of lifting and falling became almost *de rigueur* and were exemplified by companies like DV8 in Britain and Wim Vandekeybus in Belgium.

By the 1990s, however, it had become apparent that although CI was providing a thriving grass-roots practice, improvisation alone would not be able to secure a viable future for the independent professional dance scene. Although a handful of talented improvisers like Julyen Hamilton, Kirsty Simpson and Paxton himself continued to perform professionally, improvisation as an art form seemed to be in decline. Perhaps the most important legacy of the 1960s and 1970s was the principle that everyone, given the opportunity, has something to contribute, and that leadership, rather than being vested in a solitary figure, could be passed around, according to the area under investigation. A framework had been established within which different voices could be heard and different experiences valued. In the UK 'collaboration' became the buzzword for dance in the 1980s.

X marks the spot: X.24 to X6 – contemporary and new dance in the UK

> The so familiar building seemed to be in a parallel world where a wheelchair seemed totally out of place.
>
> (Celeste Dandeker, 2001)

> If one dare not invent his own dance steps, it is unlikely that he will be tolerated if he dares invent his own religious, educational, or political steps!
>
> (A.S. Neill, 1968)

As CI was evolving out of the independent dance scene in America, Graham and her technique had become part of the establishment, giving dance in America new status and providing an alternative professional training to ballet. In 1966 Graham sent the choreographer Robert Cohan to London to establish a new school. Two years later, with the support of the English businessman Robin Howard (himself disabled), the London School for Contemporary Dance took up residence in a building between Euston and Kings Cross stations. It was a building which itself boasted an unusual past, having been the headquarters of The Artists Rifles, a regiment of visual artists and musicians (and the haunt of such notables as Oscar Wilde).[34] When it had opened in 1888 the most popular act of the inaugural celebration was not a musical rendition but a humorous duet for two men, entitled X.24.[35] It seemed even then the building was destined to be the site of dance. When it reopened in 1968 as the home of contemporary dance in Britain, the name 'The Artists Rifles Place' was shortened, first to 'The Artists Place', then simply 'the Place'.[36] It was an appropriate and striking reduction and one that brings us to a crossroads in the divergent pathways of space, time and body since our starting point in Ancient Greece. Our word 'choreography' comes from the Greek *khoròs* related to chorus, as in Laban's *choric* dances, but also *khōros* which means simply 'place'.

Although completely inaccessible to wheelchair users, the Place was open, in a unique way, to new ideas and art forms, something that was encouraged by its patron, Howard.[37]

> It is important to realise that, as well as having a passion for Graham's work, Howard took a great interest in experimental work. In the late 1980s reflecting upon the development of the school, he reiterated his belief in cultivating opposition, that one of the purposes of such an institution was to stir up counter-movements in order that 'dialogue' between differing schools of thought could be kept going.
>
> (Jordan, 1992: 14)

But it would take initiatives mainly from outside of the Place to breakdown the exclusivity of professional dance in the UK. One of the key figures in this respect was Peter Brinson whose tireless advocacy, writing and teaching helped to establish the community dance movement in Britain.[38] Brinson founded Ballet for All and later as director of the Gulbenkian Foundation supported Gina Levete, one of the pioneers of disability dance work, who went on to establish SHAPE (1976), a network of dance artists (as opposed to therapists) who began to work with disabled people. SHAPE later became an organisation run by and providing training for disabled people working in the arts (see Levete, 1982).

It was Brinson who encouraged Wolfgang Stange to begin working with blind dancers in 1977. Stange, who had trained at the Place, was influenced by the philosophy and guidance of Gina Levete, yet his choreographic vision owed more to the influence of another teacher, Hilde Holger. Her own remarkable journey had taken her from Nazi Germany in 1939, via India before finally settling in London.[38] Holger offered Stange reduced fees for her classes if he would spend some time helping teach her son (who had Down's syndrome) to read and write. Holger must have sensed that Stange had a special gift for communicating and so Stange began a double apprenticeship; not only did he absorb first-hand the traditions of the European modern dance, but he began to create a relationship with Holger's son. Stange's varied experiences led to the establishment of the AMICI Dance Theatre Company in 1980. The integration of blind performers, people with learning difficulties and non-disabled dancers was the first initiative of its kind in the UK.

By the early 1970s, Fergus Early had made his way (via Ballet for All) to the Place, where he established a reputation as a teacher–choreographer with an ability to include dancers and non-dancers within his work.[39] An oft-times spokesperson for new dance in the UK, Early identified 'liberation' as a central theme of the new-dance movement. Green Candle, the community-based company he founded in 1987, was to become a vehicle for many people young and old, disabled and non-disabled to explore dance and discover themselves and their capabilities as performers. Early was part of the radical New Dance Collective that had begun to explore ideas outside or beyond formal dance technique in Britain in the same way that the Judson Church Group had done in America under the early tutelage of Robert Ellis Dunn. New Dance eventually established itself in the London Docklands, in a warehouse numbered X6; the group of dancers associated with it became known as the X6 Dance Collective. It was perhaps an indication of how disability awareness in the UK was trailing the Americans that, when the New Dance Collective moved in 1980 they adopted a building that was, and still is (at time of publication), entirely inaccessible to wheelchair users.

The year 1973 would prove to be a pivotal one in this story. It was the year that Mary Fulkerson arrived from the USA as the new head of dance at Dartington (where Laban had first taken refuge in 1937), bringing with her her release technique. Fulkerson was to influence a generation of British choreographers, further stretching the boundaries of who could and couldn't dance.

> As a student she (Fulkerson) had disliked the competitive atmosphere of her course, and the fact that she was expected to work towards a standard level of perfection rather than being taught to value her own skills and qualities. She had also felt that too many dance classes were taught by a system of repetition and imitation, so that students could not explore in detail how the body functioned – how the muscles and joints worked, how weight should be placed and how a movement was affected by tension or relaxation. Above all she had been frustrated by the fact that only certain kinds of movement were accepted as dance – anything else being dismissed as graceless or unskilled.
>
> (Mackrell, 1992: 24)

Fulkerson invited Steve Paxton and Lisa Nelson to Dartington and contact improvisation began to establish itself in England. Fulkerson and Paxton continued to have a profound impact on English choreographers and dancers of the 1970s and 1980s, particularly those who were already asking questions about inclusivity and access. In 1986, working closely with Anne Kilcoyne, Paxton founded Touchdown Dance for sight-impaired, blind and sighted dancers (see Paxton and Kilcoyne, 1993). Among those who studied at Dartington were Kevin Finnan who, with Louise Richards, formed Motion House,[40] Isabel and Lewis Jones (himself blind) who together set up Eye Contact,[41] Paul Newham[42] who went on to found the school of Voice Movement Therapy and Lea Parkinson who was to become a founder member of CandoCo Dance Company. In Germany, 1973 was the year Pina Bausch took over the Dance Theatre Wuppertal, striving to develop new work that spoke about the realities of the human condition in all its difficult beauty. It was also the year that Celeste Dandeker fell while performing in Manchester, and appeared to have ended her dance career.

In the UK the growing influence of Laban's teaching in mainstream schools, the pioneering work of Veronica Sherborne with mentally and physically disabled children, the touring of LCDT and educational programmes by organisations like Ballet for All and Ludus Dance Company, meant that the ground was set for an explosion of community dance and prepared the ground for the emergence of companies like Jabadao, Green Candle, Salamander Tandem, The Guizers, Common Ground, AMICI and Chicken Shed.[43]

In the 1980s, the experimentation of companies like Extemporary Dance Theatre and Second Stride led to further radical departures. Lloyd Newson's company DV8, and the choreographer–performer Michael Clark began to attract massive and popular followings producing work that was political, accomplished, challenging and accessible to the public in a way that much of the early new-dance offerings had not been. Like Bausch, these companies began to draw more than just 'trained' dancers onto the stage; musicians, actors, singers and even designers began to feature as clearly 'non-dancers' on the same stage as the 'professionals'. These multi-bodied, dance theatre or physical theatre companies drawing on the highly experimental, chaotic and at times 'inaccessible' offerings of new dance began to reinvent and reinvigorate mainstream dance theatre and prise open the doors of the exclusive world of professional dance.

New dance in England from the late 1960s to the 1980s was shaped by dancers like Emilyn Claid, Rosemary Lee, Fergus Early, Jacky Lansley, Sue McClennan, Laurie Booth, Rosemary Butcher, Juleyn Hamilton and Kirsty Simpson, all of whom would directly or indirectly help to set the context for the emergence of disabled dancers in the 1990s, some through their work in the community, some by the elaboration of a movement style that utilised improvisation or physical theatre and all by extending the boundaries of exactly what might happen in a dance performance (see Mackrell, 1992). By 1990, despite the successes of Graeae theatre company, no dance company of physically disabled and non-disabled dancers had yet made its way from community dance into the 'mainstream' as a touring company on the professional circuit. Consequently, there is no explicit reference to disabled performers in either Mackrell's 1992 book or in Jordan's account of contemporary and new dance (also 1992), both of which cover developments in the UK up until the end of the 1980s. This is perhaps a strange omission if we accept Early's definition of new dance being concerned with liberation.[44] Although CandoCo had yet to emerge, companies like AMICI and Green Candle were already widely known and acclaimed. It seemed that although disabled people were finding their way into dance, none was yet regarded as having made a significant contribution as an artist in his or her own right; they were still considered as 'invitees'.

In 1990, Celeste and I were struck by the continued marginalisation of many of the 'disability'-associated dance groups we saw and also in some cases by the apparently low levels of achievement expected of the performers. CandoCo, from its inception, consciously sought a place in the mainstream of British dance rather than as an adjunct, an oddity to be mentioned at the back of a dance programme under a separate heading. Following the company's first London appearance in the Ballroom Blitz festival at the South Bank, Chris de Marigny writing in *Ballett International* said

> When one enumerates the qualities of new avant-garde experimental work they might consist of the following: it should surprise; it should disorientate; it should lead one to see in new ways and it should disturb. Ideally if it is a dance work it should have technical expertise. On all counts this company succeeds, in fact in some cases reaches well beyond these definitions.
>
> (*Ballett International*, February 1993)

CandoCo soon attracted a huge following, but it was not just committed dance-goers who came to see the shows. Celeste's return to the world of dance, David Toole's remarkable stage presence and the energy of the company as a whole attracted an entirely new audience, among them, young independent disabled people who, for the first time, were seeing dance that they could relate to (see Figure 5.3). The combination of dance and physical theatre, in a company that worked with some of the country's most admired choreographers, proved hugely successful. The condescension that had on occasion clouded much early disability-related work, could now be replaced with critical appraisal, both positive and at times adverse, when the work failed to live up to its new, self-imposed standards.

Celeste recounts:

> I remember during a CandoCo performance being in the wings and watching a duet from *Between the National and the Bristol* choreographed by Siobhan Davies. I realized that what I was seeing on stage was two dancers, one of them disabled, dancing with such style and beauty that I felt spiritually moved, not in a sentimental way but in a way which the arts at their best can make you feel. They had every right to be there and it was much clearer for me after that and I have never questioned it since.
>
> (From conversations with the author)

CandoCo moved rapidly from small to middle-scale international touring, becoming the first company of disabled and non-disabled dancers to tour nationally and internationally. The message, both in performance and workshop programmes, was two-fold; not only could anyone dance, but, with sufficient talent, training (and the right choreography) dancers of all kinds could aspire to more than a sympathetic response. Young disabled people and non-disabled people, not previously interested in dance, came in droves to watch the company perform and, as a result, the demand for integrated work in Britain soared. During the early 1990s a host of community and youth dance companies sprang up across Europe, many initiated or inspired by CandoCo performances or workshops.[45]

5.3 Sue Smith and David Toole, CandoCo Dance Company. (Photographer Hugo Glendinning)

The hobbling dance

The Apollonian pursuit of excellence and the more Dionysian concerns with the 'common ground', the creative, improvisatory grass-roots of dance, are still on occasion presented as contradictory or opposing schools of thought, as if to be really committed to improvisation and access you can't be interested in professionalism and virtuosity and vice versa. I prefer instead to consider these approaches, like the Greek gods at the beginning of this story, as estranged members of the same family, adjusting to the idea that one of its number is disabled, with a body that is sometimes fallible, sometimes strong, sometimes inspired, sometimes distorted, sometimes mundane, sometimes extraordinary. A body whose greatest virtue may be that it causes us to reconsider beauty in relationship to our internal and external constructs of time and space. A body that forces us to question the origins and effects of our own perspectives and prejudices.

The tension that exists between virtuosity and communality will not go away. I find it hard to imagine community unleavened by moments of virtuosity, or virtuosity without a common ground to differentiate itself from. The fact that we may not all be standing does not take away the individual need to excel in whatever way, shape or form, in other words, to make the very most of who and what we are. Excellence requires an effort, which, as those involved in this story already know, can set us on course for the most unexpected encounters and the most exciting of journeys. This story is far from complete and there are many players, events and coincidences that I have had neither the space nor time to mention; it is a story that is still unfolding as dancers continue to share and exchange their visions and skills in countries around the world. It is a story that awaits new contributions, perhaps new interpretations and new departures.

Notes

17 Dionysus was initiated into the rites of Cybele 'the Great Mother', evidence of his links to far older female earth deities probably of African origin.

18 In another version of the story, the young Hephaestus tried to intervene in a dispute between his parents: here, he was thrown from Olympus by Zeus, landing on the isle of Lemnos, the impact shattering his legs. In other accounts he suffered both traumas.

19 (Graves, 1992)

20 In 2000 I attended a reception at S. Africa House in Trafalgar Square, with Thomas St-Louis, a black disabled dancer, part of a team working on a British Council supported project in Soweto. Although it would have been an unthinkable visit during the apartheid years, we were still barred from entering through the front door, not on the grounds of colour but because of the steps.

21 See Rowe, 2000.

22 Great expanses of the land snatched from smallholders were simply turned over to sheep or left to run wild. In the language of the day, the land was 'left to go out of culture'. A reminder that our present-day arts have their ethical roots in the sharing of physical space. See N. Davies.

23 D.H. Lawrence, 1908. From a private letter quoted in Carey, 1992.

24 The year 1935 saw the high point for alternative health practitioners – a meeting of 1,200 physicians and healers in Nuremberg (Proctor, 1988: 230).

25 A statue erected in memory of Roosevelt in Washington in 1997 caused controversy by depicting him as non-disabled.

26 For a fascinating account of Laban's complex role during this period, see Preston-Dunlop, 1998.

27 Taoism from China pre-dated Buddhism.

28 Notable among these groups was DIG (the Disability Income Group).

29 This group took their name from the Judson Memorial Church in New York where they met. A collective of predominantly women dancers and choreographers who radically challenged all of what dance stood for in the 1960s. They produced highly experimental work introducing old and young dancers, nudity and the politics of feminism and pacifism.

30 Here again we see the influence of Japanese traditions and the idea of 'kumite' or meetings between teacher and student in forms like Aikido and Shintaido. Many of the Judson Church group studied Aikido. For an excellent and detailed account of the development of CI in America, see Novack, 1979.

31 Around this time Mary Verdi Fletcher, another wheelchair user, was establishing a partnership with David Brewster. Their success as performers led them to form Cleveland Dancing Wheels in 1980 (see Albright,1997: 65–71).

32 Alessi had a sister with polio and a mother who was quadraplegic.

33 From conversations with Blackwell.

34 The imprisonment of Wilde on the grounds of his homosexuality is a reminder of attitudinal changes that have been part of the history of dance and of the Place.

35 The duet was a parody of the ballet Excelsior (Source: *Memories of the Artists Rifles* by H.A.R. May (Howelett and Son, 1929))

36 From conversations with Mop Eager, the Place administrator 1969–98 the students and staff chose its new name, (a level of involvement difficult to imagine in a dance school today).

37 Fittingly, in the year 2000, the Place in London was completely refurbished to provide access to restaurant, auditorium and most significantly to changing rooms, studios and the stage. Celeste served as consultant.

38 Peter Brinson also established the community dance course at the Laban Centre, London. See Brinson, 1991.
39 Hilde Holger taught dance to people with learning difficulties and choreographed for them, presenting work at the Sadler's Wells Theatre in London.
40 Early's sister Teresa Early had founded Ballet-makers Ltd in 1963, a dance organisation with an open-door policy and a forum for much early experimental work. See Mackrell, 1992.
41 Though committed to integrated practice in their education programme, Motion House didn't include disabled performers in their professional work. Motion was founded in 1988.
42 Lewis Jones had also established Art to Share, a national organisation creating opportunities for blind and visually impaired people to have access to the arts. Eye Contact explored movement between sighted, blind and visually impaired people.
43 Newham was the first outside director to work with CandoCo (*Resurrection Shuffle*, 1992).
44 This is inevitably a very curtailed account, there being countless other groups and individuals who contributed to this development, notably the Cholmondeleys and Featherstonehaughs.
45 Notably: Blue-Eyed Soul, Tardis, Velcro Integrated Dance Company, Independance and Stop Gap in England, Counter Balance in Eire and HandiCapace in Germany.

6 'Just' moving: ethics, integration and the discipline of improvisation

Il faut toujours rendre justice avant que d'exercer la charité. (Seek justice before dispensing charity)

(Nicolas Malebranche)

Sentimentality is a superstructure covering brutality.

(Carl G. Jung)

A bad politician confuses measurement with proportion.

(Plato)

I was once asked by a rather fierce technique teacher if improvisation wasn't 'just moving around, doing anything you wanted'. She saw spontaneity as a kind of dangerous anarchy that involved no requirement or discipline from the student and no rigour from the teacher. Improvising can lead us to unexpected riches, but its great danger as an art form (and the cause of the teacher's suspicion) was that when badly taught it can leave students 'untutored'. How then, can we approach improvisation in a way that helps us to identify and engage with problems while continuing to foster creativity and free will? How do we help students to find their edge as improvisers and think about choreographic concerns, while allowing time for the generation of new ideas and the space to develop and explore them?

It is generally accepted that creativity is not something that can be forced or 'instilled' but that flourishes when allowed to develop. Accordingly, improv teachers try to ensure unpressurised studio time (a valuable contrast to the rigorous demands of technique class) in which students can begin to broaden outlooks and refine their sensibilities to different stimuli. Here, students can explore ideas without being judged or criticised, while at the same time learning to give positive feedback and support to each other during the creative process.

Yet with all this support, too few dancers emerging from current formal training seem able to improvise convincingly. Is this because it takes a certain kind of person to improvise, or because our (dance) education knocks this playfulness and sensibility out of us? It is true that improvisation in performance often demands more of an audience than choreographed work. Watching improvisation requires a degree of openness, patience and generosity that allows time for the performers to find their way and in which exploration is an accepted part of the dance. Yet, even given this more relaxed perspective, too many dancers appear unable to sense and respond to occurrences taking place in real time when they improvise. They seem hamstrung, either within the confines of their dance technique, or they seem to inhabit a twilight world of personal fiction which fails to communicate convincingly with an audience. There are, it seems, certain underlying skills that sustain the performance of a good improviser, skills that, though not obvious, are both finely honed and reliant on a keenly developed sensibility.

In technique classes dancers are repeatedly confronted with physical challenges to be understood and mastered. Learning any technique involves a constant and disciplined attention to sets of physical tasks demonstrated by the teacher. Students then attempt to replicate the movement sequences or principles, overcoming the problems presented by their own physical condition and mental understanding. Despite the internal problem-solving that takes place, in the end the successful student is the one who replicates the movement of the teacher. A good technique teacher is looking for far more from her students in their interpretation of the material learned, yet the ability to copy, and the discipline of following instruction meticulously are skills that are necessary and highly valued in the training of professional dancers. Improvisation, on the other hand, encourages students to engage in the kind of problem-solving that leads to unforeseen outcomes, in which unique responses to different situations and stimuli are favoured. It encourages originality, free thinking and question-asking and its outcomes may be odd, idiosyncratic and unexpected.

The diversity of inclusive groups daily confronts us with problems that need solving, forcing us to clarify teaching methods in a way that may not arise in non-inclusive settings. Blind students, students with learning difficulties and physically disabled students will not thrive on woolly, esoteric or simply inexact explanations. Time and again as teachers and performers we are forced to ask 'Why is this not working – what is it that I'm missing or failing to explain?' As was discussed in Chapter 3, this sharing of time and place among 'unequal' bodies raises questions that are not just physical but also 'ethical'. If these questions are not being recognised and addressed, then the group is just a 'normal' dance group that has some disabled participants in attendance; guests to the dance world, politely included, while actually having their status as visitors subtly reinforced. Dancers who are not as fit, fast or agile will remain on the periphery of the action, the real problems of integration (and they are **real** problems) are left unaddressed and the narrow vision accepted as normality remains unchallenged. If, in addition, we begin to import charitable motives into the dance studio, the opportunity to learn from these questions in a very real sense goes begging.

Sachiko was an elderly, rather frail woman taking part in a workshop in Japan. Although able to walk, she could only do so briefly before having to sit in a chair to rest. She was always the first to leave the dance space, and once she had gone the younger dancers would continue to improvise in more robust and adventurous ways. After this had happened a few times, I asked those watching how they felt each time Sachiko left. Like me, they felt temporarily a sense of disappointment (tension falling) but each time the moment passed and was forgotten.

Sachiko said she felt as if she was 'in the way' and that she couldn't stay in too long because her legs got tired. In the improvisation that followed, the other dancers seemed more aware of her, but she appeared at a loss as to what to do and looked nervous as if she were scared of being knocked over. Again she left, but this time her departure was noticed by the other dancers and a sense of unfulfilled action occupied what was left of the improvisation; the remaining dancers now seemed to sense that an opportunity had passed them by. There was a growing awareness among those dancing and those watching that Sachiko held the key to unlocking the potential of the improvisation, yet her fragility left her isolated. In the next improv, Yukiko, one of the more experienced dancers, made a very sustained but ultimately unsuccessful attempt to dance with Sachiko; eventually, in what looked part-exasperation, part-surrender and part-traditional posture of obedience and respect, she knelt down and bowed before Sachiko. Seizing the moment Sachiko, placing a hand to steady herself, turned and with a look of relief sat on Yukiko's back. Those watching burst into spontaneous laughter and applause. The riddle had been solved and the other dancers taking up the theme began an improvisation of sitting on each other, an activity that led to those in wheelchairs also being sat on, thereby providing support for others. Sachiko was now able to sustain her presence in the group, by sitting on whoever she happened to meet, and the group was now liberated to play until the next riddle arose.

I have a sneaking suspicion that the reason I find it difficult to engage with some improvisations is not because it is art, and therefore 'mysterious' and 'difficult', but because what is taking place may not be making very much sense to those who are dancing. That is not to say we should always know what is happening in an improv; uncertainty is a vital phase on the path to new discovery and a constant companion on journeys into the unknown. The work fails to engage on the simple grounds that nothing is ever resolved because it is never identified as a problem. I mean resolved, not in the sense of being fully explained but in the sense of being revealed. How then, when there is such a need to be accepting and supportive within improvisational teaching, can we develop a more critical approach to the art of improvisation? Is it possible to acknowledge and continue to work creatively with those reservations and feelings of discomfort that occur when we watch (or participate) in an improvisation? Can we turn these 'less positive' feelings to our advantage or should we just pretend not to have them and whinge later in private?

At the end of one of the sessions mentioned above, I asked another of the disabled dancers whether she was happy with the final image or whether she felt there was something that wasn't quite right. At first she tried to identify problems with the positions of those dancers still in the space, then she suggested, rather hesitantly, that what was wrong was that there were no disabled dancers 'in the final frame', since they had, like Satchiko, retired from the improvisation. This was not an easy thing to say as up until that point everyone in the group seemed to have been working well together. Having voiced her concern, there followed an uneasy silence as the non-disabled dancers sought to understand whether they were being 'blamed' or criticised. After further discussion, several dancers admitted to having had similar reservations about the improvisation but had been uncertain what to do about it. One said that she had 'buried her feelings'.

This burying of reservations or feelings is part of an 'anything goes' approach to improvisation, which says 'If the impro ends that way . . . that's how it ends and that's fine, and anyway we don't distinguish between disabled and non-disabled people.' This is an oft-heard, rather naïve statement regularly repeated in inclusive settings. To take the last part first, if we don't acknowledge the differences between disabled and non-disabled dancers we lose lifetimes of experience and difference beneath a blanket of good intention. It is the acknowledgement of difference and the resolution or exploration of the problems that arise from it that invigorate the work. As for the ending, well, no, the ending can't be changed, it's true; the point of the question is to unearth the buried thoughts or feelings and help to identify the moment when an alternative choice could have been made that might have led to another conclusion. Asking the dancer what she felt was wrong was not so that she could blame others (or herself) but to help her to value her sense of unease. It is exactly that feeling that something is 'out of joint' that provides us with the clue, and cue, to potential action. In effect, had she accepted and responded to her feeling, she could have changed the final picture, through her own action, by making an entrance and putting herself in the final frame.

The tendency not to question or look too closely at the content of improvisations means that many moments of tension, and consequently the possibility of resolution – of looking into them more deeply, slip through our fingers. To make matters worse, there exists in some areas of dance improv, a reluctance to think critically and a tendency to avoid problems of any kind. This may be for the best of reasons: to avoid foregone conclusions, or 'a final say', and to encourage a continual Tao-like openness to the present; and yet this attempt to avoid the obvious has brought with it a number of unfortunate side-effects. There is a tendency to think that if something is resolved, it is no longer of interest. But the word resolution actually implies a 'loosening' or 'revealing'. 'Resolution' literally means that something fixed or solid is dissolved and **a new thing revealed**. Resolution allows us to move more deeply into our subject and discover deeper layers of meaning or new and unexpected details and departures. Rather than shying away, we should, like a photographer with an increasingly powerful lens, be encouraging greater and greater resolution in improvisation, but, like any good photographer, first we need to focus our attention on what attracts our interest. And this for most of us means 'problems'. All great films, books or personal stories revolve around how someone solves a problem, yet a great deal of improvisation as it is currently taught and practised seems to ignore real difficulties because we have bought into a 'theory of creativity' that allows us to dance round problems rather than value them.

Creating definite boundaries and clearly defined tasks, as in **crossing the line** (Improv 16, Chapter 19), helps us to identify and focus on these issues as and when they arise. Valuing problems means the capacity to feel that 'something is wrong' or 'out of joint' becomes one of our greatest assets. These subtle feelings of unease point us towards areas of injustice or rupture that have perhaps previously passed as 'normality'. For example, seeing someone pushed around in a wheelchair without asking where and when they want to move. Yet in many settings this sensibility is brushed under the carpet or dismissed as 'negative' or 'unhelpful'. In dance politics, or history, students are encouraged to think critically about any proposition put to them, but this capacity to think, feel and act can often go badly astray when creative dance enters the frame. This does not change the need for a positive and supportive environment, quite the contrary, but if we are ever to replace 'just moving' with 'just' movement it demands a far more rigorous and thoughtful approach on the part of those who teach. The lessons learned help us to see beneath the skin of dance to what is really taking place in front of us, and develop our critical sensibility along with our aesthetic one.

At a youth dance platform in South Africa I watched a company from Pretoria dance a very technical piece by a professional choreographer which purported to foreground the most technically able students while their 'less gifted' classmates danced in the ensemble behind them. This is the classical model of dance, which, whether one agrees with it or not, is the most widely practised model in dance schools today. It took some time before I was able to make out in the rear of the ensemble the most lyrical, gifted dancer in the group; dancing virtually in the shadows, she was the sole black student in the company. I did not have the feeling that what I was watching was 'just' dance.

I have witnessed the same principle endlessly applied to choreography on students in the UK, in which those dancers who are not 'the right shape' are given minor roles upstage while the thin, 'technical' and often far less interesting dancer is placed in the spotlight.

As a teacher or choreographer, try to notice difficulties and the tension that arises from them, and congratulate your students on their ability to do likewise. This may not always be easy: it may mean questioning a value judgment with which you have grown up, and one which everyone around you regards as normal. But you have to be able to identify the feeling that something is wrong (that's the ethics part) and if you are to succeed, to make it visible, by humour, exaggeration, creating alternative strategies, by any means at your disposal (that's the aesthetics part). This is a step that inevitably takes courage and an effort of will. It may on occasion feel akin to shouting 'The emperor has no clothes!' while those around you maintain a uniform and disapproving silence. The failure to recognise and address problems is revealed in those performances that call on the sympathy (or prejudice) of the audience rather than on a company's ability to encounter and deal with real difficulties. The dissatisfaction felt by the audiences is aesthetic, but its roots lie in the failure to confront either mentally or physically challenging material or issues; a reflection of the ethics of those who lead the group.

Clearing away misconceptions and prejudice generates the space in which relationships can be reviewed and reinvented and in which new patterns of movement can be discerned. Els Willekens, one of the dancers in *An Egg is Enough*[47], was 1. 36 m. tall, and her movement which was already quite restricted was made more so by a metal rod in her back which supported her spine. The rod enabled her to stand but prevented her either curving her spine or jumping. When lifted, she felt awkward, anxious and 'out of her element', yet like everyone else in the company she wanted to experience that glorious liberation from gravity we feel when someone fully takes our weight. The question was how to find a way of doing this that didn't deprive her of her sense of dignity; in other words, a lift that would allow her to feel fully human and not like an object being picked up and moved about in space.

We went back to basics, to the belief that meaningful movement comes from, and is not imposed on, the individual. Even though she was unable to jump more than an inch, I asked her to imagine (not jumping) but taking an elongated stride, a leap unbound by gravity, a leap of the imagination. With my arm supporting her around the waist, I then followed her 'intended pathway' allowing her to move as she might for example if she were dancing in water. This small lift fulfilled her intention. By this, I mean it accomplished the act that was being prepared for in her mind and in her muscles, but that was arrested by the rod in her back. The lift now seemed to have its very own particular kind of beauty; it was felt by her and by those watching as being 'just right'. It appealed to our common or shared sense of proportionality.

What became clear was that our earlier attempts had been imposed from the point of view of those lifting and had not arisen from dialogue or from an understanding of Els's unique situation. The feelings of unease came from the sense that the lifts were being 'done to her', they were inappropriate, or in other words, she could feel no ownership of them. There was no longer any need to fit Els into 'accepted models' of how high a lift should be. When lifted, Els remained close to the ground, but in understanding this relationship, a previously unexplored spectrum of movement became available to the group, particularly with the introduction of low-level lifts. The other dancers were drawn to work in new areas, and a whole new world of interactions opened up close to the floor, that had previously remained undetected.

Note

47 *An Egg is Enough*, Adam Benjamin and dancers. Produced by de Warande, Turnhout, Belgium, 1999.

7 The great mistake: response-ability and feedback

The man who makes no mistakes does not usually make anything.

(E.J. Phelps, 1899)

It couldn't be helped. Besides it was his step in the Dance. And yours.

(Alan Garner, 1996)

The danger of writing about improvisation is in becoming overconfident or overfamiliar with a particular 'technique' or approach, forgetting that the reason we improvise is precisely for those encounters with the unknown which challenge us to move and think in new ways. It is only the unexpected turn of events and the strange attraction of unpremeditated circumstances that actually bring improvisation to life and provide insights into new choreographic journeys.

Improvisation teaches us on a daily basis to readjust our perception of occurrences that we might ordinarily regard as mistakes or distractions. A performance I watched by Russell Maliphant at the Place in 1999, was hauntingly (and unexpectedly) accompanied throughout by a baby crying in the auditorium. It was an unplanned but beautiful soundscape, which Maliphant, an experienced improviser, seemed not only to accept but to use as part of the performance.

If some of the most exciting moments in improvisations arise from accidental occurrences or mistakes, how do we respond to a student who appears to 'foul up'? Returning to the notion of tension, if an improvisation is finely balanced and reaching some kind of climax when someone blunders in, I may feel irritated by the intrusion but there will be an instant just before my sense of irritation or disappointment takes over where the tension soars. As Keith Johnstone (1981) explains, the intrusion momentarily raises the stakes and for a split second offers the opportunity for a new and unexpected departure. As a performer, if I am to pick up on this new direction, I have to be able to let go of whatever it was I was expecting to happen and accept the new situation that is now building.

This acceptance of mistakes also has implications for how we teach improvisation. When giving feedback we can acknowledge when tension wanes or stagnates, but we can't blame dancers who make mistakes (although we can encourage them to recognise the quality and timing of their actions). When performing improvisation, I often use a three-part feedback to encourage self-criticism but at the same time keep the doorway open to accident and chance. I ask each performer (including any musicians, lighting operators, etc.) to recount:

1. One of their actions or decisions that they felt pleased with (that raised or sustained tension).
2. One of their actions or decisions that they felt unhappy with (that lowered tension).
3. One action or decision that someone else made that raised tension.

It is surprising how many of the best moments for other improvisers arise from what we consider our worse decisions. If, in our most enlightened moments, we can accept that a mistake is also a gift, then we only feel disappointment if the opportunity that it presented wasn't explored and the tension that arose from it was allowed to dissipate. It is the inability to respond to a mistake, not the mistake itself, that weakens us as performers and disappoints us as audience. This said, a student who constantly knowingly or unknowingly disrupts, and who has not yet learned how to build and sustain tension, needs guidance and tuition. (For more on feedback, see Chapter 8 in this volume.)

The ability to improvise is an important skill even for dancers performing set material. As anyone one who has spent time in the theatre will attest, the stage is a minefield of possible mishaps and upsets, and the dancer who can improvise calmly while under the spotlight can be a choreographer's saviour. In the midst of a production I was watching in France, the company were all gathering centre stage. Meanwhile upstage one of the cast had dislodged an enormous, inflated, inner tube which had been used in an earlier sequence and which now not only refused to go back in its frame, but seemed intent on bouncing downstage after her whenever she moved away. Of course everyone in the audience was now watching the real-life drama of the apparently amorous, bouncy tube and the actress. Had the company been improvisers their attention could have swung to focus on the inner tube which was so dramatically upstaging them.

Improvisation requires the flexibility to follow different initiatives by different dancers and teaches that anyone or anything (even a rubber tube with an overinflated libido) can instigate and lead the action. A car backfiring outside the theatre, a dancer stumbling on stage – all these things are possible sources of stimulation and interaction if the performer is relaxed and perceptive enough to draw on them. All too often the choreography becomes a secure track taking us from A to B until we become so fixed in our ways that we are no longer able to respond to changing circumstances.

Improvisation is one of the great levellers. In valuing mistakes and errors, any dancer, including a complete beginner, may become central to the action at any moment and discover that they are capable of providing the greatest of opportunities even when dancing with far more experienced performers. There is nothing better for the confidence of young improvisers than to be absorbed and incorporated into an improvisation in this way. The only way to teach this is to practice it, to dance with your students and be willing to transform their 'mistakes' while being forgiving of your own.

During the preparations for an improvised performance in Turnhout, Belgium, I had persuaded Ellen Vermander (then a relative newcomer to dance), to use her manual chair rather than her powered chair. Although unable to control the movement of the manual chair, she was less physically restrained and was, I felt, able to draw on a greater range of interactions with the other dancers. In one of the first improvisations I watched forlorn as she sailed off into the wings, coming to rest among various debris for the set. I had forbidden the dancers to respond to each other in any obvious ways so there seemed nothing that anyone could do. For a while I looked on with a growing sense of 'sporting the dunce's hat', but then, out of the uneasy silence that had engulfed the stage, we heard a rhythmic tapping. Ellen had reached down and begun to 'play' one of the cardboard boxes at her feet. Soon it was Ellen using the amplified sound of the box who was conducting the entire improvisation. It was an entirely unforeseen and triumphant turnabout of events. Had we rushed over and pulled Ellen back on stage she could never have exercised her ingenuity and we could have been left with the feeling that we had to 'look after' her. In fact even *in extremis* she was able to pull something out of the hat, so proving her own resourcefulness in the face of my apparent blunder. If you're going to make a mistake, make it a mighty red-nosed, loud fart, colossus of a mistake: there can be no greater gift to those with whom you improvise! Remember, that the aim of study and practice is not to rule out error but to refine our ability to engage and dance with it.

Experiences such as these can unnervingly undermine any sense of certainty about what is actually taking place at any time in an improvisation. In group improvisations many possible lines of exploration can run concurrently, and anyone can be drawn into focus by the attention and choices of the dancers. As adults, we spend most of our lives suspended in the midst of countless insoluble questions (What is infinity? What happens when we die? Why does my e-mail not receive TIFF?), all of which we ignore on a daily basis. Yet, instead of acknowledging these questions, most formal education teaches us quite simply to disregard them. This does not provide a particularly promising start when it comes to learning how to deal with the unpredictability and uncertainty of life, and it is just this that jumps up and playfully smacks us in the face when we begin to improvise. This is another way of saying improv is going to confront us with problems, and that is perfectly OK. Indeed it is a central part of our subject. This doesn't mean that improvising can't be lyrical, relaxing and harmonious; many of the exercises in Part Two are designed to be just that and they are a good place to start, but they are part of a wider subject that includes problem-solving, and paradox. It is the ability to live with uncertainty and the awkwardness of not knowing that allows access to our creativity. Improv is a return to the experience that city life and adult life attempts to inure us to, the world of the unexpected; a rediscovery of what it means to be surprised and awed, fantastic and fallible. See also Chapter 10 in this volume.

8   Tension seekers: a poet/hunter's guide to improvisation

This suspense is terrible. I hope it will last.

(Oscar Wilde, 1889)

In first-time groups I have seen wheelchair users and other dancers arrange themselves on separate sides of the studio like two completely different species, the as-yet-unanswered questions hanging thick in the air . . . the tension is almost palpable.

In our modern world, tension is something we tend to regard as related to stress; something to be avoided or released. Despite the emphasis on relaxed and natural movement in this book and within new dance generally, I would like to go some way to rehabilitate tension as a valuable if not essential part of understanding and teaching improvisation and choreography. Miss Li, with whom I studied Tai Chi in the 1980s, used to talk about the women from her childhood in China, who drew silk by hand from the silk cocoons: 'Too fast and the thread would break, too slow and the thread would sag – and break.' She explained there was an exact degree of tension which if maintained would produce the perfect silk thread (and the perfect Tai chi form). This ability to gauge tension is also vital in the art of improvisation and choreography.

We interpret dance on many levels: use of space, style, technique, timing; but behind all of these is our reading of dancers' 'presence', and the degree to which they share and sustain tension with others. Tension not in the sense of discomfort or anxiety, nor in the sense of a strained theatricality, but in the sense of how effectively and skilfully they draw and sustain our **at**-tension. Reading tension is a thing we are all well versed in. It is the means by which we make sense of our everyday interactions, the invisible thread which holds us to the world, and through which we express our connection to each other. The attention given to us as children encourages our curiosity and our ability to establish relationships with other people and the world around us. Deprived of this essential human connection, infants recoil from contact or react violently against it. It is the absence of attention that makes the images of starving street children so searing and at the same time illuminates the fragile, and often unnoticed, threads that sustain us emotionally as human beings.

I use the term 'tension' in the dance space rather than energy, when referring to how a dancer connects. I am interested in the relationship between the performers and between the performers and audience. I want to know which actions hold our interest. How the dancers' **in**tention catches my **at**tention. The Latin root of these words refers to 'holding' (*tenere*) and the word tension itself implies relationship (*tendere*) – something which is held and stretched **between two points**, like the strand of silk pulled from the cocoon.

Tension is something we all feel with different degrees of intensity and the capacity to monitor our internal sense of tension can be used when we improvise, rather like an internal barometer that alerts us to new and interesting weather systems; the chances of a storm or the likelihood of a break in the clouds. It is the ability to sense these subtle changes that allow dancers to enter new and unexpected territories. It is a sensibility not unlike that of the hunter; when others pass by an event or a location, the 'tuned in' dancer feels 'strangely attracted'[48] as if sensing something in the air. Nothing that can be necessarily explained in words but a response to an inner feeling, a subtle rising of curiosity and intuition.

Gerard Manley Hopkins[49] (1844–89) coined the word 'instress' to describe this feeling of heightened awareness, a word which clearly conveys a sense of internal tension. As a poet, Hopkins could be captivated by the outline of an old tree against the sky or by the irregular shape of a cloud. In his nature poems he returned again and again to the idea that beauty lay hidden in the most unlikely of objects, not just those that fitted the classical mould. Although he wasn't dealing with dancers, he professed an interest with 'all things counter, original, spare, strange', which, as it happens, is a fair description of an inclusive class (Hopkins, 1963: 127). Hopkins invented another word, inscape – to describe the hidden inner world of beauty captured within an object, expressing both its unity with nature and its unique individuality; in particular he used inscape to describe the beauty that seems to escape or shine out from an object, capturing the heart and soul of the observer.

> I saw the inscape though freshly, as if my eyes were still growing, though with a companion the eye and the ear are for the most part shut and instress cannot come.
>
> (Hopkins, 1963: xxi)

Hopkins's attraction to what was strange and unexpected in nature meant he was often drawn to what others passed by. Almost with a sense of exasperation, he wrote 'How near at hand it was if they had eyes to see it' (Hopkins, 1963). Sentiments not wholly unfamiliar to those who teach improvisation as they watch their students pass or disturb situations bursting with creative potential.

Perhaps Hopkins's reflections and concerns with instress can help us to understand this a little better. It is clear that instress for Hopkins combines 'seeing' with 'being seen', a kind of two-way experience in which we reveal something of ourselves in the act of seeing the world more clearly. When students in the dance studio find themselves in that intimidating position in which every action and (it may feel) every thought appears visible to those watching, it can be a disconcerting experience. They may need help to recognise the importance of such moments and be encouraged gently in future improvisations to stay longer with this new and unsettling experience. Some students may try to avoid these moments because they don't want to feel that they are 'showing off', and it is not unusual to hear students say that they thought they were getting in the way of something 'more important'. In other words, that they couldn't imagine that anything so significant could be to do with them! A rough guide, however, is, if you can feel tension rising, then it is to do with you!

On the other hand there are those who suffer from what might be described as 'performance compulsion', who might be described as attention seekers rather than tension seekers. These students, often products of dance school training, will launch into their 'improvisation routine' at the slightest provocation (being in the studio is usually sufficient) and proceed to perform, seemingly oblivious to everything and everyone around them. These are students who show everything but reveal nothing. In stark contrast, the art of improvising relies on an ability to 'listen' and respond authentically in the moment to what is taking place. In improvising, as in so many areas of life, 'less' is very often more.

During an improvisation with the de Warande group in Belgium, Els Willekens had found a spot on stage, where she stood radiating energy that seemed to fill the theatre. Johnny Schoofs approached her but she continued to stand and stare at the audience. There seemed nothing to add to what she was doing and everyone was thinking 'Don't interfere Johnny! It's already working, she's already there!' Johnny stood close by her watching, then reached out very carefully and minutely adjusted her necklace which must have become twisted earlier in the improvisation, and walked away. The tension again soared. It was a moment in which both dancers realised 'less was more'. Els by simply standing and Johnny, whose unexpected response told us he shared what we were feeling, that in effect, there was nothing to add, but also that he wasn't about to be blocked by it. Johnny's action took us a little further along the vein of exploration, the particular landscape that Els had already ventured into. Hopkins might have said that they managed to share the instress.

Moments of tension emerge spontaneously when people improvise, but we can help dancers sniff them out by directing their awareness to what they feel and sense. There is no way of knowing how these moments will be resolved, whether with humour, action, words, laughter or even tears, but there is at least a way that we can begin to alert students to their presence and this can begin in the studio in any sharing or observation periods. See **crossing the line** (Improv 16, Ch. 19) for further discussion and practical work.

Notes

48 Strange attractors: term taken from chaos theory, referring to the ordering and shaping of apparently random events.
49 Hopkins's poetry influenced the British choreographer Richard Alston. Hopkins's poem *The Windhover* gave rise to the name of Strider, which later became *Second Stride*.

9 Tension as a guide to feedback

When the movement was simple and inevitable, not to be changed no matter how limited or partial, it became what I called 'authentic' – it could be recognised as genuine, belonging to that person.

(Mary Starks Whitehouse)

Uncertainty and confusion can on occasion threaten to overwhelm those new to improvising. Feedback is one way of helping to make sense of this new experience. Telling each other about striking and beautiful moments at the end of a session can be a source of encouragement, assuring dancers that they were contributing to something that communicated powerfully to those watching. It can also provide an important means by which we can learn to remember and describe movement details. Feedback doesn't always, however, help us to understand how or why particular moments worked while other moments were less interesting, and it is just this that we need to understand both as improvisers and as choreographers.

Discussions that follow improvisations are a bit like someone who responds to a question about a new car in the following way:

'Oh it's fantastic . . . it's, it's yellow!'
'Yes, tell me more.'
'Well it's citron, more canary really, bright, beautiful, you'd love it!'
'Yes. What condition is it in?
'Oh, brilliant, highly reflective, beautifully polished . . . really, well really yellow!'

What the questioner really wants to know is what particular features the car possesses, how effective its brakes, acceleration, etc. are. Much feedback in improvisation, however, remains decidedly within the 'yellow category'.

Noticing and remembering our own sense of tension as we watch others dancing is one way of providing more useful and constructive feedback. Rather than describing or interpreting what you have seen during an improvisation, try to identify particular moments when you personally felt tension rise, drop or remain constant. For example, 'When you approached Rina I felt tension rising. When you moved past her I felt the energy drop. Did you experience anything similar?' This is a bit like learning to listen to the shifting gears in a car and understanding how the engine is functioning.

Were we studying choreography, we might explore further by saying 'this made sense to me, lets try and repeat what happened but maybe you could try staying closer and see if you feel more'.

Another example might be: 'When the three of you all stayed together without moving I felt that tension was sustained. When Noa left, I felt it dropped, rose again while she looked away, then soared when you all looked at each other. What was your experience?'

As a choreographer, you might say something like: 'Noa, let's try that again but can you wait a bit longer before you look back? See if you can feel any difference.'

This kind of feedback gives dancers detailed and useful information about how you experience their actions in space and time, and, for those interested in choreography, it provides a means of recreating and restructuring material after improvising. It is not unusual for new students to be surprised that their actions were contributing to a heightened sense of tension and this kind of feedback may help them to develop a nose for it in the future. Others may come to realise that 'overdoing it' in an improvisation may drain interest and tension and that increased activity does not always increase tension.

Improvisation is about developing individual sensibility. We can never assume that everyone's experience is comparable. For this reason, whenever dancers are providing feedback to one another I encourage everyone to talk in the first person. The statement 'I felt that tension rose when Mark moved forward', acknowledges the subjective perspective of the speaker. Whereas the statement 'tension rises when you move forward' assumes a final word on what can and can't happen within an improvisation, and is a recipe for dull puddings. What is experienced as powerful and new in one improvisation can seem stale and second-hand if repeated in the next, and then unaccountably fresh and funny if repeated a third time. There are simply no guarantees, and no short-cuts. As a teacher you can ask simply: 'Which of your decisions/choices did you feel increased tension, decreased tension or sustained tension?' And continue to encourage dancers to be aware of what they are feeling and when they are feeling it.

In more advanced or confident and supportive groups, you can ask those watching to identify moments when tension fell. Remember that a decision that lowers tension is always **necessarily** an opportunity for someone else to raise it. Saying that someone allowed tension to fall should not be used as a rod for their back but as an opportunity or a new direction to be offered to the group. More experienced dancers will begin to sense these shifts and begin to understand and acknowledge where and when they have lost tension – developing this sensibility is one way of making sense of improv. This is an approach to aesthetics grounded in everyday feelings which students are usually quick to recognise and respond to.

In **crossing the line** (Improv 16, Ch. 19) for example, a timid dancer who hugs the walls and tries always to slide out of the edges of the improvisation is in need of feedback as is the overactive dancer who always exits with a flourish, centre stage. As we have already seen, tension is not reliant merely on action but on the timing and phrasing of that action. Once timing is understood, then creeping out trying not to be seen can be an effective strategy for raising tension, **if** it is done when it is visible instead of when lots of other things are going on. Similarly, when a dancer understands the power of being positioned centre stage they will realise that they don't have to **do** so much in order to make a significant contribution.

There will be periods in improvisations when tension seems neither to rise nor fall. No particularly significant events appear to be taking place and yet interest between dancers, and between dancers and watchers, appears to be sustained; using the silk analogy, 'the thread neither sags not breaks'. The French have a word for this passage of time – *latence*, similar though more eloquent than our word latency. This kind of waiting is radically different from those moments where energy is being lost or dissipated. The latter are characterised by a lack of attention (of reaching towards, applying the mind), an absence of focus on the part of those dancing and a degree of boredom and restlessness in those watching. This kind of mental inertia is the equivalent to the land Norton Juster described in the children's book *The Phantom Tollbooth*: 'The Doldrums, my young friend, are where nothing ever changes and nothing ever happens' (1962: 20).

These periods are of interest only in as much as they **may** lead into chance encounters and new interactions, but otherwise students need to be able to recognise and find ways out of these cul-de-sacs before they begin feeling that this is what improv is about. Improv teachers, rather like seismologists, need to be able to distinguish between that which is latent and that which is dormant!

When tension leads to fracture

Although much choreography is created to play with high levels of tension, there is a difference between skilful high-speed action and recklessness. One evening I watched with an increasing sense of anxiety, as a dancer seemed to be overexerting his energy – shortly afterwards we discovered that he had seriously injured a colleague in one of the more dramatic sequences. These situations (and feelings) may also occur when teaching improvisation. Tension may be high but beyond levels of control or safety. In moments such as these, you may need to guide dancers back to basic principles, recap ground rules and set tasks which focus on spatial awareness, timing and listening skills.[50]

With experience, you may also want to try to deal with these situations by dancing them into a different conclusion: to sense a potentially dangerous situation and to diffuse it through taking the improvisation somewhere else. This may mean simply entering the improv and lying down peacefully on the floor – the solutions to such problems are not always obvious. Alternatively, as the teacher you can feed in new directions verbally, suggesting the group explore a different dynamic. There may be days, however, when you just need to call a halt gently and encourage students to talk about how they were experiencing the improvisation, so allowing overactive students to receive feedback from their peers and, when necessary, suggest alternative strategies (see **Gateway** and **Gauntlet** in Chapter 26 for exercises that deal with risk and speed). It is important to stress to 'fast movers' that high energy is a vital part of dance but that their individual task is to find when and where such activity is appropriate, so that it can energise, rather than intimidate.

At the end of a session, I often ask dancers to think of their strongest, or most positive impression and to share it with the rest of the class. I ask them not to generalise but to briefly name specific events and the people they noticed. This may mean that not everyone gets mentioned, (though it is surprising how inclusive this practice can be). What is important is that dancers:

1   get used to giving positive feedback directly to one another without embarrassment;
2   discipline themselves to look for positive elements even when improvs aren't going 'well';
3   develop the habit of remembering and retaining concise movement details when dancing and watching.

This learning is an important part of the discipline of improvisation. I have, however, heard improv teachers actively discouraging feedback and discussion as though talking about the work dilutes it and dissipates energy, using the phrase 'Don't blow it off!' This is a reflection perhaps of their own reluctance to address teaching or leadership issues or to help make sense of the theoretical as well as the practical side of improv.

There are plenty enough mysteries in the world and in dance for us to apply ourselves seriously to understanding all we can about our subject. There will always be more to astonish us without our needing to dull or cloak our critical abilities! Being able to recognise and retain movement is an important skill which can be practised in feedback sessions; it is also another way of encouraging dancers to become more aware of what is taking place around them. Once this ability to notice and remember events is developed, it can be drawn on while improvising. Borrowing and reintroducing movement material, echoing and developing it through the course of an improvisation is one way of adding texture and depth to improvisations and giving coherent structure to choreographed work, either of which may run the risk of becoming rambling, linear and incoherent. Improv doesn't require us to derive new material constantly, but to time and place material, both new and old, with ingenuity, precision and spontaneity.[51]

If a student is stuck for something to say in feedback, ask the student to look at the faces of the dancers in the group and see if this jogs his or her memory or ask him or her if, in a week's or a year's time, he or she were to think of the session, what picture would come to mind, who would be in it, and why? It can be validating for dancers at all levels to receive good feedback and I usually include myself in these sessions giving and receiving feedback whenever I dance or teach.

Notes

50 For an excellent and comprehensive account of how to deal with wayward improvisers, see Bloom and Chaplin, 1988.
51 A useful way of remembering movement while watching an improvisation is mentally to place the movement in the corresponding part of your own body, so that you can retrieve it later in feedback sessions.

10 Demons and dragons: some thoughts on becoming blocked in improvisation

There is no need for arms or physical violence, material constraints. Just a gaze, an inspecting gaze, a gaze which each individual under its weight will end up interiorising to the point that he is his own overseer, each individual thus exercising this surveillance over and against himself.

(Michael Foucault, 1980)

The only thing we have to fear is fear itself.

(Franklin D. Roosevelt, 1933)

The student hesitates not because he doesn't have an idea, but to conceal the inappropriate ones that arrive uninvited.

(Keith Johnstone, 1981)

It is not uncommon in the midst of an improvisation to feel suddenly and inconsolably stuck, unable to see a way forward (backwards, sideways?), to find oneself wishing to be anywhere but where you are at that particular moment in time. These 'blocks' to our creativity often conceal feelings that we may initially be reluctant to expose. They may arise from impatience with other dancers, irritation, anxiety or embarrassment. Not knowing what to do with such antisocial or difficult feelings, we deny them, and in the same instant find ourselves removed from what we genuinely feel. This act of denial, or refusal to accept our own creative, lively responses effectively closes the door on our imagination.

This kind of creative 'shutdown' can take hold of even the most experienced improvisers. It is as though we are caught in the gaze of some personal demon and are left flailing, grasping at anything that will hold meaning, while everything around us turns to dust. It is usually at this point that dancers 'dry up' and withdraw from improvisations. Similar feelings may also prevent us entering an improvisation, casting us in the position of frustrated observer or critical onlooker. Anything that can chase us from the dance space, or cause us to stall in such a way should excite our curiosity and attention. In loosely structured improvisations, dancers can simply withdraw and rejoin the comparative safety of those watching, returning when they feel more inspired. As already discussed, this openness is what makes improvisation so accessible, but when it comes to learning about performance skills, it can also allow us to walk away too freely when things get difficult. It is in that respect a mixed blessing.

Finding oneself creatively blocked always involves a feeling, even if that feeling is difficult to identify or accept. The problem is that the feelings that deprive us of our creativity seem to be the ones we rarely acknowledge and we are therefore even less likely to want to engage with them in front of other people. These moments of embarrassment, humiliation or anger leave us nowhere to go but behind our everyday pose, behind our social face and inwards towards those parts of ourselves of which we are less certain. Dancers who are able to stay present at these moments and resist the urge to flee, find themselves at the heavily guarded doorway to the unconscious, the threshold of what separates the known from the unknown self. Ironically, it is just here that most improvisations (and improvisers) run aground. Joan Chodorow recounts such an experience in her first class with Trudi Schoop in 1956.

> When it was my turn, I felt a moment of panic – and then hurled myself into space . . . I was shocked, almost numb. I had a terrible feeling that somehow my ultimate shadow had emerged and I hadn't seen it, but everyone else had. I felt embarrassed and awkward, but didn't want anyone to know how bad I felt. So I just kept going in the same direction, around the piano, up the steps and into the dressing room. I pulled on some street clothes over my leotards and left. It took five years of growing up before I felt ready to come back and study with Trudi Schoop.
>
> (Chodorow, 1991: 19)

Chodorow describes being chased from the space by her own particular demon. Confronting our own fears is a process that cannot be rushed or forced, but that each of us must come to in our own time. In a supportive group, with encouragement and humour, this shadowy terrain is ours to explore.

A dancer I worked with in Holland faced with **traverse** (Improv 29, Chapter 21) dropped her head and wheeled at top speed across the studio, pounding into the wall on the far side. This created a huge gap between herself and the one dancer who had come out to dance with her (and another who was still in the process of getting up to join them). She later said she had felt isolated while waiting to start, and had sped across the studio to escape the feeling. In fact had she stayed with the feeling of 'isolation' she would have also remained physically close to the first dancer, and given the second enough time to join them . . . fleeing the feeling was what left her isolated; had she stayed physically present a different situation was potentially in the offing.

Behind every 'block' is a buried or unacknowledged emotion, and every e-**motion** carries motion within it. Interestingly, when we see someone getting blocked in an improvisation it is often very easy from the outside to see that there are countless possibilities available, which the dancer seems somehow unable to notice or make use of. Accessing this movement may mean that we have to accept those parts of ourselves we would normally not want seen – not an easy demand for contemporary dancers who are often trained to remain passive and inexpressive. Dancers getting into deep water and beginning to flail need encouragement and positive feedback. Remember: it's OK to flail.

When we retreat in panic and confusion, or appear gripped and unable to move or think, it is as if we are interpreting these blocks as demons. We credit them with the power to outwit and defeat us. Perhaps we can think of these problematic encounters less as demons and more as dragons. Like demons, dragons may initially scare us but they have different origins and suggest different futures; dragons are associated in myth as guides on adventures into the unknown and, like the emotions or thoughts behind our blocks, they hate being seen (otherwise we'd bump into them every day). If we can begin to acknowledge that improvising often means coexisting with difficult feelings, if we can begin to train ourselves to stay instead of fleeing, then we can begin to deepen our practice and tap into rich areas of hidden potential. So how do we go about spotting dragons?

The use of a clearly defined entrance and exit for the improvisation represented by a line as in **crossing the line** (see Chapter 19) gives us time to reflect on our departure, for this journey out of the dance space is now also a journey 'towards'. Like children seeking the comfort and assurances of home, we travel back towards those watching, only to find ourselves caught astride a paradox. The cost of comfort means giving up the adventure.

This creation of a boundary adds an 'edge' that may be missing in looser improvisational structures. No one is ever forced into the dance space nor forced to stay in it. Students can, however, be encouraged gently to recognise moments of building tension and how they approach and move away from these situations both by developing their own awareness of breathing and tension, and through supportive feedback from the group.

Returning to the original example above, if we are more patient, if we stay a while longer in the space, perhaps we can catch a glimpse of the feeling behind that block. If we can acknowledge the feeling (despair, embarrassment, foolishness), then we can also begin to embody it, to create a form which the feeling can inhabit, and so feel what we had, crumbling like dust between our fingers, and watch it fall to be borne away across the studio on an imaginary breeze. We become the lost soul, the dying man or the fool trying to gather together broken fragments; the imagination is once again active and alive and carries us into dialogue with a new, less familiar part of our self. In the same way, the momentary flash of a clenched fist is enough to embody a feeling of anger that has arisen and led us into new movement range, or the embarrassed covering of eyes at an unintentional moment of contact can acknowledge embarrassment and, instead of freezing us, lead to a dance of awkwardness. What we feel to be our worst moments in improvising are often no more than the tell-tale signs that we are within a hair's breadth of our very best.

Welcoming those moments when we 'fail' and 'err' is vital if we are to be able to survive and enjoy the unpredictable environment of dance improvisation. The feeling of being stuck or blocked is just another image waiting to reveal itself. This does not mean that we need to lose ourselves in full-scale emoting, but implies the beginning of a dialogue between the known self and the unknown self. The awakening of tension between where I am and where I might be, but don't yet know.

As a final thought, it is worth remembering that dance is an art and is therefore deeply concerned with our internal world of images. When we attempt to make dance more accessible by using terms like dance-sport, which, particularly in the UK, allies dance with physical education, we may lose more than we gain; dragons as far as I know, don't wear Nike.[52]

Note

52 See also **Soloing** in Chapter 22.

11 Is it therapy?

> Once again we have to be 'made better' in order to paint a picture, dance or take part in drama, and once again this is an area where control of our participation lies with non-disabled people.
>
> (Donal Toolan, 1994)

> It was very important for me to learn that I had something to give to the world instead of receiving all the time. That was for me the big revelation when I started dancing.
>
> (Petra Zingel, 2000)[53]

It is not unusual to hear a non-disabled assistant in a workshop saying 'Oh I'm not here to dance, I've just come to help.' Such offers are always appreciated around issues of organisation, transport, etc., but within the studio itself, everyone must be present in his or her own right as a dancer. Those unwilling or unable to make that transition need to be asked kindly to leave or to sit out and watch. Helpers wishing to 'assist' but not participate take us back to the Greek origins of the word therapy, to minister to or to be in attendance, and will skew the work of the group by obscuring the problems that should be engaging the imaginations of the dancers themselves.

Working with 'helpers' may constitute an important part of an individual's journey towards participating as an equal at a later stage of his or her studies or career, but groups organised in this way will often attract or be initiated by those whose main area of interest is 'people with special needs', who are in all likelihood not disabled and who may well instil a caring/therapeutic ideology rather than a challenging/problem-solving one. When this happens, the time needed to develop new shared approaches to dance and to recognise the particular creativity synergy of the differing individuals within the group may be subsumed by the need to 'keep everyone involved' or to 'look after people'. The widening gap that opens between disabled and non-disabled participants is obscured beneath a cloak of good intentions. Groups such as these may do very good work but will invariably fail to attract independent disabled people as participants. It is important to distinguish when dance is being used by non-disabled people to bring disabled people together and provide them with an experience of the arts and, in contrast, when disabled and non-disabled people are meeting of their own accord to improvise or perform together. The former is quasi-therapeutic, the latter determinedly anti-therapeutic.

This said, there is no doubt that dancing makes us feel more alive, and that all of us who dance experience the benefits ourselves and have seen them in those we dance with.

Dancing is the only way that helps me to accept my body as it is. When I'm dancing I feel different (it's true that sometimes I'm jealous because I can't jump or lift) but at the same time I can explore my personal abilities, and see that there are equal or extraordinary movements that make me proud of who I am and what I can do. It is very difficult to explain this paradoxical limited experience, which coexists with longing and happiness.

(Judith Bayha, from correspondence with author)

Whether improvisers or repertory dancers, we dance to feel better and to better feel the world around us. Clearly, dance has what could be called a therapeutic effect on us, yet those of us who teach inclusive groups are not 'therapists' and those dancing in such groups do not consider themselves 'in therapy'. The determination of many people involved in dance and disability, to distance themselves from all things therapeutic arises from a number of sources:

- The recent use of dance in the West as a therapeutic medium associated with the medical model of disability – a model which considers disabled people to be in need of 'treatment' as though they are necessarily ill and need help, rather than simply being different.
- The relatively few disabled people who have graduated from dance therapy courses, making them another category of those 'treated' rather than of those participating.
- The frequent media portrayal and interpretation of inclusive dance companies as being about disabled people being helped to dance **by** non-disabled people, rather than as an exchange of equals.
- The bulk of disability-related dance books that are either therapy based or refer to 'working with handicapped people', 'special communities' or 'special popula- tions' and the absence of books in which disabled and non-disabled are viewed as equal partners in the dance process.
- The historical absence or invisibility of disabled people within mainstream dance.
- The continued lack of provision for disabled people in performing-arts training.
- The frequent unintentional or intentional inclusion of people with physical dis- abilities in activities aimed primarily at those with learning difficulties as though having a physical disability necessarily implies having a learning difficulty.

Given all of the above, one begins to see why inclusive companies repeatedly stress their distance from the world of therapy and emphasise what they have in common with other new-dance companies, notably in the way that they create work. Although it is easy to see why this position has been taken, it leads us towards something of a paradox. The integration of body and mind, which is a key component in the movement therapies, also remains central to the practice of many new-dance techniques including contact improvisation and skinner release, and these techniques which readily acknow- ledge their debt to the healing arts continue to play a major role in companies as diverse as DV8 and Siobhan Davies Dance Company. In addition, the world of professional dance is concerned increasingly with issues of health and sustainability as both dancers and choreographers become more informed of good practice relating to the body.

This complex relationship between the arts and healing is what attracts many non-professionals into the world of movement but it is also evident when we make choreographed work for the stage. Few choreographers or directors know in detail the exact movements they will use before getting into the studio to begin what is usually a collaborative process with their dancers. This often means that a very experimental or creative phase is followed by a period of structuring, which, in turn, is followed by a phase in which the material is refined and set for the stage.

Starting points for new work can come from a huge variety of sources: a piece of music, a personal story, a political or economic injustice, a poem, image or may simply be derived from movement itself. Whatever the origin, improvising invariably plays a key role in exploring and developing the initial idea. In the first phase of making, the choreographer may introduce a theme or task and then watch to see how the dancers interpret and respond. The dancers may then be encouraged to go further into themselves, to take new risks and to make discoveries that allow them to approach the work with fresh eyes. Working with a new choreographer may allow dancers to experience a different perspective, a different way of looking at the world. In the best of projects, the choreographer may play a pedagogic, at times even shamanistic role, as the dancers move beyond their habitual patterns of movement and expression, emerging from the process with a new perspective both on performance and on themselves. The experience clearly has what might be termed a therapeutic effect, extending physical ability and improving self-esteem and confidence. It may have a great deal in common with therapeutic/experiential work even though it takes place within the context of making professional dance. (It may also in the wrong hands have the opposite effect, confirming stereotypes and damaging self-esteem.)

Yet throughout this process the choreographer (and the performer) have kept an eye on the final product. As material is produced and gathered, the choreographer may take a more directorial role as she shapes and refines, cuts and edits movement to her own design. So while guiding, nurturing and often pushing the dancers to produce, she never loses sight of the goal to be achieved. At some point, the process has to transform into a cohesive and meaningful production and the dancers must begin to deal with a different set of requirements centred around the discipline of performance. This will include precision, timing, reliability, stamina, stage craft and the maturity to accept criticism and directorial decisions without complaint, even when material is cut or altered. The degree of creativity v. productivity will vary enormously depending on the choreographer, but the best of productions involve something of both these kinds of experience.

If we accept that new dance has drawn heavily on ideologies of the human potential movement, inclusive groups may be in danger of throwing the baby out with the bathwater when they push too hard to disassociate themselves entirely from these roots and present themselves as gymnastic and purely physical exponents of dance. It is worth bearing in mind that it was the breadth of improvisational work, and its openness to a whole range of human experience, that opened the doorway to current inclusive practices. Although the professional work of companies like CandoCo and Axis is clearly not of a therapeutic nature, the power of the work and its ability to integrate the public mind (of the audience) and the personal body (of the performer) allows a subtle form of healing to take place on a societal level. It is this adjustment of perception and surmounting of prejudice that might well be regarded as the soul of integrated practice.

It is only when dance begins to be something done **for** disabled people **by** non-disabled that the association with the old medical model reoccurs. Dance can be a healing experience for anyone who enters the studio. It is an activity that encourages us to learn, to grow and to surpass our limits – it does not, however, make those of us who teach into therapists, nor our students into clients.

Tears and fears

> Until the age of ten, my handicap was a real torment. The greater part of my time was taken up with reeducation. Stretching and exercise was the order of the day. At this age, I walked but fell over frequently. To prevent hurting myself too much, my physiotherapist taught me to fall. Obviously learning to fall hurt too, but my physio explained that this was for my own benefit. Hurting myself for my own well being was I confess a procedure that, at the time, escaped me.
>
> (Jacques Manceron, a workshop participant in Lyon and French horse-riding champion, from correspondence with the author)

Unlike Jacques Manceron, many disabled people growing up in physically protective environments have rarely experienced the feeling of falling or travelling at speed without associating it with great danger. It is worth remembering how often infants cry as they learn to walk and run – the tears are a part of that process. Those who have missed out on this experience may have a lower fear/tear threshold than those of us who have been thrown about and repeatedly bounced on our heads as children.

During the rehearsals for *Brooding Angels*,[54] Margit (who uses a wheelchair) had asked to work on the floor. In the midst of the improvisation that followed she could be heard sobbing loudly. The dancing stopped of its own accord and I went over and asked her if she had been hurt. She answered that she was fine, but finding herself unable to roll, she had become frightened by the proximity and speed of passing wheelchairs. (To get some idea of what she was feeling, lie on the floor and have someone come at you fast in a wheelchair.) She apologised for interrupting the session and assured me that she wanted to be on the floor, it was just that she wasn't used to the experience and couldn't prevent herself from crying. Assured that she wasn't in pain or any longer in distress I asked David Toole who was part of the teaching team to come over to where Margit was lying. Having followed what was going on, David obliged at some speed skidding his chair to a halt and then with a delightfully evil look in his eye proceeded to circle closely round her. This elicited a roar of laughter and more tears and I encouraged him to continue gently dive-bombing. Margit, now safe in the knowledge that she was not going to be hurt, enjoyed the thrill of David's attacks as though on a fairground ride. The tears and laughter were her body's way of releasing her fear, and the presence of David's chair was a homeopathic dose that ensured she got over her anxiety. Had we reacted on sentiment and thrust Magrit back in her chair, we would have deprived her of the encounter with her fears that she needed to make in order to surpass them.

When such situations arise, your priority as teacher is first to establish quietly and without fuss whether anyone is injured. If someone falls, trips or collides it only takes the nearest dancer to ask 'Are you injured?' and, if there is no harm done, the accident can be accepted as a part of the improvisation and a starting point for new ideas and directions.

At another moment in the making of *Brooding Angels*, Judith Bayha, who walks with crutches, was practising a move that involved falling backwards to be caught, while raising her crutches above her head (the material attached to her crutches would open like wings as she fell). This process began on the ground but progressed to a chair and then a table. At this point Judith, suddenly and unexpectedly, started to cry. Standing up on the table she asked me to ignore her tears, and explained that she just needed to cry to get over the fear but she didn't want to stop until she had mastered the move. Later on, in the performance itself, she was able to fall backwards off a high plinth into pitch-black and be caught by two dancers standing beneath her.

As long as no one is forced or coerced into activities that they find frightening, tears need not necessarily be interpreted as a sign to stop an exercise or an improvisation. Students need to feel in control, and be able to stop if they need to, but similarly they should be given the space and time to continue, or be encouraged to return when ready.

Notes

53 Petra Zingel is the founder of FIDODA (Federation for the Integration of Disabled and Able-Bodied People); cited in the *Documentation for Freaks* in der Kunst Festival, organised by INTAKO June 2000, Austria.
54 HandiCapace Tanz Kompanie, 1997.

12 Special schools, special students and integrated practice

One day during conversation on the porch . . . a man appeared who sat down and joined in the talk for several hours before an attendant from a nearby mental hospital reclaimed him. Cunningham was delighted that the man had fitted in so well . . . 'We'd been getting along fine,' he told me, 'mad people don't have to be shut away' – their special perspective 'can contribute a great deal to society'.

(Quoted in Duberman, 1974: 279)

It is a very grave mistake to think that the enjoyment of seeing and searching can be promoted by means of coercion and a sense of duty.

(Albert Einstein)

Can the principles and exercises described in this book be applied when working with an established group with learning difficulties? The answer depends very much on the cooperation, understanding and support of those responsible.

In some special schools there is a subtle form of coercion that arises around dance activity. It is as though the desire or need to see everyone involved outweighs the importance of individual choice. My first task is to free staff from any tendencies to bully or cajole students and to get them dancing themselves. The task of prising someone from their perceived duty as a carer is one that must be approached with tact, diplomacy and humour. For some people, there are few safer places in the world than behind another person's wheelchair and it is not a position that is always given up lightly, especially if the alternative involves the prospect of dancing. The principle of choice always remains central even in situations that are themselves far from integrated. This means that when students don't want to join in an improvisation, then I respect their decision. I may ask whether they need some kind of assistance, but otherwise I will acknowledge their decision and allow them to sit out until they choose to participate. This has on occasion been interpreted as a lack of interest or patience on my part but it stems from the belief that no one can be forced to dance, and that if what I am doing is **really** interesting, then students will want to get involved, and if it isn't, then who am I to force them? One of the phrases I least like hearing in these settings is 'Come on, come and dance a little . . . just for me.' Students entering dance through interest and curiosity are never doing it 'for me'. On the contrary, they are self-motivated, and self-determining, and that is something that is worth waiting for. What makes this difficult is the pain we may feel when we see a young student who seems not to be succeeding, and the battle we must wage with our own discomfort and desire to help. As Emery Blackwell so eloquently put it: 'Everything in life costs a little pain. If you want really to help, let me experience my own pain my own way' (*Contact Quarterly* 17(1)).

Some special schools may be very close, and in some respects closed, communities and the idea of the head or senior teacher looking into a dance session to see a helper dancing while a student sits out may run contrary to the work ethic of the school. Helpers may actually feel their job is at risk if they are not seen to be actively 'doing something'. Dance teachers are also brought up 'to perform' while teaching, the idea of letting things take place in their own time without being in the driving seat may present untold anxieties for those who have been trained within the professional world of dance and who judge success by the number of steps learned.

Learning with difficulty

Nowhere is there greater need for clarity of mind and word than around students with learning difficulties. Yet, arguably, no group in dance (and in society) receives such inadequate provision and such paucity of thought. Students with learning difficulties test our ingenuity and our abilities as choreographers, teachers and improvisers to the extreme. There is probably no more testing, nor radical terrain in all of dance. But all too often, the dance that is offered in these settings is formalised and regimented, seeming to infantalise the dancers rather than empower them; the complexity and uniqueness of dancers' movement remains untapped, and a pastiche of modern dance or disco is preferred to the more difficult beauty inherent in difference.

Some youngsters with profound learning difficulties spend so much of their time in apparent stasis that any activity is thought to be of benefit. Involving everyone in an activity might on the surface appear to be integrative, but as carers manoeuvre pupils from place to place they inadvertently, or perhaps intentionally, remove the obstacles and difficulties the youngsters face, or deprive them of the time necessary to recognise and solve them. This kind of activity may actually be about reducing the levels of anxiety experienced by the staff, who seem to be wanting to say 'Look our students **can** do this!' Perhaps there is a fear that if the pupils don't 'succeed', the school will lose your input or that the students' unresponsiveness reflects on the efforts of the carers. Let the carers know that their presence and participation is valued; if you can get the helpers interested and engaged in improvising, then their students will follow! If the helpers are suspicious or hostile, then it is most likely that the students will also resist you, or be caught in the crossfire of conflicting loyalties.

When to say 'no'

Working on a large performance project in the north of England, I tried for several days to accommodate three young people with profound learning difficulties and behavioural problems (two with autism) who, through an administrative error, had been added to an already inclusive group at the last minute. All three were disorientated, confused and disruptive, and I eventually decided to take them out of the production.[55] At this point, two younger students with Down's syndrome who had until then remained subdued and timid, responded to the changed atmosphere and suddenly started to produce the most astonishing work, one going on to become a central performer in the piece. The additional time and attention enabled us to begin working with the Simpson Board and a stunning solo was choreographed by a profoundly physically disabled woman and danced by one of the undergraduate dancers. The other university students who had struggled valiantly up until that point were released from a quasi-therapeutic task, that they should not actually have been given, and responded with renewed energy and creativity. Had we continued to try to engage and direct the three youngsters, the resources of the group would have been exhausted fulfilling a caring role that was not an objective of the project.

It is not uncommon for dancers working in the community to spend hours on the phone explaining the need for a well-balanced group to a local organising body, only to arrive and find a large group of students with learning difficulties, one or two carers and perhaps a solitary, rather confused and very pissed-off, physically disabled participant. The explanation usually proffered is that no independent disabled people could be found and so the workshop was offered to the local 'day centre' at the last minute. This kind of substitution (as though all disabilities were somehow equivalent) still takes place on a regular basis. The assumption is that if a workshop is 'inclusive' and no physically disabled students can be found, then it is OK to make up the numbers with students with learning difficulties.

It has been in frustration with this kind of situation that the many of the 'integrated' companies now in existence have moved away from working with students who have learning difficulties, choosing instead to focus on raising standards and expectations for the physically disabled and non-disabled dancers. The irony of course is that given the right balance in a group, participants with learning difficulties are capable of bringing as much to dance as anyone else. We do not have to dig much further past most people's fears of physical difference to encounter an even deeper-seated fear. The fear of those who perceive and react to the world in ways that place them outside of the norm.

It is perhaps worth remembering that the phenomena of grouping people with Down's syndrome together, (no matter how sympathetic or enlightened that segregation may be) is still based on the medical model of disability. Though these groups may currently offer more to youngsters with learning difficulties than is available elsewhere, it may be worth the effort of trying to connect with individuals rather than simply opting to work with pre-existing groups when establishing new community workshops or performance projects if your intention is to pursue an integrated practice. This means devising application procedures so that people can be selected on the grounds of their suitability for the project, and the contribution they can make to the group as a whole, rather than on the grounds that they are already a member of a club or association. This does, however, involve considerable organisation and preplanning.

Companies like AMICI and Anjali in England, Theatre STAP in Belgium and Groupe Signe and Oiseau Mouche in France have established extraordinarily high levels of involvement and achievement for people with learning difficulties, creating unique performance opportunities and backing this up with training and teaching programmes. What concerns me is that groups with less enlightened leadership can become seen as the only option. When this happens young, potentially very capable, students who might be finding their way into mainstream colleges and activities can get grouped together with older members whose needs may be very different. In such cases, students risk being drawn into a pattern of dependency and institutionalisation from which it is hard to break free.

Even within large well-run groups, the organisational demands and the need to occupy and involve everyone may mean that there is insufficient time to recognise and respond to the very individual and specific needs. I was with Bill Robbins, a student with cerebral palsy, after a performance in London when someone turned to him and asked slowly and loudly 'And . . . Did . . . You . . . Enjoy . . . The . . . Show?' Bill's deadpan response was 'I am studying choreography at Roehampton University.' Even today, with all that we have learned, it is still too easy to confuse physical and sensory impairment with intellectual impairment. In the end every teacher must develop an understanding of how many people they can deal with, and how many students with learning difficulties they can comfortably accommodate within an inclusive workshop or performance setting, that is, one that is also aimed at challenging and stretching professional dancers and dance students. This is delicate ground and the spectre of political correctness sometimes looms so large that teachers seem unable to make rational decisions when trying to determine who can and can't participate in an activity.

Those of us attracted to this work often have a deep-seated desire to include people, and this can sometimes get in the way of our work as dance teachers or choreographers. In a short 'taster' workshop I led in the Midlands in the early 1990s, two students constantly interrupted and disturbed the introductions of the opening session, making it perfectly clear they they were out to cause trouble. In response I politely asked them to 'follow me', led them around the group, out of the door and downstairs to deposit them with the project organisers before returning to lead a very successful workshop with the physically disabled, blind and non-disabled participants. This was part of a day of disability dance with teachers from a variety of different dance styles leading short taster sessions. Later in the day when the other tutors heard that I had ejected the two troublemakers from my class there was a minor outcry. Their expectation was that, as one of the few tutors experienced in working with disabled students, I should have been able to find a way of working with the two saboteurs who had run amok in every other class. The two, incidentally, had Down's syndrome. Had they been hooligans of the common-or-garden variety, I have no doubt that they would have been ejected from **every** class that day. Instead the youngsters' behaviour was confused with their disability and as a result they were tolerated. In fact what they needed was to be treated normally and, for once in their lives – thrown out on their ear.

Disruptive students or those simply unable to engage with the objectives of a dance project need provision that is more therapeutic or remedial in nature (or they may need to be playing football or climbing mountains). We need to be able to recognise what we have to offer as dance teachers and acknowledge our own limitations rather than trying to be all things to all people. The alternative is that we lead a group who silently resent the constant interruptions, who thank us at the end of the class, politely wave goodbye and resolve to stay away from anything to do with disability and dance in the future.

Note

55 It did not necessarily mean that they were incapable of being involved in dance. Isabel Jones has pioneered methods of working creatively with students with autism – what is important is setting the context for a particular approach (see Jones, 1998) and Salamada Tandem (Appendix 1).

13 Lost narrative

Despite my personal reservations about placing students with learning difficulties together as though this will somehow improve their learning possibilities, I have often taught such groups, and am still asked for advice by young teachers faced with similar challenges. The exercises and improvisations in Part II have all been used successfully, sometimes with adaptions, with students with learning difficulties. I had been teaching for several years when I was fortunate enough to watch Isabel Jones spinning a web of improvised magic with a group in Scotland. I had never been so caught up in (and convinced by) an improvised dance experience aimed at young students with learning difficulties. So what was she doing, how was she doing it, and why do those trained as professional dancers find it on occasion so hard? Taking the last part of this question first, despite the inroads of physical theatre, contemporary dance training continues to deal confidently with abstraction, space, time and form but leaves most students virtually incapable of dealing with narrative and story. In that respect we remain very much Cunningham's children.

Create some abstract movement material, however, and the majority of students with learning difficulties (and the majority of the public) spontaneously create story-lines around what they see. They want to know why someone is doing something and who is doing what to whom.This way of perceiving human movement is exactly what Cunningham purposefully fractured in his experimentations with random positioning and chance events. Cunningham freed dance from a slavish adherence to emotional story but the aesthetic values he championed have influenced dance training to such a degree that, returning to work in the community, dancers often find themselves ill-equipped to converse with people whose primary interpretation of the world is through story. As Matthew Hawkins has pointed out from working with Anjali Dance Company, the Anjali dancers resist dance, or dance structures that are broken into component parts, and are most at home when dealing with whole concepts, be it in the rehearsal process or in their understanding of performance.[56]

Many dancers emerging from contemporary training will actually freeze if asked to tell a story, but it was clearly here that Isabel Jones seemed most at home. She was able to improvise a story drawing on the suggestions and actions of her students as she went along, so that every participant was able to contribute and understand the journey they were making, without any fear of 'getting it wrong'. It was an approach that I subsequently used in a variety of settings and later developed in different directions with the storyteller Danny Scheinmann in the Stare Cases Project (see **narrative traverse** in Chapter 21). As improvisers, this kind of experience is invaluable in teaching us to move from one idea to another with fluidity and a certain kind of mental 'grace'.

Improvising narratives liberates us from becoming fixed too rigidly to any one particular thematic line or outcome and teaches us to accept suggestions and new directions that are offered by those around us (see Johnstone, 1981).

With one school group, I had proposed a trip to 'anywhere in the world'. 'Disney World!' and 'India!' were offered and I opted for the latter (OK, no one is completely impartial). At one point in this adventure, as we made our way on a raft (everyone holding onto the two young students in wheelchairs) across a vast ocean (an adaption of **traverse** – see Chapter 21) we came across Barry, an autistic child, sitting alone in the middle of the studio. When I asked the group what he could be doing there, one of the group called out 'He's on an island!'. When I suggested that maybe we could all take a rest on Barry's island, he, uncharacteristically, allowed us to crowd around him (Barry would never have accepted an invitation to join such a group). At a later stage when we were all in an aeroplane that was looping the loop, Barry came over, never looking directly at us, and lingered 'Outside the windows', again he got caught up in the narrative – 'Barry's wing walking!' and for a moment he became the hero of the children's story. There was no attempt to force Barry into dance drama, because he would simply have screamed and recoiled, but the story that was being created was always able to accommodate his appearances. Barry was obviously aware that something interesting was happening and was able to gauge his own proximity and involvement. He was exercising his choice just as the others were. In this kind of inclusive setting there should be space for every student to engage at his or her own level and, like the best of children's stories, the work should be capable of being read and danced at many different levels simultaneously. There is no need for condescension if the group leaders are working at the very furthest reaches of their imaginations.

People with learning difficulties have unique perspectives and insights that can, on occasion, stop us in our tracks: towards the end of a hot and tiring day's teaching in France I asked one of the members of Groupe Signe rather tersely, whether or not he understood the object of the exercise we were doing. Philippe, who had Down's syndrome, responded 'I too have an object; it is fragile and easily broken.' Suddenly I was being told that my ideas and exercises did not give me the right to be short-tempered. In other words to treat someone's feelings as though they were 'an object'. One of the countless times I have been given cause to reflect on a 'teaching difficulty' by a student with a 'learning difficulty'. We are still far from a shared understanding of the role of those with learning difficulties in today's society, but the arts, and dance in particular, provide an environment where current prejudices might be undermined and new perspectives received and explored.

As teachers, it is important that we compose groups that allow us to work effectively, whether as a teacher or choreographer. We need to recognise also that not everyone is either at ease or effective when working with groups of students with learning difficulties. In my own work, I like to ensure that there is always a space for any student with a learning difficulty who has expressed an independent wish to be involved. There is still too much that I don't know to risk closing a door on new perspectives, new possibilities and new learning. (See Jones – Salamander Tandem, Appendix 1)

Note

55 From lecture demonstration at the South Bank, London 2000.

14 Access v. excellence

Many people would sooner die than think. In fact they do.

(Bertrand Russell)

Setting up

There is a widely held and largely erroneous belief that integration will somehow magically occur if the doors of the studio are thrown open and anyone and everyone is allowed to enter. Within any dance setting, the number of individuals participating will have an effect on the quality of teaching that takes place. Large groups may work well on occasion, under the eye of an experienced director/teacher, but initially it is probably better to start small and invest in the patient development of a committed core group. CandoCo, for example, emerged from a once-a-week class barely topping ten people for nearly a year. This unpressurised beginning allowed for the development of experience and skills among the dancers **and** teachers and, in particular, the development of a 'problem-solving' ethos, which would influence all that followed. Some of my most important lessons during this period came from two students, one disabled (Bindi Sharer) and one non-disabled (Victoria Jane Marks) who had grown up playing and dancing together. Their familiarity, ease and playfulness with each other was a constant source of information and inspiration as I found my way as a teacher in what was still relatively unexplored territory.

In groups that become too large too soon, there is a danger that the development of dance and performance skills (in other words the pursuit of excellence) may become outweighed by social or 'care' priorities. In these situations, if teachers are over-stretched, experimentation and risk-taking can begin to be interpreted as 'showing off' or 'attention seeking' – active and energetic students are discouraged rather than praised and either remain in the group as underachievers or leave to seek challenges elsewhere, for example in the field of sport, where a more positive approach to risk-taking is encouraged. Keeping a project small may prove hard for teachers and administrators, particularly when there is often a huge demand for work open to disabled people. At times saying 'no' may place you in just the position you set out to avoid: that of excluding a disabled student. But if you are to secure an environment in which creativity and experimentation can flourish, then this is a word that you might do well to practice. Defining the aims and objectives of each project will also help you answer questions about the number of students you can successfully accommodate.

An integrated group does not handicap its non-disabled dancers

If either non-disabled or disabled students in your group are underachieving, then they must look elsewhere to fulfil their potential, leaving us with the uneasy equation that inclusivity equates with access for all, but at the price of individual excellence. It implies that inadequate provision is being made for those capable of outstanding performance and that, most importantly, no way has been found in which the spectrum of skills within the group might successfully coexist. The litmus test is whether those with most experience are having to lower their standards, or whether they are being pushed to extend their range in meetings with different bodies and different ways of perceiving. To put it very simply **integration implies an approach that demands the best from everyone**, not just the disabled members. The realisation that, as a teacher, you may not necessarily be able to work with everyone, is the first step in generating a successful, creative and productive group for yourself and your students, one which fosters growth and development, not dependency.

It becomes increasingly clear that the pursuit of integration makes very particular demands on those leading; it requires a thorough knowledge of dance and people, a high degree of communication skills and a willingness to engage publicly in unknown territory. There are as yet very few maps. Defining your particular methods and areas of interest and expertise will create both the boundaries and the space for you to put your dance skills to best use and create guidelines for those wishing to participate.

There will always be new problems emerging from inclusive groups, but you must ensure that you have the personal and professional resources to engage creatively with them. Here are some of the questions that you might want to ask in setting up a group:

- Is the group to be inclusive? Will it have an open-door policy or a selection procedure? What will your selection criteria be based on?
- Is it a social dance group with the emphasis on access, inclusivity and involvement? What kind of dance structures do you intend to use?
- Is it a disability-specific group? What do you hope to achieve by narrowing down your field of exploration? Will the group focus on training and development and/or on performance?
- Is the group to be led by disabled, non-disabled or jointly led by disabled and non-disabled teachers? If non-disabled, what provision will be on offer to train disabled people as leaders?
- Are you intending to create a performance group geared to devising, rehearsing and showing? What level of performance are you aiming at? Community sharing or professional stage?
- If you are intending to be a performance group, what is the choreographic background/experience of the leaders? Make sure you are prepared and trained for the job you are about to take on. Many people who want to make work for inclusive groups have little or no professional choreographic experience, which raises the question 'why should inclusive work be any less demanding than making work for non-disabled dancers?'
- What links do you have to local education network? If you are working within a school or centre for disabled people, are there links that can be made with nearby performing arts courses?
- Can you organise/ask for 'supervision' or feedback from other professionals?

Selection criteria

Until the end of the 1990s very few disabled people in the UK had received professional training in the performing arts, and this remains the case in many countries today. What then are the criteria for selecting disabled dancers or those without performance experience, for example in auditions for new work? Consider:

- stage presence;
- an aptitude for learning movement sequences;
- stamina;
- versatility;
- a range of movement appropriate to the piece being made or an individual suitability to the ethos of the company;
- other experience in performing arts;
- an understanding of stagecraft and performance skills.

Much will depend on the intention and areas of interest of the choreographer, balanced with the requirements of the company itself. Is it a touring company with a heavy schedule or a short-term local production with no touring?

There is an increasing tendency among inclusive companies to look for what might be called the sexy/sporty disabled dancer. While making the face of disability acceptable and consumer friendly, this tendency to favour the more marketable face/body of disability will inevitably avoid some of the harder issues we face as individuals and

14.1 Andualem Kebede and Junaid Jemal. The Adugna Dance Initiative Addis Ababa, 2001. (Photographer Adam Benjamin)

as a society, and which are raised by those whose body renders them less 'marketable' or less sexy, less attractive. On the other hand we may be accused of voyeurism, exploitation or 'victim art' when more profoundly disabled people appear on stage. The issues, in the end, are not about the nature or the degree of the disability or the classicism or otherness of a performer's body; rather, they are about the intention of the choreographer/performer and how they address themselves to the art of communicating with the audience. There are, in short, no easy answers, only questions about our own motivation, our own desires and a constant demand on us as dance artists to say something about life that might causes others to reflect and reconsider what it means to be a human being.

Part II

Exercises and Improvisations

15 Working against resistance: an introduction to the improvisations and exercises

> When we desire to encourage the growth of the human spirit, we
> challenge and encourage the human capacity to solve problems.
>
> (M. Scott Peck)

The improvisations and exercises described in this book are suitable for any group of dancers or dance students; they have been used successfully with professional companies like Scottish Dance Theatre, Vertigo Dance Company (Israel) and DV8 (UK) as well as with groups of beginners with no dance experience at all.

Although a varied repertoire of exercises is essential for every teacher, I still today find the best way to begin a workshop (or new piece of choreography), particularly with an unknown group, is to arrive early and watch as people come in. This period of quiet observation lets me absorb something of the nature and composition of the group, discern any particular dynamic that may be in the air that day, and notice anyone who might present particular challenges to me as a teacher. In this way I am able to shape the session, laying in a structure for success rather than sticking doggedly to a pre-existing plan that may simply set up unnecessary resistances and obstacles. Ongoing groups and classes will need a greater degree of planning and organisation, but this becomes easier once you have begun to understand the group you are working with and their particular needs.

The difficulties we encounter in teaching are often in reaction to the words we choose or the way we treat people. Intelligent and creative dancers can be reduced to sullen indifference in response to the wrong words or in reaction to those who underestimate their capabilities. Talking about the 'troubles' for example, may go down well if you are teaching in a Protestant neighbourhood in Belfast but will instantly distance your students in a Republican one, where the events of history have led to the use of the term 'the struggle' (see Parker, 1993). I mention this because the resistances we encounter are not always obvious ones: they may have been set in place long before we arrive or we may carry them with us through our own shortsightedness or prejudice. In my first teaching post in a mainstream college in North London I tried for two arduous weeks to get through to the students I had inherited. Finally, exasperated, I stopped mid-class, sat down with them and asked what it was they felt I was doing wrong. It was only then that the students opened up and told me that they had had a succession of dance teachers and none had stayed more than a term. They had assumed that they were unteachable and that I would leave like all the others. Having gained their trust, I was able to see them through to graduation, during which time the dance department became a place of humming activity and, thanks to the rekindled enthusiasm of the students, I was able to cut my teeth as a novice choreographer.

These are not examples that have anything to do with disability other than those which we all share at times, the problem of clear communication. Teaching dance is always more than simply fitting exercises to body types. It is an art form which involves the body and the mind. At its best, it is an exploration and an adventure in which you, as the teacher, are an intrinsic part. You are never outside of the process. As a teacher especially of inclusive groups, you will constantly be encountering new problems; solving them contributes to the store of knowledge you carry with you, but for the most part your learning takes place with and in front of your students. Unlike some forms of dance, you demonstrate your craft by learning and by making mistakes in the presence of those you teach. This is perhaps the hardest concept for many would-be teachers to grasp. Being prepared to go into undetermined situations and not always come up immediately with an answer seems to run contrary to everything we are taught about teaching, yet this is part of the creative process and cannot be hidden if we want to teach what it is really like to be an artist. This is what distinguishes the best in the field, those who are able to say 'Well I'm stumped! Let's take a break and see what emerges when we come back.' Or 'Has anyone else got an idea we can try?' When Siobhan Davies came to work for CandoCo[57] she was tremendously open to everyone's ideas, and very up-front when she didn't know where to go with a movement. It was precisely this openness that allowed her to draw ideas from everyone and then shape this material into a beautiful dance piece. It was as if she didn't burden herself with 'being creative' but worked rather like a gardener – allowing for growth and abundance which she then shaped into astonishing pattern.

Choreographers have shown time and again that successful choreography is not dependent on highly trained 'technical' dancers. Great work like Christopher Bruce's *Ghost Dances* (1981)[58] can be made on bodies of all shapes, sizes and ages, while dreary and uninspired work can (and frequently is) made on the most technically accomplished of companies. If body type (and hence movement style) no longer defines what makes for good dance theatre, then there remains a number of elements that can be investigated with some degree of precision, and which will remain central whether our interest is in understanding choreography or improvisation. They are our use of space, our understanding of time, the quality of our actions and behind all of these, the clarity of our decisions. In one way or another, these will be the subject of the exercises and improvisations that follow.

Notes

57 *Between The National and the Bristol*. Choreographed by Siobhan Davies, for CandoCo Dance Company, 1993.
58 Christopher Bruce was directed towards dance as a child to help deal with the disability he carried as a result of childhood polio. Bruce was to become both an exceptional dancer with Ballet Rambert and later one of modern ballet's outstanding choreographers. Interestingly, his work would frequently address political and social issues.

16 An unruly location[59]

and she concluded that freedom and order were not mutually exclusive, but essential preconditions of each other.

(Louis de Bernières, 1995)

GROUND RULES IN THE STUDIO

The sense of freedom and mysterious order that on occasion reveals itself when we watch dancers improvising is no more entirely chance than the massed, aerial choreography of birds in flight. What prevents the individual birds in these groups constantly bumping into each other is a particular kind of awareness and an adherence to a set of embodied rules. The better these rules are incorporated, the greater the freedom of the individual to soar, to dive and to take part in the spectacle, and on certain delicious and unexpected occasions to lead the kaleidoscopic movement of the entire flock.

It is the relaxation and confidence which come from this kind of shared physical understanding that generates such playfulness, originality and spontaneity when dancers improvise. It is an

16.1 Freedom and order. (Photographer Adam Benjamin)

understanding based on a few simple agreements. The agreements set out below are for basic improvisations, particularly those which involve any kind of contact work with inexperienced groups. They are essentially about respecting individual freedom. Rules within more advanced improvisations are constantly being subverted and overturned (as human beings, we have more options open to us than your average seagull). However, before it is possible to break a rule with any degree of wit or skill, it is necessary to understand its purpose. If there is a tendency to emphasise the ground rules in this book, it is to ensure that those new to improvisation do the learning necessary to become successful and ingenious rule-breakers. The ground rules are designed to encourage cooperation, safety and respect within an unpredictable environment, without denying the possibility of individual freedom and creativity. Everything in this book arises from and returns to these basic principles. They can be summarised as follows:

  i   Take responsibility for our own body.
 ii   Whenever possible, avoid the use of force.
iii   Avoid injury to yourself and others.

Just about everything else falls into one of these three categories. We'll take a look at each individually.

Taking responsibility for your own body

The first rule means that we should take time before each session to inform each other about any movement that is dangerous for us or that is likely to lead to injury, be it through a temporary injury we might be carrying or due to a physical or sensory impairment. Failing to communicate this information may result in injury to yourself or worse still cause someone else to injure you. Young students with vulnerable conditions may need to be reminded to speak up at the start of every new session.[60]

As a teacher you don't need a full medical history of everyone in your class, but you need to ensure that dancers take responsibility for themselves and let you know important information.

As a dancer, you are responsible for informing those you dance with of particular health/safety concerns for you that day. If you have particular requirements around communication, try to advise teachers **before** taking a class or workshop so that they can come prepared. Otherwise, take the time to explain your needs before the class begins.

For example, if you use a voice simulator you can prepare for sessions by asking tutors ahead of time about questions and subjects that might be raised in class, and pre-program answers into the computer memory. This can save valuable time when you and everyone else could be dancing. Don't allow yourself to be handicapped by your own lack of foresight.

16.2 Workshop with HandiCapace Germany. (Photographer Claus
      Langer)

The first rule of taking responsibility for your own body also
covers the principle of choice or choosing to take part. Within a
dance improvisation class, students cannot be forced to participate, only invited. Dance by duress is no longer dance. This takes
us to our second ground rule.

Whenever possible, avoid the use of force

It is not uncommon to see inexperienced dancers grabbing and
pulling each other around in improvisations. In groups where the
range of physical strength may vary considerably, avoiding the use
of force needs to be quickly understood by everyone. Grabbing
the hand of someone in a wheelchair and dragging them around
may give the impression of a duet but is more likely to be the
manipulation of an unwilling or unwitting partner. Offering
an open hand to someone in a wheelchair, however, allows the
invitation to be accepted or refused; this principle can be carried
over into other areas and leads to far more interesting outcomes.
If we allow someone to take our wrist, then they can come with
us for as long as they wish and can leave when they choose. Taking
control of someone's wheelchair (e.g. from behind) is ruled out
for the same reason, as is pulling or pushing someone out of an
improvisation against his or her wishes, or moving a blind dancer
around without his or her consent.

If you are seated in a chair (regardless of whether or not it has
wheels) and someone comes and moves that chair without asking
you, you would have every right to complain. A person can make
choices, a chair can't, so, whenever possible, work with the person,

not the chair. There maybe occasions when control of the chair is taken by other than the occupant, especially when a profoundly physically disabled dancer is involved, but there are still many ways of negotiating this, through indicating location and direction with eyes and head or through pointing with a finger. These negotiations must involve a rigorous exploration of the use of 'language' in its broadest sense; verbal, visual and tactile. Time may need to be set aside to establish these channels of communication so that the intention and significance of signs can be agreed and learned. Once this level of accord is reached, such cooperation and understanding can lead to great freedom of movement and can be subverted to great theatrical effect in choreographed work. For example, Jon French's manipulation of his assistants in *Trades and Trusts*[61] and Ellen Vermander's misinterpreted directions in *An Egg is Enough*.[62]

We also rule out lifting by force, rather than through offered supports – as grabbing and hoisting someone into the air restricts that individual's freedom (to travel) and more importantly, if the lift is a bad one, his or her freedom to fall correctly.

Avoid injury to yourself and others

This really comes out of the first two ground rules, but it means that everyone should be conscious of creating an environment where basic safety precautions are understood and respected. It lies with the teacher to reiterate the ground rules when they are being disregarded. This third rule also means that, on occasion, force can be used if it is to avoid injury. Grabbing and holding may be appropriate if it is to prevent injury. I have on more than one occasion been forced to leap to the rescue of a hapless couple, when one of the pair has unintentionally sat on the chair's joystick and the partner and their chair are careering out of control across the studio! These rules present the minimum accord of respecting certain basic human rights – those of freedom of expression and freedom of movement. Our journey, renewed and expanded every day in the studio, is a study of how we negotiate and reinterpret this passage between freedom and order, chaos and pattern, without injury to our self or others.

A cautionary note

Every care has been taken to explain the exercises in this book. Some involve risk. If you are uncertain, then progress carefully and when in doubt contact an experienced teacher for guidance (see Appendix 1). That said, every exercise can be drawn on (with patience, thought and consideration) and adapted for any level of student. The author cannot, however, be held responsible for accidents arising from misapplication of the material contained in this book. When in doubt, err on the side of caution, there is no better guide than your common sense.

THE DANCE SPACE

If the studio is to be a place in which creativity and ability are valued and in which dancers (particularly beginners) feel both relaxed and secure, it needs to be an area safe from interruption and distraction. Preparing a studio for inclusive groups needs additional thought, for example the dance floor needs to be suitable for both feet and wheels.

- The studio needs to be a space over which you have some control. Be clear that other people using the building cannot wander in and out during sessions.
- Ideally, it should be easily accessible, warm and light with a floor suitable for dance.
- A sprung dance floor is ideal with mats available for those who need them for floor work.
- Make sure that the floor is cleaned before each session. Encourage wheelchair users to check that tyres are clean and dry before entering the dance space. It may be useful to have some cleaning materials, dry rags or newspaper, available – particularly in winter.
- It is a myth that wheelchairs damage dance floors; a good dance floor is made to withstand the wheels of theatre equipment, far heavier than someone in a wheelchair.
- Carpeted spaces, which, for some unaccountable reason, get repeatedly proposed for inclusive projects, are not recommended. Carpets slow down and impair the manoeuvrability of wheelchairs, and do pretty much the same for ambulant dancers, they can cause friction burns and are to be avoided whenever possible.
- Stone floors are the only option in some countries – but they are far from ideal and in the West at least should really only be considered for outdoor performances, or site-specific events; they transmit sound vibration poorly for deaf students, and if uneven can create unpleasant vibration for wheelchair users; they are hard on ambulant dancers and make floor work unappealing. Wear trainers if necessary. Spills from chairs are to be avoided!
- Visually impaired dancers will be able to locate you more easily if you wear clothing that contrasts with your surroundings. Think about how you position yourself in relation to available light when talking and demonstrating, especially when you have students who may be lip-reading.

- Hearing-impaired students will benefit from a space with good acoustics, bad acoustics is a distraction and will severely handicap blind and visually impaired students who are dependent on hearing verbal instructions clearly.

Given all of the above, inadequate buildings have long been used as an excuse for doing nothing. Remember problem-solving is central to an integrated approach to the arts! The Stare Cases Project purposely perform in unlikely and inaccessible places – like stairs in the Royal Festival Hall in London's South Bank Centre. It is up to you as a teacher (or group) whether you refuse to work in 'inadequate' spaces or decide on occasion to use your ingenuity and turn them to your advantage. Finally, be prepared to learn what works from your students. Ask them what they need in order to get the most from each teaching situation.

WHEELCHAIRS, SAFETY AND ETIQUETTE

The fate of Isadora Duncan is a reminder of the incompatibility of fashion accessories and wheels in motion![63] Ensure that loose necklaces, watches, scarves and other fashion items are removed before each class.

- Keep passage-ways clear. Try to keep all bags, trainers, etc. off the floor or placed out of the way. This is good practice for any dance studio but is particularly important when wheelchair users and visually impaired dancers are using the space.
- Wheelchairs used regularly for dance are subject to more than average stress on their component parts and so should be subject to more frequent servicing and maintenance. Tyres must always be well pumped and brakes kept in good order. Try always to know where the nearest wheelchair repair centre is – particularly if you are away from home.
- Uncluttered, wheelchairs can have a particular, functional beauty of their own. Ensure that bags and panniers are removed (it can be a disconcerting sight to see someone improvising with a week's groceries swinging from the back of their chair). Apart from bags and holdalls there may be panels and appendages that serve no useful purpose and merely add weight and reduce the possibility of contact with others. Lose them!
- Check chairs for sharp edges and dangerous attachments or fittings. Unused and unnecessary fittings can sometimes be sawn off with a bowsaw and smoothed down with a metal file, or capped with foam and gaffer tape to prevent causing injury.

16.3 CandoCo Dance Company 1996. Charlotte Darbyshire, Lea
Parkinson, Helen Baggett, Jon French, Kuldip Singh-Barmi.
(Photographer Anthony Crickmay)

- As a point of etiquette and hygiene, chairs should be kept
  clean. There is nothing more disenchanting than coming away
  from a class with the residue from the underside of someone's
  chair all over your favourite sweatshirt. If you can't clean your
  chair yourself, be prepared with cleaning materials and ask
  someone to give you a hand. Any time spent tinkering with
  chairs is a valuable source of learning and everyone in an
  inclusive group should know how wheelchairs function/come
  apart/go back together.
- Wheelchair users involved in full-time dance practice may
  consider having a set of (quick-release) wheels kept at the
  studio to be used solely for dance.

See overleaf for 'Avoiding Injury'.

16.4 David Toole. (Photographer John Cole)

HARD METAL, SOFT BODIES:[64]
AVOIDING INJURY

> It's not enough to say: I've made a mistake; one has to say how
> one has made the mistake.
>
> (Claude Bernard)

How do we avoid injury when our dancing often involves hard
metal and soft bodies travelling at speed, and when the spontaneous
invention of improvisation involves a high degree of unpredictability? The plain answer, as anyone experienced in this field knows,
doesn't exist! Dance, like any other physical pursuit involves risk
and that means accidents do happen. The way forward is through
careful, researched, exploration where new and possibly dangerous
moves are tried slowly at first, with plenty of protection before
being attempted full out.

What distinguishes the approach to dance proposed in this book
is that those participating take full responsibility for their involvement. As already discussed, it is up to each of us to to provide
important information, for example 'I have a condition which
means I should not tilt back suddenly' or 'I have brittle bones,
so cannot take much weight on my legs.' In many dance settings
in the past, this information seems to have prompted dance
teachers to embalm would-be disabled students in great swathes
of cotton wool. The fear of a disabled person getting injured in
their class smothers all possibilities of risk-taking and with it go
any chances of experimentation or growth. It is one of the lingering
reasons why many disabled people are reluctant to talk about their

disabilities and resist the idea of dance as a serious physical pursuit. In the approach outlined here, safety dictates that information is shared but for a quite different end. The dancers' agreement to participate might be expressed:

> Having given you this information I now wish to be as fully involved as possible and to take whatever risks I choose, providing all sensible precautions are taken to avoid injury to myself and others.

These are the same conditions that apply to any physical pursuit that involves risk. In many cases when someone falls out of a wheelchair there is a greater risk of heart failure in those watching than of any serious damage to the person who has just been ditched. While taking sensible precautions around students with fragile conditions, as teachers we must weigh up the damage we do to a student's growth and development by excluding risk-taking as compared to the pain of the occasional bruise or abrasion they may receive from hitting the dance floor.

If you are not a wheelchair user and have a real fear of having someone fall out of their chair while you are teaching, spend whatever spare time you can in a wheelchair yourself and set up a safe situation in which you can feel what it's like to tip up (see **tilts** in Chapters 23 and 24). It does feel scary but as you will soon discover, in most cases, the world does not come to an end. Without this information you are in a position of teaching someone to ride a bike, without having ridden yourself.

It is not uncommon to see the most creative and energetic movement in disabled children vanish (or on occasion be banished) by the arrival of a dance teacher. When teaching in schools, take a surreptitious look at playground activity to gauge whether the programme you are offering comes anywhere close to tapping your students' real physical potential. I have seen young blind students, tearing around with complete abandon, bouncing off each other and the walls during their playtime, only to be reduced to cautious, hand-holding temerity once inside the dance studio.

When accidents occur, we need to be able to find out why and encourage students to learn from their mistakes rather than punishing them by forbidding 'speed' or 'risk'. In this way, safety measures become understood and self-monitored. Some of the most exciting choreographic ideas have come from reconstructing the events that led to an unexpected fall or collision, and then (assuming that no one was mortally wounded) finding a safe way of achieving the same result! The key issues are responsibility, both personal and collective.

This said, as teacher or dance leader, be aware of students who try for the spectacular too fast or too soon. This may be the overspeedy wheelchair user or the would-be acrobatic dancer. Sensitive students become aware of the anxiety they generate in others, those who don't may need to be reined in from time to time. There are dancers with remarkable sensitivity and ability who can achieve extraordinary connection very quickly, but it is best to err initially on the side of caution and move gradually from simple exercises to more challenging material.

If someone is seriously injured during a session, quietly but quickly call a halt to whatever is in progress while you assess the situation. Utilise support that is available within the group (know who your first-aiders are) and seek external assistance if required to take care of the injured dancer. If necessary, call for a break so that you can focus your attention where it is needed. It is always a good idea to know the whereabouts of the nurse or the medical cupboard (and ice) before starting a new project. Don't assume that the organisers already know.

HELPING YOURSELF: TEACHERS' SUPPORTS

Those who teach in the community daily charter unknown territory; it can be exhilarating but also demanding work. Try to make time in your schedule to take classes with other teachers or ask to sit in and watch. You may also find it beneficial to share some of your teaching with other practitioners and schedule time to provide each other with feedback about what worked, what felt difficult and possible alternative approaches.

Working with the help of experienced assistants also reduces the pressures involved in more challenging situations so that you have someone on hand to troubleshoot within a workshop setting . . . and so avoid becoming bogged down or sucked into the demands of a particularly needy or demanding student. Over the years I have been assisted by a succession of wonderful trainees and student placements, many of whom are now working professionally in different parts of the world. All too often, young teachers graduating from courses are thrown into teaching situations with little support or supervision. Just having another person to talk to, even to let off steam with, can make a huge difference.

The best teaching teams for inclusive work are those that consist of a disabled and non-disabled leader who are already familiar with each other and with the many issues that may arise around communication and access in inclusive groups. Establishing this kind of partnership before setting out as workshop leader is time well spent and will be essential if the group is to continue to attract both disabled and non-disabled participants.

Invite feedback from colleagues and students as to what is working for them, what excites and involves them. Remember that solving problems is central to integrated practice, so be forgiving of yourself when you encounter difficulties in your teaching practice and remember that the problems are there for you to learn from.

Notes

59 'An unruly location' is after Albright, 1997.
60 Further information may be required when working in school settings or with younger students, and schools should have details of any counter-indicated movement. It is good to be forewarned of such details, as younger children may not always remember to let you know.
61 CandoCo Dance Company. Choreographed by Guilherme Botehlo, 1997.
62 Adam Benjamin and Dancers. De Warande, Belgium, 1998.
63 Duncan died when her trailing scarf became entangled in the wheel of her open-top car.
64 With acknowledgement to Stephen Hooper.

17 Introductory work

Because the approach to dance proposed in this book seeks to reach across the traditional structures and hierarchies of formal technique, it is not always possible to say 'this is a beginner's exercise and this an advanced exercise'. Clearly, some dancers will have progressed further in their explorations than others and will therefore be more confident, creative and accomplished, and eager to seek tougher challenges. Ultimately, the 'advanced' student is not someone who is merely possessed of a strong technique, but is able to extend their range and sensibility to dance with an absolute beginner or a seasoned professional, and who, perhaps most importantly, is capable of translating improvisatory experience into convincing performance or shape it into choreographic form.

The improvisations in the first section are suitable for introducing dance to newly formed or inexperienced groups, but they may also be used as warm-ups for established groups with advanced students. The approach here is not anti-technique. Indeed the understanding of ground rules and the applications of the principles contained within these exercises could be considered in a broad sense a highly flexible dance technique, which equips us to deal with the uncertainties of improvisation and provides insights into the challenges of choreography.

Each improvisation includes a brief summary of the areas of exploration and a recommended number of dancers. Exercises differ from improvs in that they require a more disciplined attention to detail and are concerned with developing specific skills (ie wheelchair tilts). Most improvs and exercises are preceded by a paragraph or two under the heading **Introduction**. This is to give a little information about the sources of the improvisation or ways into the subject, and as a reminder that the stimulus for creating your own improvisations lies all around you, not just in books. The practical instructions for each improvisation are headed **Directions**. There are also **Teacher's notes** and possible ways of extending the exercises under the heading **Options**. Lastly, **Examples** are accounts from real teaching situations that describe how the improvs have been used in practice.

IMPROV 1: STRETCHING A POINT

> Joindre les mains c'est bien mais les ouvrir, c'est mieux
> (Holding hands is good but letting go is better)
>
> (Louis Ratisbonne)

A good exercise to begin a workshop
It is non-threatening (most people have shaken hands before)
Introduces skills of 'listening' and 'letting go'
Connectivity
Breathing with awareness
Up to 30 dancers – then pairs

Introduction

Shaking hands in England can range from the hand-crushing, power grips of those out to impress to the disdainful contact that seems to say 'You may touch the tip of my fingers . . . briefly!' I was teaching in Senegal when I experienced for the first time what it means to shake hands and where the current western gesture probably has its origins. It was in fact not a 'shake' at all.[65]

Every morning the members of the project would meet at the dockside in Dakar and wait for the small boat that would take us to the island of Gorée where we were working.[65] On the first morning I was greeted by Oumar Diop, the project organiser. Omar, who was a huge man, took my hand as we began to talk. Five minutes later, still talking, and with beads of sweat beginning to break out on my brow, I was no longer really listening, but merely wondering in a very English kind of way when, if ever, he was going to give me my hand back. By the end of our stay in Senegal, however, I had been converted. There was nothing more reassuring than to hold hands and listen to each other's words at the beginning and end of each day. Oumar Diop's greeting was like having your battery charged; conveying a sense of strength and companionship that would last until the same gesture was shared again at the day's end. Returning home, the English handshake seemed atrophied and impoverished by comparison. (See Appendix 2 for an account of the project)

Directions

a. First simply move around the space on your own and without speaking. Take (don't shake) the hand of each person you encounter. (To see how to make this work if someone is in a wheelchair and needs help moving, see Improv **Flock** below.) Notice the unique quality of each meeting, its duration, sense of connection, its ease, its hesitancies, awkwardness or intimacy. Notice each tiny aspect without judging and then move on to greet someone else.

b. Many people unconsciously hold their breath during this exercise, so while the face seems to be communicating 'Hello, its great to see you!', the internal reaction may be saying something quite different, more along the lines of 'You could be emitting poisonous fumes and I'm not going to take another breath until you let go of my hand!' Try to breathe naturally as you move and greet others.

c. For each encounter try to learn/intuit as much as you can. If they were a colour, what would they be? If a fruit, what fruit? If a kind of weather, animal, element? This is just for your own sense of how you perceive – you don't need to tell them!

d. You don't need to stare meaningfully into each other's eyes, in fact you may be able to sense/feel if you 'rest' your eyes. Try to keep your arms and body relaxed. Pay attention to what is happening to your breath and to the sense of connection or resistance that you feel.

e. Can you sense the moment when it feels right to separate and move on?

f. Continue moving round the space meeting new people. Be aware of your own reactions and the subtle information you receive from each contact. Just notice what you sense, don't make any value judgments about it.

Partner exercise

a. Now take a partner and hold hands. Notice the quality of the connection you make. Notice the temperature, strength and, less easily defined, the 'energy' or sense of communication that you share through this contact. When you feel that you have a shared focus, a clearly defined point of contact, very gently release your hands and draw them apart. Separate them only as far as you can without losing that sense of connection, drawing the point out like a stretched thread between you (See Figure 17.1). This may be only a few inches to begin with. When the connection threatens to fade or be overstretched, follow the connection back to its point of origin until you are holding hands again. Keep your hands 'alive' and open.

b. Don't try to invent or be creative, just let your hand 'listen' and respond to what you are really feeling. If you feel that you have a very strong connection see how far you stretch the distance before you follow the feeling back to where it began. You can do this seated, sitting on the floor or standing.

17.1 Stretching a point. Tshwaragano workshop, 2000.
    (Photographer John Hogg)

Development

- When you have got the hang of this, stop briefly and discuss what you have just done. What did you notice? Then start again with the same partner. Establish your initial connection and make three or four separations and returns. Now, without stopping, close your eyes (both of you). Follow exactly the same procedure, separating and returning. Stay true to what you feel. If you miss each other on your return, keep your eyes closed and seek each other by gently sweeping the air with your arms (lightly, like cobwebs). When you find each other, begin again.

- Now try stretching the connection just that little bit further. Be prepared to go into that place where it feels that you are in danger of 'making a fool of yourself'. Stretch the limits beyond where you feel confident of success. Congratulate yourself equally whenever you 'foul up' as well as when you 'succeed'. The good improviser needs to grow accustomed to this upturning of events, and this exercise is a simple intro- duction to the transition from mastery to mockery – enjoy it.[66] It is possible that you may feel like 'giving up' if you are unable to relocate your partner. If you become lost, try opening your hands as though expecting (or offering a gift). See what comes your way. (See Improv 8 below, **open hand**.) You may not get your original partner back but you might find a new one!

- Now is a good time to divide into two groups as this is a fascinating improvisation to watch. What moments did you find most engaging as you watched? Why? What does this tell you about choreography?

IMPROV 2: FLOCK – IN SEARCH OF A 'COMMON SENSE'

> The most precious thing in speech are pauses.
> (Sir Ralph Richardson, attrib.)

> Motion multiplies inscape only when inscape is discovered, otherwise it disfigures.
> (Gerard Manley Hopkins, 1963)

Group timing. Beginnings and endings
Spatial awareness (the sense of what is going on around you)
Collective awareness
Particularly valuable for groups with blind and deaf students
For upwards of 3 dancers. (The most I have tried this with is 80)

Introduction

Make a list of all the events that you can think of that begin with silence.

- storm
- argument
-
-
-
-

Directions

a. Take time to find the place in the studio where you feel right (see Improvs 16 and 17 and **Crossing the line** in Chapter 19). Don't just assume that anywhere will do. Move around the space until you feel you have found the place that is right for you. Now stand or sit quietly, breathing naturally. Take your attention inside for a while, be aware of the subtle movement of your own body. Be aware of the pattern of your breath, the inhalation and exhalation. Close your eyes. Notice the contact your skin is making with the clothes you're wearing and how this shifts as you breathe, notice any contact you have with the floor or chair, be aware of how your weight falls through your body through your legs or through the seat and frame of your chair into the floor. Be aware of any small or subtle shifts in your musculature. Finally, notice the movements of your thoughts as they pass through your mind. Notice the

energy of these different aspects of yourself at rest. The way
you are always subtly in motion, the way different thoughts
change the level of energy you feel in your body.

b. Open your eyes and take your awareness to those around
you. Look closely. How still are they really? Can you detect
the movement of their breath, the small shifts they make to
counter gravity and maintain balance. Are you able to detect
the energy of a particular thought?

c. If you become aware of (see, hear or sense) a small movement,
it might be someone yawning, flicking a fly, scratching or
stretching, copy their movement as though you were a reflection or echo of the original, then simply let it go and return
to rest. Does something else catch your attention? Copy, echo,
and this time slightly amplify it, then let it go. Always aim
to participate in the feel or energy of a particular movement
rather than trying to make an exact replica.

d. As more movements arise, accept them and make them your
own. For example you can take a movement someone is
making with their leg and transfer it to your arm. A tilt of the
head might be interpreted as a tilt of the back, an arm reaching
might become a leg stepping. Continue to amplify movements
until you find yourself travelling around the space.

e. Synchronising your breathing with those you meet as you
travel round the studio will serve to open the door to a shared
experience of dance rather than the experience of creating
adjacent solos.

f. Maintain an awareness of detail even as you become more
mobile and free-ranging in your own movement. Be prepared
to let go of a movement when it no longer interests you and
return to stillness.

g. Now, if you notice a dancer who is at rest, even for a moment,
allow yourself also to become still, wait and allow this stillness
to spread to other dancers. See how long it takes before
everyone notices and ceases their activity. When everyone has
settled, begin again by noticing and echoing any small gesture
(intentional or otherwise) made by another dancer.

h. Continue to repeat this cycle until the whole group begins to
share a 'common sense' of the shifting phases of activity and
rest.

Teaching notes

*   Encourage dancers not to freeze when they notice others have
stopped but to find their own individual pathway to stillness,
like geese settling down out of the sky onto a lake. Similarly,
when beginning to move, try not just to start but to 'be moved'
to start by something you see, feel or hear. Recognising
stillness and silence is an essential practice in dance. Try

to end this (and every exercise) with an awareness of calm returning to the body and to the group around you.

- The initiating gesture in **flock** (Improv 2) may be a tiny movement made for example by a profoundly disabled dancer, so the group needs to recognise what it means to be really quiet to begin with. Dancers can often lose the sensitivity needed to notice really fine movement detail because they are too busy being creative.
- If a wheelchair user (who is unable to move their own chair) has come to class accompanied by a carer or assistant, separate them and let the group find a solution to how the disabled dancer gets round the studio. Rule out a single dancer who simply replaces the carer.
- Encourage the student in the wheelchair to offer a hand or foot to the other dancers as an invitation to be pulled, rather than waiting passively for another dancer to move the chair. Whenever possible, the **person in the chair should take hold of the hand or wrist being offered** to him or her rather than being grabbed and pulled around passively – this ensures that the individual is making choices about where and when he or she moves. This offering and accepting of offers can be taken up by others as part of the improvisation.
- Make sure anyone in an electric chair puts their speed on 'slow'.

Option 1

If there are blind dancers in the group, what senses will they have to use to notice the group's activity?

Get the whole group to try the exercise unsighted. You won't be able to work with everyone blindfolded if the group has electric-chair users **and** deaf dancers in it, but see if you can come up with your own variations on the theme. For example, you could use **leading and following** (see Improv 9 in Chapter 18) partnerships and work with **flock**.

Option 2

Try encouraging dancers to settle not just in isolation but also in clusters, like piles of leaves, gently supporting each other. Younger students may enjoy creating shapes that can snag or hook other dancers. When everyone is hooked up (perhaps using counter-balances, see Chapter 24) and the group have sensed a shared stillness, allow the connections to melt and gently release dancers into the space again.

Option 3

Divide up into small groups of three or four. Try working so that each group finds its own stillness and movement independent of the other groups. Then try working, but with small groups paired, each following its own pathway through space while coordinating moments of stillness. Create your own variations on this theme.

BREATH, PROXIMITY AND DISTANCE

> We would feel our proximity with our finer senses. As, for example, one of two, lying still in a dark room, knows when the other is awake.
>
> (Marilynne Robinson, 1991)

Introduction

A dispirited dancer is rarely a creative dancer. To be dispirited is literally to be separated from our breath, the word *spiritus* in Latin means 'breath' (see also Improv 4). The spirit (or breath) of adventure is a vital ingredient to improvisation and without an awareness of how the breath ebbs and flows in response to our actions, much within improvisation will remain a mystery. Because we live the greater part of our lives breathing unconsciously, this is a skill or a sensibility that comes slowly. Initially it may be an unexpected or dramatic turn of events, or a shift in atmosphere, that brings our breath to conscious awareness.

As we become more aware of the breath's natural rhythmicity and its many qualities, we also come to realise that there are times when we seem to imprison or 'hold' our breath. This should concern us on a number of levels. First, if we are not breathing, we are not gaining the oxygen we need in order to dance and, second, if we are capable of breathing without effort (i.e. when asleep) then we must be using unnecessary muscular effort in order **not** to breathe.

IMPROV 3: SPIRIT LEVEL

Awareness of breath
Proximity
Space
Up to 30 dancers

Directions

a.   Take a moment before you begin to move just to notice your breathing. Make a friend of this gentle rising and falling of the rib cage and the passage of air to and from the body. Notice where each breath begins, and the way the breath rolls over from inhalation to exhalation. Be aware that this simple rhythm has accompanied you throughout your life, every night you have slept, it has gently rocked you, every day it has brought essential oxygen to your system. Make a habit of tuning into your breath, wherever and whenever you can.

b. Now begin to travel around the studio moving in and out of spaces that open before you. Move naturally, keeping alive to your breathing. Don't make eye contact with other people, use your peripheral vision and keep your attention on how you feel both inside and on the surface of your body. Notice without judging any changes that occur in these subtle sensations or 'body charge'. Be sensitive to the shifting of tension inside your body as you move past and are passed by other dancers and of any tendency you might have to hold your breath.

c. Now take turns to remain still and close your eyes, while the other students continue to move around the space. Feel the energy of those moving past you. Notice how the proximity of others influences what you feel and how you breathe. Spend a few minutes being aware of how you, and your breath, respond to movement and sounds occurring around you. When you are ready to move again, make sure you open your eyes and sense what is happening around you before moving off. Remember, someone maybe blocking your way or about to pass you at speed! If you are travelling around the unsighted dancers, do so without touching them. Try to:

- Move past at speed.
- Place yourself immediately behind, in front, alongside.
- Wave your hands around them creating drafts.
- Place a hand close to their face, but not touching.
- See if you can make them aware of your presence without moving.

d. When everyone has had a turn with eyes closed, the whole group comes gently back to stillness. Notice the shifting rhythm of your breath as the body slows down.

e. Together discuss what you experienced during the improvisation, with particular reference to what you felt happening to your breath. Julyen Hamilton has a beautiful variation on this: dancer A repeats a simple motion (an arm waving back and forth), dancer B observes and then begins to play in the spaces created by the motion. Dancers A and B monitor their breathing and the changes that take place. See also Improv 10 **interloper** in Chapter 18.

IMPROV 4: BREATHING SPACE

Breath
Proximity
Use of space
Up to 30 dancers

Introduction

One of the most frequently criticised aspects of contact improvisation comes from students who have found themselves glued to an overenthusiastic partner who has been given permission to roll all over them. It is an unenviable position and one which has frightened off many a sensitive soul, and left many feeling that their personal space has somehow been violated. Contact makes little sense without first considering how we approach one another, and how we negotiate our use of time and space. In other words, our freedom to arrive and depart. Feeling uncomfortable or pressurised when we improvise with someone is our body's way of asking for space.

Directions

a.   Imagine your breath is a fine filament connecting you to the space around you. The breath may be held but it never loses its sense of direction or motion. Your breath always wants to move, either in or out, towards or away.

b.   Allow your breath and your feeling to lead you on a pathway around the studio. Don't force your breathing. If you lose your way, simply stop and notice what your breath is doing, then start again.
      Breathe space into you, allow space to attract you. Allow mass to affect you.

c.   Continue to play with proximity and distance in order to alter your breathing and that of other dancers in the space. Notice changes that occur as a result of your shifting spatial relationship to others.

d.   Without any physical contact, begin to play with changing speed and levels, action and stillness. It is important not to start 'acting'. Remember, here we are working simply on proximity, and sensing the changes that arise from altering distance and position. Try to alter consciously the breathing of other dancers through your movements. For example:

•   Try moving slowly towards someone.
•   Sit at someone's feet.
•   Move quickly towards someone.
•   Lie down next to someone.

- Move with someone.
- Position yourself quietly close to someone.
- Mirror or track someone at a distance.

e. Notice how another person's movement (be it a gesture or a shift in direction) affects how you feel and breathe. Allow yourself time to feel fully the effect in your own body. Often we respond before we have fully perceived the totality of another person's movement. Imagine you are a pond and that the movement of another dancer is like a handful of paint powder thrown into you. (Next time you take cream in your coffee, look at the movement that is created before you stir it.)

Teaching notes

- It is not uncommon to see dancers stuck in a face-to-face 'stand-off' apparently unable to move. It is clear that neither is particularly comfortable, but, like two cats unexpectedly bumping into each other, they wait for the other to give way. Often in these circumstances the situation resolves awkwardly and the moment is then forgotten. It is amazing how often these problematic vignettes arise within improvisations and yet when I ask about problems, students rarely seem able to recall them. It seems that we have a device for temporarily blotting out such moments. Essentially all these minor confrontations invite us to change our status. And this may seem hard when we are just beginning to enjoy the freedom of moving in the space – to be feeling our first sense of dignity and freedom as a dancer only to be suddenly confronted with someone else equally convinced of their own rights.
- Remember the task of the improvisation is to notice changes in breath and to find ways of altering another person's breathing pattern. These head-to-head moments are when neither person can find a solution, both cease to notice their breathing and become physically stuck.
- Remember, there is no winning or losing, only an enjoyment of the various shifting patterns of movement and breath. If someone solidly blocks your way, breathe, relax, then use them as a support, or drop to another level and curl up at their feet. Remain flexible, seek solutions, be soluble.

IMPROV 5: SEAWEED EXERCISE

Receptivity and passive movement
Relaxation and concentration
Balance
Centring
2 or 3 dancers

Introduction

This is an exercise taught in China and Japan as a means of improving a balanced stance. In the Chinese art of Tai Chi Chuan it is used to develop Tsou – yielding or 'leading by walking away'. In Japan it is sometimes called Wakame Taiso[67] (seaweed exercise). Wakame seaweed grows in long strands, rooted firmly to the seafloor. Its fronds sway in the tidal currents, providing a model of earthed and yet pliant movement.

Preparation

Bring in illustrations, photos, etc. which you think help to illustrate structural and flowing energy. For example, pictures of water and pictures of skeletons or architectural features.

Directions

Passive 'seaweed' dancer

a.   One dancer is the passive 'seaweed', the other is the active 'sea'. The seaweed dancer works with eyes closed. If standing, begin with your feet shoulder-width apart and with your knees slightly bent. Imagine your skeleton inside, spaciously supporting your body upwards towards the sky, energy moving up through the bones of your body and penetrating the crown of your head. Imagine the soft tissues of the body flowing down, energy releasing in a relaxed, cascading stream in and around the joints of the skeleton and flowing out through the soles of your feet deep into the earth below you. Spend some time sensing these two directions through the body.

b.   Now imagine that the centre line of the body is open to both directions simultaneously. Downward grounding energy and upward floating energy. You are anchored and at the same time buoyant. Knees slightly bent, pelvis and pelvic floor relaxed and crown of the head floating upward. Allow your body to be passive, but if standing, keep sinking your energy into the floor as though your feet have taken root. Your aim is to allow your partner to generate your movement while you float like seaweed in the tide.

The 'sea' or active dancer

c. Position yourself behind or close to your partner. When your partner has settled into a relaxed position begin to push lightly and manipulate your partner's limbs. If your partner is standing, you can push gently on the muscle masses on either side of the spine to encourage the spine to rotate. Keep your hands soft as you work, relax your arms and as much as possible use the shifting of your own body, forward and back, to move your partner rather than just using your arms to push.

d. If your partner is very relaxed, you can try generating more movement. If your partner looks like toppling, slow down and let him or her find his or her balance again. You can nudge your partner behind the knees if he/she is standing, or if your partner's knees are bent, try pushing down firmly on his/her hip; the pelvis should have the feeling of a buoy or beach ball floating in water.

e. Like many exercises, this needs to be adapted to individual physicalities, but with time and patience the principle can be applied to many different situations and partnerships. Remember the key is to explore passive movement and natural breathing – so that your partner comes to the realisation that he/she can be moved without expending effort and is able to receive different movement stimuli without the need to hold tension or hold his/her breath.

Option 1

When everyone has understood the two-person exercise, create an open improvisation with 'seaweed' dancers positioned in the studio and others circulating around them.

Teaching notes

•   If a student is unable to stand, you can explore the same themes lying down. Gently lift and rock arms and legs. Remember never to use force but to encourage movement as though your hands were waves massaging your partner.

•   Always try to support joints when lifting arms and legs and try not to drop a limb onto the floor or onto part of a wheelchair; this will make your partner anxious and therefore generate tension in the muscles, which you will then have to work to undo.

IMPROV 6: LINEAR PATHWAYS EXERCISE

Giving an impulse
Initiating movement
Interpreting an impulse
*Perceiving the completion of a pathway through space from A
to B*
2 or 3 dancers

Introduction

Linear pathways works at the simplest level of our understanding
of movement; a simple outward impulse away and into space. Its
simplicity means that it can be explored by dancers in any situation
if appropriately applied. It has often provided keys to unlocking
apparently intractable difficulties particularly in working with
students with learning difficulties (see 'The woman who imprisoned dancers', p113).

In **Seaweed** we looked at passive movement around a centre. In
linear pathways we explore passive or undetermined pathways
in which the centre moves through space.

The idea of 'centre' preoccupies dancers in every field; be it
Graham, ballet or contact improvisation, it is a perennial theme.
We experience centre in many different contexts, but it is made
most evident in a common everyday experience. It is possible,
for example, for a large person temporarily to lose his balance
when bumping into a much smaller, lighter person. This tells us
that balance is not reliant solely on weight, but on something less
tangible; in the example above, the smaller, lighter person has
inadvertently disturbed the larger person's centre of gravity, and
this is what causes him to lose balance.

When standing, the body simultaneously accepts and defies
the force of gravity. Balancing over the feet, the body constantly
readjusts to maintain balance. As with a tree that has been cut at
its base, it only takes a slight nudge for the trunk to begin to go
out of balance and begin to fall. This balancing act and the body's
capacity to remain upright is further explored in **reaching** (see
Improv 36, Chapter 23).

In Tai-Chi the basic standing position (which we approximate
in the **seaweed exercise**) is called 'the stance of the child' because
it approximates to the earliest standing posture of most infants.
The body is relaxed and without tension, the pelvic muscles
relaxed, and the knees are bent dealing with the new experience
of gravity and balance. Having achieved this remarkable feat, the
infant spends the next few months of his/her life falling over.
(Fortunately, at that age, bones are soft and pliant and it's not
far to fall.) Then, one day, something quite remarkable happens.
Instead of falling to the ground, a foot reaches out. The fall is

The 'sea' or active dancer

c. Position yourself behind or close to your partner. When your partner has settled into a relaxed position begin to push lightly and manipulate your partner's limbs. If your partner is standing, you can push gently on the muscle masses on either side of the spine to encourage the spine to rotate. Keep your hands soft as you work, relax your arms and as much as possible use the shifting of your own body, forward and back, to move your partner rather than just using your arms to push.

d. If your partner is very relaxed, you can try generating more movement. If your partner looks like toppling, slow down and let him or her find his or her balance again. You can nudge your partner behind the knees if he/she is standing, or if your partner's knees are bent, try pushing down firmly on his/her hip; the pelvis should have the feeling of a buoy or beach ball floating in water.

e. Like many exercises, this needs to be adapted to individual physicalities, but with time and patience the principle can be applied to many different situations and partnerships. Remember the key is to explore passive movement and natural breathing – so that your partner comes to the realisation that he/she can be moved without expending effort and is able to receive different movement stimuli without the need to hold tension or hold his/her breath.

Option 1

When everyone has understood the two-person exercise, create an open improvisation with 'seaweed' dancers positioned in the studio and others circulating around them.

Teaching notes

*   If a student is unable to stand, you can explore the same themes lying down. Gently lift and rock arms and legs. Remember never to use force but to encourage movement as though your hands were waves massaging your partner.
*   Always try to support joints when lifting arms and legs and try not to drop a limb onto the floor or onto part of a wheelchair; this will make your partner anxious and therefore generate tension in the muscles, which you will then have to work to undo.

while others will need more energy to get them moving. Listen with your hand to sense how they respond to your impulse.

d.   At first try to send him/her as you would a toy boat onto a pond. Not so fast as to create a bow wave, but with just enough energy to make some headway. For heavier dancers, it may feel more like sliding a heavy object gently over ice. Try to give the clearest, straightest direction possible without 'shoving'. Observe closely how your partner receives and responds to your impulse. The push should never feel uncomfortable, even a strong push should have that feel of, for example, when your anorak gets caught in a strong gust of wind and you are bodily 'lifted' forward.

e.   If you are receiving the impulse, you may want to try travelling with your eyes closed, responding only to the directionality and energy that you feel rather than where you think your partner wants you to travel.

f.   A strong push will not necessarily send you a long way. Does the push carry you in a straight line? Does it turn or spin you? Does it create a disturbance and generate erratic movement? Does it give you a clear sense of directionality? Does it make you glide or rock?

g.   Breathe naturally and try not to pre-empt the journey you are about to take.

h.   Respond to the push in the most natural way you can. Don't invent or embellish, simply go where and as far as the push takes you. Stop where you stop as opposed to where you think you should stop. This can be beautifully demonstrated by students using manual chairs – when and where the chair stops *is* where and when it stops. If you are receiving in a chair, allow your upper body to respond to and enjoy the feeling of gliding.

Option 1

When receiving, try placing your attention in different parts of your body. How does this affect the way you travel?

Option 2

As you progress, try to follow accurately the energy of the push. Does it move you in a straight line or does it turn you? How does it end? Where does the impulse leave you? Does it peter out or ebb back at the end like a wave rolling back down the beach? (See Improv 8 **open hand** below.)

Option 3

For power chair users

It is difficult though not impossible to work this exercise from a heavy powered chair. Giving the impulse from the chair is usually not a problem, and can be done with the arm or legs or head, but receiving and interpreting an impulse can be. Often the chair back prevents contact and the pushing impulse must be translated through the manual controls into a mechanical movement.

- The 'pusher' demonstrates a push in space. Try to understand its direction and strength. You can ask to see it several times. Now adjust your chair speed to correspond to the energy of what you have seen. Finally, combine your partner's action with your movement following its direction and dynamic into the space. Get feedback from your partner and those watching to see how well you are interpreting the move. Try the combined actions with and without making physical contact.
- Alternatively, work in or out of your chair on much smaller impulses and tiny journeys with hand, wrist and head. Don't forget you may be able to combine these smaller movements with the larger travelling pathways, for example, if your chair starts and stops abruptly explore how this creates movement in your body. Now get your partner to pick up on these movements and include/introduce them in their pushing action.

IMPROV 7: RECEIVING – STOPPED IN YOUR TRACKS

Arresting the movement of a travelling dancer
Initiating movement
Groups of 3: one sender, one receiver and one traveller

Introduction

The principles of catching or receiving are best understood by considering the different mechanisms involved in arresting objects in motion. What is the action of catching a cricket ball or a rugby ball falling from a great height? How do trampolines or the buffers on the front of a train function? In each example, the person or material doing the catching reduces the effect of impact by absorbing the incoming energy and gradually increasing resistance until the object is stopped.

Directions

a. To begin with, dancers should work quite closely so that the travelling dancer moves only a short distance from the moment of being sent to the moment of being caught. This can be explored initially as a traditional trust exercise. For students who can't step, the exercise can be interpreted as falling and catching or can be explored as an exercise on the floor – rolling and stopping.

b. An effective way to stop a dancer travelling towards you is to reach out to him/her and make contact as early as you can (the buffer effect). Place one hand on the dancer's hip and one on the shoulder and cushion him/her into your body by gently dropping your elbows, so your arms can hinge and act like absorbing springs. You may find that by transferring your weight from your front leg to your back leg as you do this will add to the buffer effect.

c. A similar technique can be used for receiving someone travelling towards you in a wheelchair. Placing a hand on his/her shoulder while the other makes contact with the knees will prevent the dancer from pitching forward.

Option 1

For power chairs

Receiving someone when you are in a power chair may cause greater problems and requires a greater sensitivity on the part of the traveller. You still need to think about the best surfaces of your chair and body to use. (Remember to check your chair for any sharp edges or points – these need masking, see Chapter 16.) Discuss with your partners where you are able to take weight, and then think about how you can control or disperse weight so that you can still take part in the improvisation.

Option 2

For power chairs

If the group is warm, the exercise can be played in a freer way. A single power chair user can drive into a group of standing dancers who interpret the 'collision'.

Watching dancers call 'Freeze!' and 'Go!' to capture held moments of impact and dispersal, and 'Reverse' in order to watch the process rewind!

IMPROV 8: OPEN HAND

Directing your energy
Giving
Receiving
2 dancers

Introduction

Open your hands as if you are offering someone the most precious gift. Make it the best thing you can imagine. Have the sense of this gift moving out of your hands. Notice how that feels. Now, without changing your position in the slightest, imagine you are receiving the most precious, wonderful gift, the best thing possible for you in this moment. Notice how that feels. Now, again without changing your physical position, swap between giving and receiving. What do you sense and feel in your hands as you change from one image to the other?

Now try **linear pathway** again with these two images in mind.

It is a good idea to space pairs out and have everyone working in parallel to avoid collisions.

Sender

When you send your partner forward keep your focus on them and keep your hand open with the feeling of 'giving' while your partner travels away from you. As your partner comes to rest, keep your hand open and directed towards them but now think of receiving, almost as if you were inviting your partner back. Don't give up if nothing happens. Just invite them with your hand open with the expectation that he/she will come back.

Stay in the same position as long as possible (only shift your position to catch or retrieve your partner at the end if you have to). If your partner doesn't return, simply go and join them and try again.

Traveller

Imagine you are a wave rolling up a beach (as you are pushed) and then, instead of just stopping, see if you can feel a return or ebb phase (that carries you back to your partner), like the wave sweeping back down the beach to the sea. Try travelling with your eyes closed. Try not to invent this. If it doesn't feel real, then don't pretend. But do stay alive to how the energy of the push dissipates (does it just go, or does it go somewhere?) and be ready to follow any direction that arises. Hint: keep breathing as you get to the end of the outward journey.

The elasticity or sense of a return phase in a linear impulse gives us many new options when we come to improvise. A strong impulse away from someone need not be taken as a final rebuff or rejection, if we remain open and flexible it may in fact be inviting us back.

Example: the woman who imprisoned dancers

On a week-long project with Janet Smith's Scottish Dance Theatre, in Dundee, a compact little woman with a seemingly profound learning difficulty appeared unable to engage with the dancers. There was even some discussion as to whether the project was actually appropriate for her as it involved an improvised performance at the end of the week, yet when asked she was quite clear that she wanted to take part. Despite this, she initially seemed to exhaust everyone who worked with her, offering very little physically and often chattering away inappropriately. She seemed to imprison or block even the most able and inventive members of the company.

When we tried linear pathways she seemed unwilling to push her partner, while her constant chatter kept everyone at a distance. Because she was quite robust and cheery, I was encouraged to explore a more playful approach. I got very close to her and virtually stood on her toes, at which she exclaimed 'Get off a me yer great elephant!' and gave me a vigorous shove. The energy of the push had a clear return phase to it and so I bounced back towards her to be met with another push, and an animated cry of 'Off yee go!' She was now enjoying herself, and the energy of her pushes was clear and easy to read. Her cry of 'On yer bike!' became the catchphrase of the residency and her delight in the improvisation meant that she eventually led a vocalised section in the performance in which other dancers called out to each other as they pushed. Noticeably through this engagement she found her place in the group, and from being an outsider at the start of the residency she had become known and warmly valued by the end.

Notes

65 Project sponsored by HandiCap International and the British Council. See Appendix 2.
66 This transition from known to unknown, from mastery to mishap, is beautifully illustrated in the mirror image of the two Hebrew words, Melech (king) and Lemech (fool).
67 From the Japanese movement school of Shintaido founded by Hiroyuki Aoki.
68 In Tai-Chi the return to this original posture is part of a process of re-education in which the act of walking (by falling) is replaced by 'stepping' through shifting weight, so that the centre is never off balance.

18 Listening through touch

I listen like a person telephoning in the dark.

I listen like the ornithologist who unwraps bird bones from tissue paper.

(Stephen Kuusisto, 1998)

'It was a knowledge that became embodied through my hands, which "listened" avidly to his in order to move with him, reading the energy pattern manifest there and following it, absorbing it, reflecting it as movement dispersed throughout myself, up my forearms and down into my feet, seeping from the distal ends towards my centre of gravity' (Ness, 1996: 135). This quote from Sally Ann Ness describes her experience of being led into a Philippine rural folk dance/game by one of the performers. It beautifully describes the sensation of following a partner through the sense of touch, into unknown territory. To those new to dance, the idea of listening through touch may seem strange, but it is in fact based on 'sound' physiology. If you are hearing sound as you are reading this book it is due to vibrations in the air 'touching' your ear drum; in just the way that a stretched goat skin on a djembe is played by the beating hands of the drummer, so your eardrum is being played (touched) by the percussive action of atomic particles formed into moving patterns or sound waves. The eardrum itself is highly specialised skin, which passes information to the brain like the skin of the rest of the body, by responding to pressure. So although you may 'feel' some part of the seat you're sitting on and 'hear' the sounds of people moving around, these are both communications from the skin responding to different kinds of pressure, one on a macro and one on a micro level. The human ability to listen to others allows us not only to be touched but also moved.

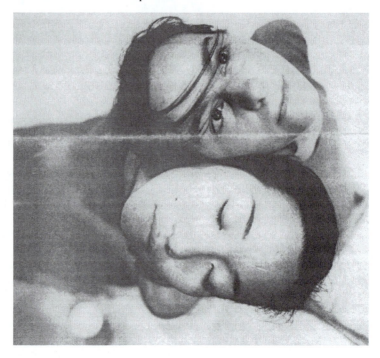

18.1 Chisato Minamimura and partner, CandoCo Summer School, 2000.
(Photographer Kalpesh Lathigra)

LEADING AND FOLLOWING

> When eyes are blind, the mind seeks new ways of seeing. My
> fingers look not with two eyes but with ten eyes, and the whole
> body is alert to perceive and hears the voice of life.
>
> (Helen Keller, 1968)

Introduction

It has often been stated that CI eliminated the idea of leader and
follower, so it may seem strange that so much of my work focuses
on identifying the distinctive qualities of this polar relationship.
Within a good improvisation, leading and following are in
constant flux. However it soon became clear to me that many
people (including students of CI) are not always able to distinguish
clearly between the two roles. People often think they are following when they are actually leading and vice versa. Teachers in
particular, often have a hard time learning to listen and be led
by someone else, particularly when they might consider that
person to be less experienced. In Improv 9 **leading and following**
the two roles are purposefully distinguished in order that each
is increasingly understood and experienced, thus avoiding any

tendency for the faster, stronger or more experienced, dancer always to be in the driving seat.

Because partners exchange roles, we get to experience the joys and frustrations of both sides of the leader–follower, teacher–student relationships and in the process begin to identify and solve problems that arise in each area. It is a refreshing sight to see an experienced professional being led by a young disabled student into a whole new movement world. Later on we come to realise that leader and follower are two sides of the same coin, the white and black interlinking 'tears' of the Tai Chi symbol, and the idea of leader–follower if not eliminated, is at least expanded: leading manifests itself as the ability to listen to, understand and therefore at first guide and draw out the best in our partner, while advanced following skills arise from an ability to understand the intention of the person leading and therefore to make the very most of what they are offering.

Leading and following grounds us in the essential skills of listening through touch. It demands on every occasion that we listen as though it were our first meeting. It is an exercise that can be constantly revisited and researched as a source of new discoveries. It is an ideal warming-up exercise, though it can develop into a fast and dynamic dance, but, more importantly, it is an ideal way for dancers to attune themselves to one another. Just as two musicians, say a cellist and a guitarist, will tune their instruments to establish the same harmonic range, so dancers in **Leading and following** tune their movement to a shared harmony as a prelude to the more complex movements that follow.

Stealing, freewheeling, interloper and **cascade** are all improvisations based on problems encountered in **Leading and following**. Remember, finding a difficulty in any of the exercises is an invitation to create new solutions.

IMPROV 9: LEADING AND FOLLOWING

'Education?' said he, meditatively, I know enough Latin to know that the word must come from *educere*, to lead out; and I have heard it used; but I have never met anybody who could give me a clear explanation of what it means.

(William Morris, 1890)

Leading skills
Listening/following skills
2 dancers

The exercise below is described for two dancers who are both able to use their hands and arms but can be adapted for just about any dancers regardless of their physicality (see Figure 18.2).

Directions

Working in pairs, position yourself facing or alongside your partner. Decide who will lead and who will follow. If leading, offer the back of your wrist to your partner (as though you were showing him/her a wristwatch). If following, place your palm on your partner's wrist. Relax your arm (elbow pointing down) so that there is just a little weight on the point of contact between your palm and his/her wrist.

Teaching notes

- Before thinking of moving, notice your breathing and that of your partner. Listen to your partner intently through your point of contact. Notice the imperceptible, subtle movement that already exists and, if you can, try to draw this movement out, inviting them gently, gradually into an ever wider and more dynamic range. Always go slowly at first, especially if you are using the exercise as a warm-up. When travelling, keep your eyes open (see notes below for visually impaired leaders) and lead your partner into space and away from obstacles.

- If you go too quickly, you will either feel your partner beginning to 'hold on' or you will lose your partner – either way you are going too fast too soon. Your goal as leader is to create movement that is stimulating, varied and at times challenging, without inducing panic in your partner. Learn something new about your partner. For example, are they happier moving forwards or backwards? Where do they become hesitant? Can you encourage your partner to explore these spaces without forcing them? Notice the expression on your partner's face. Do they look relaxed, engaged, excited, frightened or bored? Your partner's expression and breathing pattern will give you valuable information that will help you maintain a lively and animated connection.

- If you are uncertain how to lead, try some of the ideas below without actually speaking:

  - describe the landscapes of different countries;
  - show the way different animals move;
  - prepare a cordon bleu meal;
  - describe the passage of the meal through the body (yes, all the way through!);
  - write your partner's name and address in space;
  - conduct an orchestra playing a selection of your choice.

- On occasion, try returning to stillness; if your partner is really listening, they will also become still. If your partner continues to move, wait until they register your stillness . . . see how long it takes. When you have worked for a while, you may find that your arms begin to tire – can you change arms without breaking contact? You can do this by gently bringing your free hand or arm up underneath your partner's to lift your partner lightly away. If you can't use your hand, try changing to another part of your body.

- Take time to slow down. There is no need to think 'I'm going to stop.' Remember you were already in subtle motion before you began. Simply observe your body's unique pathway back to resting, keep breathing and be aware of the ever finer quality of your body's movement until you register a sense of stillness inside yourself. Notice the different sensations now that your body is no longer 'actively' moving.

Notes for followers

- Keep your eyes closed and imagine that your palm is an ear following a melody. Try not to use your fingers or thumb to grip or hold onto your partner but use the ability of your skin to feel and follow.
- Notice the smallest of movements and begin to follow your partner as they move.
- If you lose touch, keep your eyes closed and wait for them to come back to you.
- Breath easily and naturally throughout the exercise.
- If it is hard for you to keep your eyes closed, use a blindfold.
- If you have poor balance, you may want to try following with both hands (see Figure 18.5) or work from the floor or seated.

To conclude, the leader returns to a centred balanced position and waits as the follower lightly breaks contact. Try to lift your hand away so that the leader doesn't feel you leave (try to lift, rather than slide off). Finally, open your eyes and don't forget to thank your partner. It can feel quite rejecting if either partner simply walks off and talks to someone else after an exercise like this that involves close, mutual attention. Traditionally in countries like Japan the 'harmony' of these exchanges (particularly in the martial arts) are recognised by politely bowing before leaving, though a smile or a 'thank you' will serve the same purpose.

Leading from a manual wheelchair

- Ensure you have plenty of space. When you first start leading, work from the spot with your brakes on. The reason for this is twofold. Initially, try to control the movement of your partner towards and away from you. This gives your partner time to begin to sense the presence of your chair in relation to your body and to develop an internal image of its location.

By working on the spot you make this easier for your partner and cut down on the number of cracked shins in the process. You will also discover that, by working on the spot, it is still possible to take your partner on a wild and engaging journey by using your own body more imaginatively than you can if you are occupied with steering. Remember that, when you lead, you are in the teaching role, and that means helping your partner to learn – something they will not be able to do if they are: (a) anxious; (b) in pain!

- When you are both feeling more at ease, experiment with travelling – try replacing the leading wrist with your head or shoulder. Now you are free to use your hands to control your chair and will be able to work on travelling and speed. It is important for the safety of your partner that you do the preparatory work first.

- It is quite possible for one wheelchair user to lead another, though negotiating the movement of two chairs can be confusing, so, again, begin working as leader with your brakes on.

Following for manual wheelchair users

Having said 'don't grip' there may be occasions where a different kind of contact is going to be useful. If you are working with your brakes off, you may still find that it is difficult to move your chair to follow your partner, especially if your partner travels quickly across the floor. In these situations you would normally need both hands to propel your chair and so lose contact with your listening hand.

- If your partner begins to move out of your range, then you can hook your hand over your partner's wrist and take a free ride. To slow down, stop or move backwards, the point of contact can be used to offer resistance. All of this can be done without actually gripping and greatly extends the dynamic possibilities of the improvisation.

- If you are leading someone who is using a wheelchair, you can similarly offer to hook and pull, in which case your partner is free to accept the offer or not. This is completely different from grabbing your partner's hand and pulling them around, which may seem at first to extend the range of movement but actually rules out the element of choice (see **ground rules**, Chapter 16).

Blind dancers leading

- Because of the initial danger of followers bumping into each other, blind or visually impaired dancers leading can be positioned in an open space and work from the spot. In this way whoever is leading is 'tethered' and the follower is able to explore freely in a 360° extended circle without fear of hitting walls or other dancers. His/her presence also serves to remind other leaders to make use of the space. Leading from a fixed location is a good test of ingenuity for anyone, so try it!

Teaching notes

• Try to ensure that the whole group starts from a shared stillness. Encourage dancers to sense this among themselves and to find their own beginning when they sense that everyone in the space is quiet and focused. This common or shared sense is part of the group's learning (see Improv 2 **flock** in Chapter 17).

Problems and solutions

In 1997 I was teaching at a school for deaf students in Tokyo. My words were being translated into Japanese and then into Japanese sign; the student's sign language was translated into spoken Japanese and then into English. This in itself demanded an economy of words and a reassessment of teaching methods. Try stopping a studio full of deaf students, who don't speak your language, half of whom have their eyes closed, and all of whom are concentrating intensely on dancing with their partners; it is quite obvious, in the way it can only be on the metro on the way home, that this was a problem I should have considered before starting.

In response to this problem I introduced the idea of **flock** (see Improv 2, Chapter 17). A single leading student was able to take a signal from me and bring her partner to stillness. The other leaders gradually became aware of this couple who were no longer moving and stillness spread effortlessly through the studio. This method encouraged us all to be aware not only of the bodies moving in space but also of the space itself.

Having taught dance to deaf students, the Austrian teacher/dancer Brigitte Jagg was faced with the problem of a large, noisy and unruly class of 5- and 6-year-old hearing youngsters. She told them about her work and then conducted the entire class without speaking. The children followed her directions in rapt silence.

Try teaching a class yourself, without using words.

In South Africa on the Tshwaragano project we experimented with deaf dancers signing while their partners 'followed' their hand movements through touch. We found this most effective when the signing was large and slow.

18.2 Two leading. Vertigo Dance Company workshop. Israel, 2000. (Photographer Michal Chitayat)

Option 1

Two leading

Try following two dancers at the same time (see Figure 18.3).

Begin with one dancer leading gently on each palm and allow the movement to build in complexity and speed.

If you become dizzy or disorientated, simply slow down. Remember that your leaders cannot travel any faster than the speed at which you follow. Going faster is not the goal; learning to listen is. Discuss any new discoveries before changing roles.

Option 2

Profound physical disability

If your movement is severely limited or restricted, you may find it more effective when leading to hold your partner's fingers in your hand and to lead by turning and twisting your grip. The fingers are sensitive and are capable of 'hearing' and transmitting articulate movement to the rest of the body; a huge range of movement can be elicited in this way.

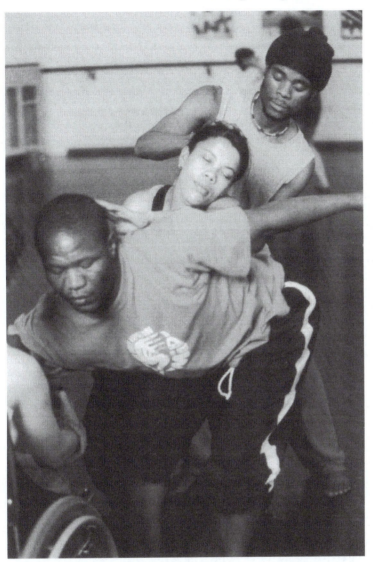

18.3 Tshwaragano workshop. One leads, three follow. (Photographer John Hogg)

If your partner is profoundly disabled, and is working with you as just described, take time to listen to the energy of the contact you are making with each other. Movement may be very subtle (like the first unfurling of a butterfly's wings). Allow what you feel to move you. It is important not to invent movement. If you can't feel anything, listen for a while longer, allow whatever you feel to resonate or echo through your body. Use yourself as a sounding chamber that amplifies the finest impulses and makes them visible. Above all else, keep 'listening' and be true to the impulses you receive. When your leader is still, return to stillness. Talk about how it felt, and particularly try to identify moments when you felt connected or moments when you felt you were 'faking it'.

For students who have virtually no voluntary movement, try following and leading using eye direction.

- Move whichever part of the body your partner's gaze falls on.
- Do the same but with a second dancer mirroring
- Add a third dancer moving in opposition
- Create your own variations.

See also the **Simpson Board** for choreographic work using the eyes (Chapter 4).

Option 3

Profound physical disability

1 dancer leading
2, 3, 4 or more following

The initial leader–follower partnership is established, but a second follower 'listens' to the first follower. One hand is placed on his/her hip, the other very lightly on the back of the head in order to follow the movement of the spine. A whole chain of dancers can be added (see Figure 18.4). This exercise can be tried with non-disabled dancers leading through minimal movement, i.e. just the hand, and no movement of the arm or body.

Option 4

The dancer on the end of the chain can begin to **freewheel** (see Improv 12, below).

This is a bit like a tail that is being wagged, and the last person on the chain is like a fly on the end of the tail (can be tried eyes open or closed). Develop as an improvisation with the end dancers interchanging between different groups.

Examples

With good 'listening', someone with very limited movement can lead an entire company of dancers. Aislinn Lewis, one of the members of the Velcro, Dance Company began one of the company's pieces by moving one dancer with just her fingers; this dancer being followed by a second who was being followed by a third, until twenty dancers were in motion, undulating like the surface of a still pond into which Aislinn had dipped her hand.[69] In order to prepare for this kind of work, the whole group had to recognise an impulse and understand when that impulse had ended so that stillness could return. Without the ability to return to a state of quiet listening, the system becomes full of 'noise' and the original connection and impulse lost.

Equally, there are some profoundly disabled people whose movement is very dynamic, active and powerful. This range of movement also presents challenges in listening and in following. Dancers who have developed advanced listening skills will delight in the kinds of duet work that can arise from such partnerships.

The often chaotic, random and seemingly violent movement that is familiar to some people with cerebral palsy can transform itself in the most extraordinary way when listening skills are developed sufficiently. I have often found that this random and spasmodic muscular activity will resolve itself into recognisable patterns (ellipses and figures of eight for example). This might mean following using both hands in order to provide stability while allowing the chaotic activity to guide both partners. It is a bit like plugging one's hands into an electric current, and having one's upper body literally thrashed about, while the lower body maintains a stable base which serves both dancers. Here, although the dancers are holding hands, the support is flexible, allowing for a wide range of movement.

To enter into the movement world of another person and to experience the full force of the body's energy in this way can be both exhilarating and exhausting. On ending a duet, my partner turned to me and said 'Now you know what my life is like!' It is still almost inconceivable to me to understand what it means to be wrestling with this kind of energy, twenty-four hours a day. What was clear, however, was that the movement was not random – it was what scientists today call 'chaotic' (see Gleick on chaos theory). In other words it was disguised pattern, and by 'joining with it' instead of standing back, the hidden pattern became evident. In fact, the dance that arose between us on this occasion had a rhythm not unlike jiving and was followed by a rare moment of complete physical and mental relaxation.

Sometimes inexperienced students will blame their partner for 'not doing it right' as though there were only one way of interpreting the exercise. Clearly, certain elements and principles improve the skills of **leading and following**. Relaxing the arm and hand, not gripping, breathing naturally; these are all techniques that can be developed in class. The more experienced a dancer becomes, however, the more they should be able to adapt the technique to dance with any partner. It's a bit like learning a foreign language; an expert is not someone who can only speak with other experts but someone who can talk to children, academics and everyone in between.

A student in Kobe, Japan, complained to me that her partner wasn't following her, and in one sense it was true, his contact was very light and he wasn't managing to drop his weight into her wrist. The question that faced her in that moment, however,

18.4 David Fumbatha leads Gladys Agulhas in a workshop demonstration. Johannesburg, 2001. (Photographer John Hogg)

was whether to spend the session feeling frustrated or to seek
to understand and dance with his energy. When I asked her to
describe his touch, she said he felt 'Like a small bird learning
to fly'. With this image in her mind she was then able to 'loft' his
hand up and enjoy the freedom of her own movement before
his hand floated down to rest on her wrist again. Once she shifted
her attention away from blaming him, she was able to find a
dancing solution to her problem. In the process she had made
her own discovery of the improvisation called **freewheeling** (see
Improv 12, p. 127).

This principle of invention is essential to integrated practice for although in the example just recounted, the dancer was eventually able to learn how to sink his weight more effectively, there are many people whose bodies are not able to adapt. That does not mean they are 'doing it wrong' but that we are faced with making the exercise relevant to whoever we are working with. In an orphanage in Ethiopia a very young boy, clearly afraid of contact, allowed me to make only the lightest contact with him and them moved his hand away, twisting and flicking his wrist. His hand fluttered about like an injured moth. To follow this fragile and broken dance I gently cupped my hands around his, so that his dance was not restricted but was somehow heard; in this way, allowing his movement to guide me, his story seemed gradually to unfold in my hands and I was led to a new understanding of his dance and his character.

IMPROV 10: INTERLOPER – INTRODUCING THE THIRD PERSON

> The two body problem is easy. Newton solved it completely. Each body – the earth and the moon, for example – travels in a perfect ellipse round the systems joint centre of gravity. Add just one more gravitational object, however, and everything changes. The three body problem is hard, and worse than hard.
>
> (Gleick, 1998)

Negotiating spacing and timing
Entering and leaving duets
3 dancers

Introduction

A development of **leading and following** in which a third dancer combines with the initial duet. The central principle is still about listening and harmonising but to understand the 'three-body problem' there needs to be a greater emphasis on freedom (space), choice (time) and rhythm (space, action and time). This relationship is also dealt with in **stealing** (see Improv 13, below).

Directions

The first two dancers (the primary couple) simply repeat **leading and following**. The 'follower' still works with eyes closed and remains in contact with the 'leading' dancer. The third dancer is referred to as the soloist or satellite.

Notes for satellites

- While the primary couple get ready, place yourself in the studio so that you feel connected to them in some way. This may be nearby or at a distance. It may mean reflecting the position or spacing of the dancers, or may arise from your sense of how they are breathing or it may be something quite unique and unexpected that leads you to feel a sense of connection.

- As the primary couple begins to move, try to gain a sense of any rhythm in their partnership and begin to move with them. It may help to imagine that the whole dance is taking place in water, or in some medium that swirls and glides around you. Explore the wider movement sweeps (like the wake of a boat) as well as the more intricate patterns (eddies and whirlpools) that are thrown up around them. The latter represent opportunities to introduce more subtle detail into the improvisation. Remember that you are still trying to understand and reflect the energy of the initial partnership and to stay connected, so try to let their motion move you. Don't be overly creative! Make sure you all take a turn in the position of soloist.

Option 1

Add a fourth (and fifth) dancer so that there are additional satellites following the duet. The satellite dancers now have to respond to the primary pair and to the pathways of the other soloist(s). Allow any natural moments of contact between any of the dancers.

This improvisation can be combined with **traverse** (see Chapter 21) particularly when using two or more satellite dancers.

Teaching notes

- This can initially prove a difficult improvisation. In Belgium we named it 'spot the steklbee' (spot the gooseberry) as there is a tendency for the third person to get disconnected and to wander about like an embarrassed chaperone. It may help the soloist to place their focus on just one dancer at a time, or shift focus from one to the other, whichever draws the attention. Alternatively, work with the spaces that open and close around the duet.

IMPROV 11: DEPARTURES

Separation
Breaking contact
Breath
2 dancers

Introduction

You may have found that when you are following your partner
in **leading and following** that there are certain moments when
you accidentally lose contact. As already explained, this is a good
opportunity to notice your body's reaction to the unknown. You
may feel yourself tightening up and notice that your breathing has
temporarily halted. These are common reactions but ones that are
important to recognise if we are to go beyond them. Holding our
breath is a response to anxiety or alarm – just noticing that you're
not breathing is often enough to allow a return to a more relaxed,
responsive state.

Directions

Dance **leading and following** but begin to be aware of these
minor separations. As the leader, explore how you can facilitate
them; as follower, begin to enjoy the moment of departure. At
what moments do they occur? What does a 'natural' separation
feel like, as opposed to a forced one? After each separation, the
leader returns to, and reconnects with, the follower. The follower
continues to dance with eyes closed. Now explore **freewheeling**
(below).

IMPROV 12: FREEWHEELING

> The universe is full of matter, and matter warps space–time so
> that bodies fall together.
>
> (Stephen Hawking, 1999)

Creating openings within a duet
Awareness of breath
Listening skills
Spatial skills
Timing
2 dancers (leader with eyes open, follower with eyes closed)

Introduction

Freewheeling addresses the frequently asked question: 'How long should I stay in a duet and when or how do I leave?' This improvisation needs plenty of room. It is often worth splitting into two groups to ensure enough space in the studio and to benefit from the opportunity to watch each other dancing. In **leading and following** and **departures** you will have become aware that there are moments when you come close to losing your partner, or times when your partner is on the verge of breaking away from you. **Freewheeling** utilises these moments by: (a) allowing a natural separation to occur; or (b) by actually giving your partner a slight impulse that sends them away from you.

Directions

Notes for leaders

a. Begin in the same way as **leading and following**. Remember your partner's eyes are closed so that you must work more consciously to lead into space before releasing your partner and ensuring that they do not collide with anyone or anything.

b. As you release your partner, keep breathing and don't inhibit your own movement. Continue to move with and around your partner until you find a natural means of reconnecting.

c. At the moment of release, try not to become a static 'observer'. Your partner's departure should also give you new impulses and information. Try to respond to these and to continue to move. Imagine an apple falling from a branch: the re-adjustments that the branch makes to accommodate its new condition. When we give something away or when someone leaves us, there is always something to be felt. As leader, the moment of separation not only determines the pathway of the follower but also provides information about your own journey. So long as your partner isn't in danger of colliding with anyone, see where your pathway leads you.

d. Keep a sense of where your partner is but don't feel that you have to stare fixedly at them. Remember that your relationship to your partner is based on what you feel, it is three dimensional rather than two dimensional. Don't restrict your movement through overvaluing what you can see. Your eyes only hold part of the picture.

e. Try to be as clear as you can about the source of movement that sends your partner away.

f. Given time, you may begin to find that your pathways lead you naturally back together. If this doesn't happen simply return to them calmly and begin leading again.

Notes for followers (unsighted)

a. Try to avoid freezing up as your partner releases you, but, similarly, as you have your eyes closed, you will need to gauge the range of your movements to suit the size of studio you're dancing in. Try not to be overly creative, simply respond naturally to the impulse your partner gives you.

b. The moment of release is full of information, and the more you attend to this the easier it will be to make sense of the journey. Watching this done well there is a real sense that the 'freewheeler' is still following some line of tension that connects to the leader.

c. If you are finding it difficult to find your way back, you may need to make sure that you establish a real connection before you separate; spend longer with your partner and try to take shorter separations. The initial journeys can be tiny (as in the beginning exercise of **stretching a point**: see Improv 1, Chapter 17).

Development: up to 16 dancers

• Freewheeling can be used as a large-group improvisation with the unsighted dancers being picked up and led by different partners. Such a group might have 3 or 4 unsighted dancers and 9 to 12 sighted at any one time. The unsighted dancers can start with a leading partner or alone in space, and wait for the leaders to find them.

Option 1

An advanced exercise to be tried with plenty of space

Dancers who have mastered this exercise can try freewheeling with both dancers working unsighted. It is a good idea to have only a few couples working at a time. Dancers working in this way tend to monitor their own speed and accidents are a rarity. Nonetheless, if you are concerned, you can place additional bodies around the periphery of the space to guide the dancers away from walls or other potentially dangerous objects.

This is a fascinating improvisation and can lead to the most unexpected and beautiful dances. It can also be attempted by experienced sighted improvisers with blind partners. You may wish to revisit **stretching a point** as preparation (Improv 1, Chapter 17).

Give dancers time to discuss each improvisation and to identify interesting and challenging moments. **Freewheeling** can be used in conjunction with, or as a development of, **stealing** (Improv 13, below) and **interloper** (Improv 10).

IMPROV 13: THE ART OF STEALING

> It is harder to crack a prejudice than an atom.
>
> (Albert Einstein)

> They do not keep clocks in their houses. Instead, they listen to their heartbeats.
>
> (Alan Lightman, 1993)

3 dancers
Intercepting
Timing
Use of space

Note

Only to be attempted when you are comfortable with **interloper** and **freewheeling**, and are at ease with travelling around and in and out of a moving duet without interrupting or disturbing it.

Introduction

I am often asked why so many improvisations I use involve at least one person dancing with their eyes closed. The reason is not, as is often thought, to overcome prejudices about disability nor to discover what it would be like to be blind. It is to address a far less obvious prejudice, that of how we perceive space and time. Like most other prejudices, it is neither readily acknowledged nor easily relinquished.

In the following improvisation we will look at some of the problems that arise when we confuse 'mechanical' time with the more human quality of timing. It is quite common in **stealing** to see dancers, trying to solve the problems presented by stopping, metaphorically (or literally) scratching their head, trying to work things out intellectually, or circling the studio with their eyes glued to the action. In either case their primary reference is visual, they are looking at a three-dimensional, moving problem as though it were a two-dimensional picture. This visually loaded approach locks the body into a 'front on' position with the eyes always directed forward and the body trailing behind like an obedient though hapless servant.

The emphasis on 'unsighted' work in this book is designed to disrupt our tendency to regard the world as though we were viewing images on a screen. It is a re-education and a relocation of the mind in its proper home, the body. Through the repeated experience of being deprived of the sense of sight (and by maintaining first principles: not to hold physically) we gradually let go of our habitual means of registering and controlling the world around us. Through a process of initial disorientation, we become aware of sensation on, and space extending from, all surfaces of the body, and begin to experience ourselves as participants in a three-dimensional world, in which we are moved as much as mover and in which pathways open as we travel along them. It is through learning to complement what is seen with what is felt, that a sense of personal, spatial orientation is gradually developed. This body learning refines and sharpens our senses and develops our intuition, so that as choreographers we begin to understand moving elements and as improvisers we become adept at integrating ourselves into the moving picture.

Directions

a. In just the same way that you swapped hands in **leading and following** when your arm got tired, here, the soloist aims to move into a position so as to replace the hand of the original leader who then moves out of the duet and takes up the role of the satellite.
b. When this exercise is mastered, the follower may remain unaware of the transition from one leader to another (though hairy arms are usually something of a give-away!). Take turns at following so that every member of the group experiences the different aspect of the dance: leader, follower, soloist.

Option 1

Round Robin

A single unsighted dancer. The satellite dancer replaces the leading dancer who becomes the satellite, and then exits to be replaced by a new satellite, who replaces the leader . . . and so on.

Option 2

Stealing for wheelchair users

If you're using a wheelchair, you may initially find it difficult to get close enough to make a steal without endangering the safety of the 'blind' follower.

Start by working at a distance so that you are in sympathy with the primary duet. Sense the rhythmicity of their movement and the way they open and close, be aware of the entrances (spaces) that they create in their dancing.

Begin by simply playing in and around them, as if afloat on a wave that carries you in and out of a rocky coastline, i.e. as if you were practising **interloper** (Improv 10, above).

If you are using a manual chair, experiment with gliding past with an arm free and outstretched. Don't get discouraged if you don't manage a steal, keep physically offering opportunities and remain alive to the movement of the duet. It is not unusual to see less experienced soloists 'hanging around' the duet, a kind of 'lingering with intent' dance, which tends to close down the space available. This comes from a sense of urgency or in other words through overemphasising the 'mechanical' element of time. When we take away the pressure to come up with a result, the central duet will experience more space in which to move, openings become apparent and the satellite dancer can then find the appropriate moment to enter and steal. Time is replaced by **timing**. Engaging in the flow of movement around the duet, we are guided to the appropriate place to receive the follower (this is the art of stealing).

It is important to make the leading dancer aware of your presence. If a leading dancer is unaware of the approaches of other dancers (particularly those using wheelchairs), feedback from those watching will help to clarify this situation. However, try to avoid manufacturing the exchange, stay involved in the energy of the dance as opposed to the energy of rather stilted negotiations. It is worth waiting for a genuine steal, you will be able to feel the 'rightness', the effortlessness of it in contrast to the 'tackiness' of a set-up exchange.

The proximity of wheelchairs is an additional incentive to the follower to really follow and not invent movement, and to those leading to control and guide the directionality of their partners with clarity!

The skills being learned are those of manoeuvrability, proximity and connectedness – **dis**possession rather than possession. Notice how your internal energy and thought processes change as you come close to making a steal; notice the shift in mental attitude of 'I want this to happen', or 'I didn't manage to make it work.' Notice changes in your breathing. Watch these shifts as you move in and out of the central space. See if you can negotiate transitions without holding your breath. Is it possible to come away with a new partner without having 'wanted' or 'needed it', but simply because you put yourself in the right space for it to happen?

IMPROV 14: CASCADE

Group cooperation
Teamwork
Timing
Ground work for lifting
3 to 5 dancers; 1 guided, the others guiding

Introduction

This can be a deeply moving improvisation, having what might be considered a therapeutic effect, but it demonstrates a radical departure from therapeutic work in its requirement that the guides are also dancers whose task is to interact with each other and the space, while continuing to ensuring the safety of one of their members.

Preparation

Take time to set up well-balanced groups (ideally, no more than a single wheelchair user in each). Allow between 10 to 15 minutes for each person in the group. You may need to come back to this improvisation over a number of sessions. One dancer is guided by the others in the group. This is at first very passive, as in a gentle massage/manipulation, and the guiding dancers are relatively stationary. The improvisation grows so that there is more movement in both the guided and guiding dancers. For the latter, it raises the issue of care and responsibility v. freedom and self expression. For the guided dancer, it is about how to use support, find freedom and gauge one's activity in response to an unknown environment.

With practice, this can become one of the most profound, moving, reassuring and, at times, exhilarating exercises. Some people connect very deeply to this improvisation and it is worth allowing for time to absorb and talk about each improvisation.

Cascade can be adapted for any dancer, with or without wheelchair. Remember to discuss any safety measures that might need to be taken into account before you start the exercise.

First phase

- This may last around five minutes as the group grows accustomed to the way your body works and to each other as a team. Take a little time to discover what works for you and in the early part of the improvisation be prepared to talk to those working with you: lie on the floor with your eyes closed (use a mat if necessary) and allow yourself to be gently rocked and cradled by your fellow dancers. Give the weight and movement of your body over to those around you allowing yourself to be entirely passive, as if you are floating in the shallows at the sea's edge, with soft sand just beneath you, gentle waves lapping against your body. Try one person cradling your head while the others support and move your arms and legs.
- You may find that too much disparate movement prevents you from relaxing and that a more coordinated and balanced

approach by the group may be easier to absorb. This involves the group listening not only to you, but to each other.

Second phase

- Allow yourself in a relaxed and unforced way to begin to roll with the movement that is being created. In particular, allow your spine to become engaged with the movement of your limbs so that your torso can respond and follow. Don't use any great effort, but try to ride the movement that is being given to you, extending easily with the directions of impulses offered.
- It is now even more important that those moving you begin to orchestrate their impulses so that you are able to follow and respond to clear directions. The group's task is one of understanding and cooperation.

Third stage

- The group begin to introduce vertical impulses. You begin to move from rolling into sitting and even standing (according to your readiness). Again, try not to force your movement but take advantage of the impulses and support that are being offered. The group may now be using different parts of their bodies to support you as you extend more fully. Now begin to initiate your own directions through reaching and extending your limbs.
- It is up to the entire group to find a pace that is right, and to recognise and back off when too much effort is being expended. Remember there is no hurry, no prize for going fast and always plenty of time simply to rest and relax.
- If you are one of the guiding dancers, allow yourself to be responsive and alive, able to move into and away from the 'unsighted' dancer. So long as she is in no physical danger, then there is no need to be constantly at the unsighted dancer's side. Remember that you are there to dance as well as guide.

Fourth stage

- The 'unsighted dancer' begins to take impulses and travel with them. This again is done very simply by authentically responding to impulses and directions given by the group without adding superfluous movement. There may now be movement that travels and rests, both into and out of the floor.
- Progress gradually through each stage so that by the time you come to travelling the group has developed an understanding of your particular dynamic and is able to guide you safely and contain you within the space, while giving you the freedom to find a real sense of abandonment in your dance.

- Complete the dance by returning through the earlier stages until you return to a place of rest. This is often lying cradled among the bodies of your fellow dancers. Take time to talk about your experience.

Teaching notes

- The essential element with **cascades** as with **aerial pathways** (Improv 15, below) is that those who are leading understand and follow the intention of the 'unsighted' dancer. It is the movement of the 'blind' dancer that orchestrates the whole improvisation.
- The most common difficulty for those sharing the supporting role is finding how and when to be involved and how and when to move aside. The group's task is to find a way in which every member can play a part. This may be fairly straight forward in the opening stages but can become more elusive as things get faster. It is not uncommon at this stage to see dancers hovering frustrated at the edges of the action or frozen in a state of defeat while one or two industrious individuals monopolise the centre ground of the dance. The key to undoing this quandary is the principle that is explored in **interloper** (Improv 10, above) and developed in the sections on time and space.
- Some dancers may need to be gently reminded that they are part of a dance improvisation and are not leading a one-on-one bodywork/therapy session; that the time to move away and dance is as important as the time they spend guiding the 'unsighted' dancer. Some people seem to feel responsible for 'taking care' of the dancer who can't see, unable to see that they are busily excluding everyone else in the group from participating. Remind the guiding dancers that travelling away does not mean losing contact with the flow or pace that continues at the heart of the group. They can take and stretch the energy in the studio, refreshing themselves, and then returning to the shared task of guiding.

IMPROV 15: AERIAL PATHWAYS

Timing
Lifting skills
Group and soloist
5 to 7 dancers

These notes are meant as reminders for experienced groups. Work that involves lifting is best learned in the studio with an experienced teacher rather than from a book.

Introduction

Aerial pathways is a development of **cascade** (Improv 14, above) and of **placement replacement.** It extends the supporting role of the group into lifting. It often arises spontaneously when experienced dancers are working with **cascade.**

Directions

a. With sufficient supports being offered to the central dancer, dancing with eyes open or closed, he/she may gradually be able to give all (or most) of his or her weight over to the supporting group. Once suspended in this way, the supporting group may circulate, offering supporting surfaces and moving away when their support is no longer being used.
    Remember, the supporting group offers planes of support and does not try to hold, grab or lift.

b. The supported dancer can indicate direction by extending a limb into space, a sign that a support is required. Seeing this, dancers respond by placing supports under the outstretched limb like a step that magically appears under a raised foot, or like the back of a sofa that appears under an extended elbow. Supports are proffered and the central dancer makes use of them by softening into, and then extending onto and over them. Lifting arises from this mutuality of offered and accepted supports.

Notes

69 Velcro Dance Company. Circling the Square, 1996

19 Making an entrance in time and space

Because our presence is noted publicly, there is no place that I am going to walk in the door and not be noticed, it isn't going to happen. People will notice me, they will ponder me, they will think about me, they will note my presence. If I do anything physically, their eyes will come back to me immediately. I've become a part of the landscape that they are paying attention to.
(Bruce Curtis, attributed)[70]

Our respect for each other demands of each that we take our freedom when it comes.
(Brian Keenan, 1993)

INTRODUCTION

On my first visit to Japan, in 1996, I was impressed with the students' ability to listen to each other, a quality that seemed an essential part of Japanese culture. What I offered in the workshops seemed to be quickly absorbed and understood, and yet returning to England I had the uneasy feeling that I'd somehow missed something essential. The following year, while teaching at the Aichi Arts Centre in Nagoya, I found the answer to what had been troubling me.

It was a roasting hot, ozone-holed afternoon and I was standing with a small group of pedestrians across the road from the centre, waiting for the street sign to change. It was some time before I noticed that the road we were waiting to cross was all of two paces wide, 'A tiny-bloody-road!' I thought as the sweat trickled down the inside of my shirt and I stared longingly at the cool shadow of the Arts Centre opposite. To make matters worse, not a single bus, car or bicycle passed us as we slowly cooked by collective accord. Despite the searing heat, no one moved until the 'walk' sign turned green. By the time it took to cross the road, get changed and enter the studio I had formulated a response to the question that had been troubling me since the previous year.

Japanese society places great emphasis on conformity and I realised that while most Japanese will do anything not to draw attention to themselves, disabled people cannot help but be different and be noticed. I realised that I could not begin to get the non-disabled dancers to understand their disabled contemporaries if they were not able to step out of line, to understand difference themselves.

The essential idea of **crossing the line** (Improv 16, below) is not new, indeed it is an often unacknowledged part of most improvisations. What was exciting at that moment was how the experience on the street brought its possibilities to life for me as a teacher. Entering and leaving the space across a clearly defined line initially presented huge problems for the students in Japan. Forbidden in the studio to move across the line as a group, it became quite clear that some had to overcome enormous barriers in order to enter the dance space 'in their own time'; several were reduced to tears of frustration and, later, joyful discovery as they engaged in the improvisations. It proved to be powerful, uplifting and in at least one case life-changing work. One of the students announced at the end of the workshops that she had been moving when other people had told her to do so all her life. She had decided to leave her job and follow a new career. Suddenly the workshops in Japan found their edge and led to a reappraisal of my teaching on many different levels. We were, in the best traditions of 'exchanges', learning from and influencing each other.

By defining the dance space with a line or boundary and by placing ourselves outside of this boundary, we bring into sharp focus a further essential element to our understanding of dance; hard on the heels of time comes that very human element of 'choice' or, in other words, timing. At which moment do we enter? How long do we stay? When do we leave? These are all temporal considerations that become heightened when we define the physical space within which we dance and begin to explore our relationship to it, and from it.

The first to venture across the line cannot help but be noticed. It is a chance to speak with movement to all those present, to 'step out of line', so it helps to have something engaging to say in movement terms, or at the very least to be conscious of the gift of attention available. The empty space presents a heightened level of focus and attention in which timing becomes an almost tangible quality. The timing of those who follow the first dancer may add to, or detract from, the initial sense of tension that has been created. Dancers who monopolise being first in (or last out) will discover through feedback that they are decreasing tension rather than building it. No matter how 'original' a dancer is, if she is always the first to move or the last to leave the space, she eventually loses originality and becomes predictable. The aim of feedback is to encourage new development and departures and to allow reflection and analysis on what actions or decisions serve the improvisation by sustaining or raising tension. Interestingly, this awareness will gradually bring into attention the 'non-achievers' in the group, those who always remain somewhere in the middle of things, because everyone, no matter what they do, raises and lowers tension. Once students recognise this extra-ordinary fact – that they are all actually influencing proceedings regardless of how hard they try to remain invisible, they can begin to see, feel and enjoy the effect of their actions. Their contributions come more clearly into focus and they begin to move with less apprehension and more freedom. This is the moment when impro-vising becomes addictive.

The last few dancers to leave the dance space will also experience a growing sense of tension as will those on the outside, watching. There are at least two reasons for this. First, our fasci-nation with human relationships makes us ask 'Who will leave whom and how?' Second, the pathway out has become one that leads towards all those who have already departed. The last dancer to leave must navigate this transition from the empty space towards all those who have already left. The heightened focus and tension has been bought at a price. Leaving now is not as simple as it would have been earlier in the improvisation when fewer people were watching. The beginning and endings are rich opportunities for improvising and for gaining feedback because of the concentration of focus available. Those who abuse these positions by staying too long or by throwing away opportunities do so witnessed by the whole group. Feedback should be given with patience and humour. Students need to be encouraged to take the risks and not feel punished or humiliated when things don't work. Be prepared, when teaching inexperienced groups, to call time or introduce a time element when dancers look as if they have become stuck in the space (or see also Improv 21, **vocal scores**, below).

See lessons in non-competition below, for further discussion.

IMPROV 16: CROSSING THE LINE – 'INSCAPING' NOT ESCAPING[71]

> Art, like morality, consists of drawing the line somewhere.
> (G.K. Chesterton, Orthodoxy, 1908)

> When a person leaves a room, he becomes the topic of conver-sation for those remaining. It is a human preoccupation.
> (Brian Keenan, 1993)

Timing
Individual choices
Decision-making
Improvisation/performance skills
3 to 20 dancers (can become overlengthy for larger groups)

Introduction

Think of situations where you have done something, said something or placed something, and have felt satisfied, not triumphant, or smart but that your actions were appropriate and perhaps filled a real need. Perhaps a well-placed vase of flowers, a timely joke, a reaction that pulled someone back from danger, a well-timed departure before the weather changed, or perhaps a decision to do something or go somewhere that for some reason felt right at the time and led to an unexpectedly positive outcome (see Chapter 9).

Within any given physical area, be it a room, studio or a landscape, there will be a spot or a location which draws our attention, it may be because of the quality of light, because of the view, the form or structure or perhaps some less definable aspect which arouses our curiosity. If we go there, we may feel a mood change that leaves us more relaxed, confident or expectant. In some unique way we get to feel that we are better for being there.

Directions

a.   Agree a line which separates you from the space in which you are going to dance. This may be an imaginary or actual line on the dance floor. Make sure its position is clearly understood by everyone. You may want to draw a chalk line or put down some tape.

b.   If you are a large group, make sure that everyone has easy unobstructed access to the dance floor across this line, i.e. ensure that any wheelchair users or unsighted dancers are not caught behind a row of non-disabled dancers sitting along the line. The line now represents the sole entrance into and out of the dance space.

c.   Take time as a group to survey the empty space in front of you, notice its features, its colours, its areas of shade and light. Notice any particular features or areas of the space to which you are drawn. The start of this improvisation may on occasion have the same sense of alert attention that a conductor of an orchestra commands when he taps and raises his baton before the music begins.

d.   In your own time make your way across the line and into the studio towards the spot which most attracts you. Make sure that the decision to move is yours and comes from your own desire to move, and is not at someone else's request or suggestion. Beginners may at first try to make a pact to go with someone else. Encourage dancers to trust their own timing and to enjoy the sense of empowerment that comes from making their own decisions.

e.   Having reached the spot you were drawn to, see if you need to be in a particular position or facing in a particular direction.

You will know when you have found the right place and position because you will feel 'right'. If you feel uncertain, continue to search until you find a location and position that suits you. Allow time for everyone to settle before seeking the moment to leave the space. Now make your own way out again across the line. No command or direction should be given to leave – it is up to the dancers to feel when the moment is right.

f.   Sound can be used to guide or 'call' visually impaired dancers out of improvisations and then become the basis of new rhythms or musical improvisations (see Improv 55 **calling** in Chapter 28).

g.   Discuss what you have just done, any moments of interest that arose and particularly any moments in which you felt noticeable shifts in tension.

For individual consideration

- Ask yourself whether you were you satisfied with the following:

  - the moment you chose to enter;
  - the duration of your stay;
  - the time you spent travelling;
  - the moment you chose to leave;
  - how you chose to leave.

- For each of these questions did you feel you were too early, too late or just right?

Teaching notes

- Finding the right place to be in the studio in **crossing the line** is not always as simple as it first appears. By the time you arrive at your chosen spot, other dancers may have placed themselves nearby, changing the 'landscape' or the feel of the location.
- Remember, the idea of the perfect spot is what starts your journey but the journey itself may change your needs and feelings. The journey and the pathway you take will effect what you feel on arrival and how long you stay, it may even lead you to a new, unexpected location.
- How you approach the improv defines what you find when you arrive. If, for example, you see a group of butterflies drinking around a pond you would need to approach quietly and cautiously if you expected to share that spot with them.
- Dancers new to **crossing the line** often travel along linear pathways and leave the space in a similar fashion. Encourage more elaborate journeys. See Chapter 9 for further discussion.

LESSONS IN NON-COMPETITION: HUBRIS AND NEMESIS

Sometimes in **crossing the line**, the last dancers in the space get involved in what seems like a 'competition' to stay in longest, as if endurance were the sole objective of the improvisation. This competition may temporarily raise tension, but if the dancers become locked in a battle of wills, where obstinacy outweighs wit, those watching will quickly lose patience and tension will dissipate. The dancers can become trapped in what feels like a goldfish bowl, where every move they make is placed under the microscope.

These lock-horn situations often arise when dancers are unwilling to lose face. In these contests there often appears to be a winner and a loser. We may experience the apparent triumph of the final dancer, but that dancer is also now confronted with having to find a way out of the space. Unless she acknowledges the competitive manoeuvring in which she has been involved, we may notice a subtle lowering of tension as she departs. When someone stays at someone else's expense, there is often a paradoxical lowering of tension. On such occasions the final dancer can seem to be stalked out of the space by her own dark cloud.

It is important to ask dancers to remain aware of their sense of felt tension rising and falling throughout their improvising, right until and after everyone has left the space. A dancer noticing changes in tension, even if they are falls in tension, is always to be congratulated.

Real positive or raised tension experienced in an improvisation will seem to exist in the space after all the dancers have left and has a way of carrying over into the rest of the day. A momentary triumph will leave the space feeling empty and its effects will quickly fade. This is a reminder that the tension and changes we explore are not imaginary but a very real part of how we understand and deal with the energy available to us. Every dancer is seeking to find an exit which raises or sustains tension, but not at the expense of another dancer. It is an 'inscape' rather than an escape from the dance space. (See Chapters 8–9)

IMPROV 17: CROSSING THE LINE ON TIME

> 'What shall we do with our spirit?' said his fingers. 'Our piece of Time is not used, our step not ended. Where shall we walk?'
>
> (Alan Garner, 1996)

Directions

a. Read sections on time and space then try **making an entrance** with some of the following conditions:

Dancers must enter and leave:

   i Within five minutes (timed).
   ii Within five minutes (estimated).
  iii Within the playing of a well-known piece of music.
  iv Within the playing of an unknown piece of music.
   v Within the playing of an improvised score.

b.   Agree the length of time of the improvisation and have some-
     one call time intervals, for example:

   i every five minutes in a 25-minute improv
   ii every minute in a five-minute improv

Discuss how temporal considerations affect your experience
of dancing.

ARCH ENEMIES AND RITES OF PASSAGE

> I had discovered the miraculous possibility that art holds out to
> us: to be part of the world and to be removed from the world at
> the same time.
>
> (Sirgid Nunez, 1995)

The postmodern and new-dance dancers in the 1960s and 1970s
rejected the idea of the traditional western theatre space as the
sole venue where dance might happen, and laid claim to countless
alternative settings for performance (see Chapter 5). Although
many theatres and much dance practice changed as a result of
this movement, the divide between audience and performer, once
epitomised by the proscenium arch, continues to be a subject of
lively debate in the dance world. Although in many modern dance
theatres the proscenium arch and the raised stage are things of the
past, the ghost of the proscenium still seems to haunt us. Many
productions are still criticised for their remoteness and inaccessibility, as though they are taking place behind a glass screen.

    Contact improvisation, perhaps the most influential dance
form to emerge from the 1960s, succeeded in creating a more
human relationship with the audience by taking dancers off the
stage and presenting them as real people, doing real things. This
was achieved in part by focusing on the practicalities of how
human bodies functioned physically without concern for creating
a layer of illusion or make believe.

    The accessibility of today's dance world owes much to these
proscenium 'arch' enemies. Yet the passage from one space into
another remains a fundamental human concern. The two worlds
that the proscenium divided were not just those of the professional

dancer and the spectator. The arch came to represent a far more
profound passage, that between the objective, watching, critical
mind and the imaginative, creative, fantastic mind; a doorway
through which the imagination was invited to journey, and, as
such, a powerful symbol of the unconscious.

No matter how infuriatingly inaccessible they may prove at
times, doorways are an essential part of our inner world and outer
world, revealing themselves in the work of artists and in the
individual rites of passage that mark our lives. From birth, through
each initiation in life until the moment we die, we enter and leave
through physical and psychological doorways.

IMPROV 18: MAKING AN ENTRANCE –
A DEVELOPMENT OF CROSSING THE LINE

Personal timing
Understanding tension
Up to 24 dancers

Introduction

* Make a list of doorways as rites of passage.
* Make a list of dances as rites of passage.
* Consider doorways as symbols in writing, poetry, songwriting,
  art (see the god Janus).
* Recall significant moments you remember waiting outside a
  door.
* Recall significant moments in your life when a door was shut/
  opened.

Directions

a. Choose a line in the studio, or imagine one. Imagine that the
    line marks the base of an entrance. This time, before you cross
    the line take a moment to consider its significance for you
    right now. What does it represent at this moment? (Your first
    thoughts are usually your best.) What are its dimensions?
    Is it a door to a room, to a hall, an opening to a cave? What
    is it made of? Is it immense, rising to the sky, or is it a tiny
    crack that you must squeeze through? Is it made of stone? Is
    it hard or soft? Is it cold on the far side or warm? Where have
    you come from? Who is waiting for you on the other side?
b. As you enter the space, show through your movement and
    feeling how you perceive the entrance and the change you
    experience as you move from one space into the other.
c. Continue your journey embodying any images that arise
    from your initial experience of entering and incorporate these

feelings into your journey towards your place of rest. Be open to the changing circumstances you meet on your journey.

d. As you approach the resting place of your journey, ask yourself if it too has an entrance that you must approach in a particular way, direction, level.

e. Once everyone has entered the space and found their place, wait until you feel the right moment to begin your 'homeward' journey. Again, be aware of what you feel as you cross the line from one space into another.

f. If you find it hard to imagine an entrance, here are some suggestions for entering the improvisation.

  i Enter the space like the first person to venture out onto a frozen lake in the early morning.
  ii Enter the space full of wonder and risk.
  iii Dash in as though the bearer of desperate news.
  iv Enter backwards as though leaving another room still in conversation.

Option 1

Allow the improvisation to develop as in **crossing the line** so that dancers begin to interact rather than following their own images in isolation.

Teaching notes

In feedback, dancers need never feel pressured to reveal the images they have been working with.

IMPROV 19: ENTRANCE/EXIT

Timing
Entering and leaving the space
2,3,4 or 5 dancers

> A beginning is an artifice, and what recommends one over another is how much sense it makes of what follows.
>
> (Ian McEwan, 1997)

Introduction

Sometimes an event in time seems to cast a shadow across the space, somehow depriving subsequent actions of light and tension. When dancers choose to move in these 'overcast' moments their actions may fail to register or, worse still, detract from the resonance of the previous action. Learning to feel when we are in the shadow of an event and when we are 'lit' is an important skill both for the improviser and for the choreographer who wish to understand how actions communicate.

Directions

a.   One dancer makes an entrance into the space and the other (one or two) dancers leave. This may be simultaneously, immediately afterwards or after a pause. Try each separately. Keep alternating, one dancer entering as the others leave.
b.   Develop this idea into a larger group improvisation involving more dancers.
c.   Discuss the effect of timing: which moments had tension and held tension?

IMPROV 20: ENCOUNTERS

The initial explorations of **making an entrance** and **crossing the line** should be explored with the focus mainly on time and space. Once these elements have come more clearly to the fore, the element of relationship can be looked at with greater clarity. In reality 'relationship' has been there all along, for even the first person to enter the space must make a decision 'in relation to' all the others who have not yet moved, and will inevitably effect the timing of all who follow. Our ideal spot becomes changed by the presence of others and (like people choosing places on a beach) we must constantly accommodate ourselves and our sensibilities to those around us.

Encounters allows these relationships to become clearer, through an increased emphasis on the dancers' proximity to each other. As duets and groups evolve and are explored the improvisations may take longer to resolve.

Option 1

Agree the length of the improvisation and have someone who is not dancing calling time: 'You have 15 minutes, 10 minutes, 5, 4, 3, 2, 1, 30 seconds, 15 seconds, 5 seconds, Time.'

- Without any physical contact.
- Allowing light contact.
- Introducing the elements of weight sharing and lifting.

IMPROV 21: VOCAL SCORES (FROM AN ORIGINAL SCORE BY LISA NELSON)

Timing
Phrasing
Clarity
Voice
5 to 20 dancers

Introduction

Sometimes improvisations like **crossing the line** and **traverse** can become too long and uneventful (see Chapter 9). One way to inject new life is to call succinct instructions. It need not be just the teacher/leader who does this but, once the directions are clearly understood and agreed, any of the watching (or dancing) group can try. Make your voice clear and easily understood (though an inventive improviser will make something even of a partially heard or apparently incorrect instruction). Initially restrict yourself to the agreed word. Remember, it is important to understand the rules before bending or breaking them.

The simplest example of a vocal score is to call 'End!' This can be called by anyone at any point in a **traverse** or free improvisation. When 'End' is called the dancers should hold their position for a few seconds and then leave the space, making way for a new beginning.

Option 1

Introduction of commands called by the watching dancers

- **Hold**: everyone freezes.
- **Replace**: dancers watching replace those in the improvisation.
- **Replace from within**: dancers replace each other's positions within the improv.
- **Play**: dancers unfreeze and continue.
- **Eyes closed**: dancers continue but with their eyes closed.
- **Eyes open**
- **Rewind**: dancers reverse their actions as far as they can remember.
- **Only men move**
- **Only women move**

Option 2

Falling

For wheelchair users familiar with tilting who are working in groups and who have a high level of trust.

19.1 Makhotso Sompane and the author during rehearsals of *The Querist's Quire*. Tshwaragano, 2001. (Photographer John Hogg)

This can be called even by a wheelchair user who is unable to put on his or her own brakes. The command is a sign to other dancers to put on the brakes and set up a tilt or balance; or 'Tilt!' can be used to the same effect as long as everyone knows that the brakes must be applied first (See Chapter 24).

- **Catching!**: this command tells a dancer that it is safe to proceed from a tilt or balance into a fall. It is called by a dancer or dancers who have positioned themselves ready to catch. Or as an invitation to a dancer to fall.
- **Falling!**: this can be called by a dancer in a chair both for

theatrical effect and to alert anyone else that a fall is taking place. A wheelchair user who has executed a fall in this way can right themselves by offering or reaching to other dancers, or simply be returned by the dancers who caught him/her. This score should only be used by groups who have thoroughly understood the physics involve in wheelchair tilts!

- 'Falling!': can also be called by **any** dancer in the space prior to or after 'Support!' has been called.

You can create your own scores to adapt to different situations.

Notes

70 Bruce Curtis, dance artist and disability rights campaigner.
71 See p. 53 for a discussion of inscape.

20 Con-temp-lation: thinking about space, time and centre

And when I happened to read that sentence of Albert Einstein's: 'There are no fixed points in space', I thought, indeed, if there are no fixed points, then every point is equally interesting and equally changing.

(Merce Cunningham, 1988)

Each person who gets stuck in time gets stuck alone.

(Alan Lightman, 1993)

This section is a departure from the previous improvisations and discussions, and presents, by way of a guided fantasy, a consideration of space and time.

A MEDITATION *IN SITU*

Imagine you are alone in a beautiful open moorland under a wide cloudless summer sky. Ahead of you the land slopes away gently into a valley. On the floor of the valley, lying like a giant coin that has fallen from the sky, is an immense, circular arena. As you approach, you realise that the arena is made of a single, colossal flat stone, several hundred metres wide. Even more remarkably, this beautifully crafted stone is sunk into a shallow depression, also of stone, so that it lies at the same level as the surrounding ground.

Making your way onto the disc, you cross a narrow gap filled with water. The water seems to be very slightly disturbed as you place your weight on the stone.

As you venture out into the arena, you feel a deep sense of calm and peacefulness. When you reach the centre, you decide to rest, closing your eyes you settle down and enjoy the warmth of the sun on your face. As you relax you wonder what civilisation could have created such a structure, and with such thoughts in your mind you drift into a pleasant sleep. Before long, you rouse yourself and notice that the sun which was shining into your face is now behind you. You check your watch but realise that you have only slept for a few hours. Not long enough for the sun to have journeyed so far across the sky.

Suddenly you realise that the enormous disc has been imperceptibly rotating. You are thrilled by the discovery even though you still have absolutely no idea how the disc came to be there, who made it or what its function might be. All you know is that it is the most extraordinary discovery and one that you would love to share.

After a short time, you see some travellers approaching and head towards the edge of the disc to talk to them, but when they arrive you discover that you have lost the power of speech. They seem in no hurry and, having looked around the site, they settle in the grass not far from the disc. You think 'If I sit on the disc next to where they have camped, after a while they'll notice that I've moved and so they'll come to understand that the disc is turning.' Satisfied with your plan, you settle down on the disc close by the visitors and wait for the rotation to carry you away. After a couple of hours have passed, the travellers pack up their picnic and wave goodbye, leaving you still sitting exactly where you were before they arrived.

As you move off again you notice that the water in the crack at the edge of the disc seems to move. Now you come to realise something else about the disc. You intuit that the disc is perfectly balanced at its centre and is sitting, like an enormous top, on a fine cushion of water which circulates under the base causing its mighty mass to turn very, very slowly. You now understand that it was your own weight at the edge of the disc that had caused the disc to go off balance, touch 'ground' and so stop turning. Finally, you understand how the disc moves and, even though you have no idea what purpose it serves, you still take immense delight in your discovery and want to share your insight into the mysterious nature of the structure.

Being at the centre of the disc as it moves seems to make you feel good. Your point of view constantly changes and new vistas constantly open themselves to your gaze. Despite the fact that you still seem to be without speech, you decide to stay on the disc to show people who visit just how the disc works.

Now you have a number of problems to deal with. A single person who stays exactly at the centre of the disc long enough would, like you, notice that his point of view or perspective had changed, but it soon becomes apparent that very few people have the time to spend alone in contemplation, and few stay long enough at the centre to be able to perceive the movement.

When someone on the disc seems to be in need of help and you rush over to them you create a slant in their direction, and if you stay with them your combined weight prevents the disc rotating. The more time you spend on the disc, the more difficulties you discover. To counter-balance someone on the disc, you must move to a place diametrically opposite that individual; when they move, you must also move. Now the disc is turning, but they larger movement means they are unable to perceive the subtle and very slow rotation of the disc.

WHAT IS THE POINT OF BALANCE?
THE DISC AS ANALOGY FOR INTEGRATIVE DANCE TEACHING

As a teacher of dance, your aim is to encourage all students to move, to explore space, to exchange places and experiences and ideas. To do this you must constantly readjust your position in relationship to them (the disc maintains its balance and movement). A movement teacher not only has to provide a centre for learning but must try to embody that centre. The word 'centre' comes from the Latin *centrum*, the still point of a compass. Your dance is defined by your relationship to all the individuals in the space and to the centre of the space itself.

In this analogy, there is no stable 'right position', no single method, no recipe and no safe, easy answer. The pursuit of balance within a constantly shifting environment instead allows us freedom to move in any direction but favours those pathways that most benefit the movement of the entire group as a whole. Keeping the disc balanced and turning serves me as much as it serves anyone else. If my intention is to keep the disc balanced and a person is stuck on the disc, he effectively traps me (in a position diametrically opposed) on the far side. His discovery of movement means that I am then also free to move. Put another way, his freedom liberates me to dance.

When the focus of an inclusive group is shared among all the members of a workshop, the real subject of integration can be addressed: how each of our pathways helps the movement of the entire group; and it is this subject that is explored through our use of space and time. We can use the image of the disc grinding to a halt to represent our intuitive feeling that something is not quite right, that something, somewhere is wrong even if we are unable to identify it. If, for example, I give all my attention to disabled students in a workshop, the non-disabled may remain silent out of politeness but there will be a growing sense of 'injustice' (and vice versa). It is this sense of injustice or of 'wrongs' that leads us to question our actions and our movements.

The analogy also throws up a number of features characteristic of improvisation: such as avoiding the obvious. This means that moving in the direction of a perceived problem will not always bring a solution. This is explored in **more time** and **the great mistake** (see Chapter 27).

EXERCISE 22: PIVOT – AN INTRODUCTION TO PLATEAU

Balancing the space
2 or 3 dancers

Preparation

- Take some time to understand or explain exactly how a fulcrum works. Make a simple see-saw out of a ruler and a pencil. Look at how proximity and distance affect balance.
- Get out of wheelchairs (or stay in them) and explore points of balance (see Chapter 24).
- Make a wobble board out of a board or tray and a tennis ball – balance on it!
- Find examples of balances in the local playground. Play on them!
- Consider the idea of balance in different works of art, sculptural and two-dimensional.
- Look at the balance of Zen rock gardens and megalithic stone circles. If possible, visit one.

Directions

a. Start the improvisation by agreeing a pivot point midway along a line marked on the studio floor, i.e. a straight line balanced at its mid-point. Place yourselves according to your individual weights so that you feel the imaginary 'see-saw' will balance. For example, a dancer in an electric chair would need to be closer to the pivot point than a dancer of a similar body weight without a chair, who would have to be positioned much further out in order to balance.

b. Either dancer can shift position at will and their partner must respond by adjusting so that the see-saw comes back into balance.

c. Once you have understood balancing along a straight line, you can progress to **plateau** (below).

EXERCISE 23: PLATEAU – A PRACTICAL EXPLORATION OF IDEAS RAISED IN THE DISC ANALOGY

Balancing the space
Balancing groups of dancers
2, 3 to 5 dancers

Introduction

- Imagine that the entire dance floor is finely balanced on a central pivot. Anyone entering the space causes the floor to begin to tilt.

Directions

- Start by introducing 2 students to the 'plateau', one of whom intends to keep the floor balanced, the other who is free to move anywhere.

a. Freeze the dancers on the plateau from time to time by calling 'Hold!' and ask those watching if they think the floor would balance. You can then call 'Play!' to continue, or 'Replace!' to introduce new dancers. The exercise can build by adding one or two dancers to either side (team). If the dancers get confused, call 'Hold!' and then 'Reposition!' to give them time to reconsider their placement.

b. Try introducing 2 dancers who must keep in contact, or stay close together, whose aim is to tilt while the others try to keep the plateau balanced. Create your own variations.

IMPROV 24: BALANCING THE PICTURE – AN ADVANCED PLATEAU

Introduction

Artists like choreographers balance images in a variety of ways. Take a trip to the local art gallery to look at how two-dimensional images are balanced. What is it that makes a picture balanced or unbalanced?

Directions

a. Working in pairs to begin with, one dancer moves through a series of poses or still postures. Without making physical contact, try to find a shape or gesture that you feel somehow offers a balance to what they offer. Use either their physical form or your sense of the emotional content of the posture that is being offered.

b. Don't stay longer than about 5 seconds in any one posture. If you are unable to see/feel a response, try to make any response rather than waiting for the next one. Push yourself always to make some kind of reply even if it is just a shrug of the shoulders. Take it in turns to observe couples working together. See Improv 35 **contradiction** in Chapter 22 for development.

c. Now return to the idea of **plateau** and encourage dancers to use freer interpretations so that the overall energy of the dance space is balanced. Here students can interpret 'balance' more freely and be less concerned with the notion of a physical pivot and be more creative with what they offer. For example, can you make the other dancers move by changing how heavy you 'feel' instead of by changing location?

d. Have students watch and give each other feedback. The vocal score used in **plateau** can be used to good effect here too.

ORDERING SPACE

We live in a world of spaces defined by codes of behaviour. Home, college, work, play. We share yet larger, often invisible, boundaries, which define our society, cultures and religions. These amorphous spaces envelope all aspects of human behaviour. Indeed each of us, even at our most solitary, carry or inhabit our own personal space envelope within which strict rules of engagement, language and ethics apply.

Looking into a school playground we see an apparent chaos of interactions in which myriad groups and individual children are following their different games, apparently oblivious of one another. Along with the mastery of various social rules and hierarchies, the children are also learning to master 'space' in just the way that birds navigate the spatial relationships within a flock. Without this skill, the world would be full of people and animals constantly bumping into each other. Although it is quite clear that status plays a vital part in how individuals negotiate space, the mass movements of flocks and shoals would fall apart if every individual within the group were responding solely in relationship to its status with its immediate neighbours – it is quite clear that other ordering principles are also at play.

Most of us are already well versed in the codes and regulations governing use of space according to status. The choices of where we sit in a café, studio or indeed any space, will be defined according to strict yet unspoken rules. Most of these choices and decisions, however, go unnoticed, until the code is challenged or disrupted.

Set up a train or bus improvisation in which people take their seats according to the remaining spaces available, or use a table and have people bring their own chairs. There will be a remarkably predictable sequence of choices made. We are all acutely sensitive to those who disregard these rules, and who sit too close to us or who take someone else's designated place. What tells us something is out of place is the tension we feel as a result. Learning about space entails a recognition of the rules to which we all adhere on a daily basis. These rules can be upturned and subverted to great effect in improvisation, as well as in choreographed work.

IMPROV 25: PLAYING FOR SPACE

> I could be bounded within a nutshell and still consider myself
> master of infinite space.
>
> (Shakespeare, *Hamlet*, 1600–01)

A simple exercise in space
Improvisation
Non-contact
Position and focus
Up to 24 dancers

Introduction

Look at the spaces that the group is creating right now. Discuss
where the 'live' spaces are, i.e. those which everyone is aware of.
For example, perhaps you're all positioned in a circle as you talk.
Looking 'in' may feel very comfortable, but see what it feels like
for one dancer to move out of the circle and face towards another
direction. Look around to see if there are any 'dead' or unused
spaces. Get someone to bring a dead space alive by changing their
position or focus.

Directions

a. Allow the space around you to contract or collapse by dropping your focus.
b. Expand or create space around you by raising your focus and
   changing your stance or position.
c. Direct your gaze in a particular direction, hold it until another
   dancer becomes aware of the space you are indicating (bringing to life) and occupies it.
d. Resonate or emphasise the space someone is indicating by
   positioning yourself alongside the individual and share the
   direction of their focus. (Like looking at a view.)
e. Reduce the space someone has created by placing yourself in
   front of the individual. (This may feel confrontational at first.
   Don't worry, the objective is just to alter the feel of the space,
   not to become involved in a stand-off!)
f. Disrupt the space between two people by entering it.
g. Get onto the floor to play with spaces and perspectives that
   are not used in everyday activity.
h. Explore different spatial relationships. Low v. high. Diagonal
   v. cardinal. Horizontal v. vertical. Feel the particular qualities
   of each.

Teaching notes

Initially, spatial relationships are more easily identified if you hold your focus steady rather than glancing around. Keep your face open and relaxed, don't get into staring matches, and don't forget to breathe!

IMPROV 26: RESTING IS DANCING

> The muscular system, which is said to function with the contraction/extension duality, also includes a relaxed state – it is a triad, not a duality.
>
> (Paxton and Kilcoyne, 1993)

Advanced group improvisation

Introduction

Inexperienced dancers often generate endless amounts of movement material when improvising, yet still struggle to communicate their ideas or feelings with clarity. The space is full of activity, yet like poor choreography, there is a certain sense of relief when it is over. In contrast, dancers often seem to be at their most relaxed and natural when watching each other in class or rehearsal.

There is a quality of open engagement and unselfconsciousness in their bodies which seems to make them as fascinating in repose as those exerting themselves on the dance floor. It would be misleading to call this state 'neutral' as it is not devoid of feeling, it is when we feel no need to make something happen but feel curious about what **may** happen. It is a restful but alert state of mind and body. Unfortunately, many students confuse inaction with inertia and therefore avoid stillness at all costs, so although full of energy, they are often unable to pick up on subtle, whimsical, original and often more outrageous lines of exploration.

Movement, like music, must embrace stillness if it is to communicate. If our motions and emotions are to be understood they need to be given shape, form and structure. Without silence, music deteriorates into noise. Without stillness, dance becomes equally unreadable and will eventually exhaust both dancer and watcher.

Directions

a. Create an improvisation that has no allocated place for watchers anywhere in the studio. Everywhere is part of the dance area and anywhere can be used for watching.

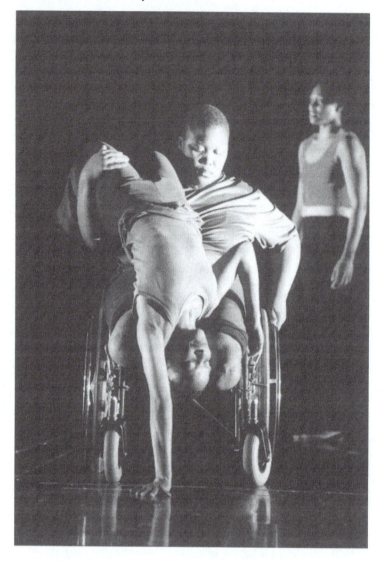

20.1 Tshwaragano. Makhotso Sompane, Caroline Mofokeng and Gladys
      Agulhas (background). (Photographer John Hogg)

b. If you become tired or simply want to observe, then do so
    wherever you happen to be. You are not allowed to say to
    anyone that you are resting (and therefore not dancing).
    In this improvisation resting **is** dancing. In this way, dancers
    at rest may frame or counterpoint action, they may become
    the focus of sculptural forms.
c. As no one in the space is an observer, you will need to agree
    a signal to end the improvisation.
d. Give feedback about what it was like to rest in the space
    and about what you experienced and saw. Particularly try to

identify when a non-moving dancer contributed to tension rising.

IMPROV 27: FREE IMPROVISATION IN THE STUDIO

From natural movement into dance movement
Advanced group improvisation

Directions

a. Needs to be organised in advance. A date, time and location are agreed for the improvisation and a time or signal is agreed to mark the end.
b. As in the previous improv there are no boundaries between watchers and dancers. The key difference is the improvisation begins the moment the first student enters the studio. Don't forget to organise a prearranged sign to signal the end. If the improv starts as dancers enter, and ends as they leave the studio, it is important to arrange a place where you can meet for feedback.

IMPROV 28: IMPROVISATIONS AND THE ENVIRONMENT

> We keep passing unseen through little moments of other people's lives.
>
> > (Robert T. Pirsig, Zen and the Art of
> > Motorcycle maintenance, 1974.)

Advanced group

Introduction

I have sometimes improvised in public spaces with experienced groups without prior permission, but some spaces like galleries or museums may require permission, or you may find yourself improvising answers to local policemen or gallery attendants.

Directions

a. Agree a location. This may be a studio and college grounds, a park, a station, a beach, a café, a museum, indeed anywhere where the entire group feels safe to improvise.
b. Agree to abide by certain ground rules, i.e. not to use force, not to intimidate members of the public!

c. Agree a period of time.
d. Agree a place to begin and a place to end. Feedback and discussion is important in this kind of improvisation.

Examples

Tskuba City, Japan, 1999

Tskuba City is an hour from Tokyo. It is a very modern city that has been built rapidly and imposed on an older village system (a bit like Milton Keynes in the UK). The Tskuba City Arts Centre is one of those architectural landmarks that speaks of civic pride and high-art ideals. It is set in its own grounds with an impressive plaza. I had been invited to lead a five-day workshop by Hiroke Koike, the dynamic artistic director, who had inherited this impressive but unwieldy building.

The theatre itself was not available and I was offered the choice of two studios. The first resembled an aircraft hangar, a massive space which doubled as a sports arena and rehearsal space for the town's marching band. The second was a 'purpose-built' dance studio, containing mirrors, bars and piano. Like most such spaces, it had no natural daylight and was far too small and claustrophobic for a week's workshop.

My whole feeling about the centre was that it was not designed to accommodate creative arts practice. In fact the whole building seemed to say 'Keep out'. The interior studios felt 'locked away', hidden from sight and offered no sense of belonging or identity, they could have been in any building anywhere in the world. Returning from the dance studio, we passed through the foyer area. It was the first space that seemed to have any life or light, and I immediately requested that we work there.

Hiroke Koike (also artistic director of PapaTarahumara) had recognised that there was a very real problem in getting local people involved in the arts, which was one of the reasons why he had invited me to work there. Because of the way the 'modern' city was dropped on the older villages, there was a lasting feeling of resentment against the 'university world' of which the arts centre was a part. The issue of integration at Tskuba was not specifically about disability (the arts centre was highly accessible), it was about how the building could open itself to local people and how the arts themselves could be made more accessible.[72]

I soon decided to extend the work out onto the plaza, so that our improvisation would begin to interact with the local environment and local people. As soon as this was agreed, I was astonished to see a team of eight cleaners emerge to sweep and wash down the plaza. In the unlikely event of having asked for such a thing in England, I am sure it would have taken at least a week to organise. Here it was done immediately and without request, yet the arts programmers had virtually no budget for community projects, no education officer and no support other than the determination of Hiroke Koike to make things happen. After the first day's work, I returned to the centre at midnight. Deserted and under a starry sky it looked beautiful and austere with its high columns and formal gardens and it struck me that this is how the architect must have envisaged it; like the whole of modern Tskuba City it had been conceived and imposed without reference to, or dialogue with, local people.

The next day our decision to work in the foyer began to signal that something was happening; that a creative activity was taking place in what had up until that point been a dauntingly impersonal building. The dancers and those who visited to watch began to feel and look at ease. It was quite clear that in future they would be able to return to the building with a sense of ownership, no longer intimidated but with the feeling 'I have danced here, this belongs to me.' The week consisted of an introduction to improvisation using many of the exercises in this book. The final day saw an improvisation in which the dancers who had first found their spot out in the grounds of the building gradually made their way into the foyer The audience were seated inside the foyer looking out, initially not knowing who were dancers and who were members of the public. The dancers performed without music, taking their timing from each other and the passing pedestrians and cyclists crossing the plaza, while the audience seated in the foyer, listened to Albinoni as they watched the improvisation through the arts centre's massive glass windows. Once inside, one of the dancers, with his eyes closed, played blues harmonica and was swept up in a **traverse** (see Chapter 21) which moved past the audience and on, disappearing down a corridor into the interior of the building.

The problems inherent in the building led us towards the structure for our improvisation. Recognise the problems and you are more than half way to creating a solution. The following year the idea of dividing sound and vision, inner and outer worlds, was further explored when the deaf dancer Chisato Minamimura joined the group. This was one of the few occasions in Japan when I have been able to develop work in the same location in consecutive years.

Ethiopia: to dance or to dig?

On my first visit to Ethiopia to work on the Adugna Dance Initiative[73] I visited a number of different schools, hospitals and remedial settings. One of these visits took me to Ledita (residential centre for the care of physically handicapped) in Addis Ababa. The road to the centre was so uneven that our four-wheel drive could manange no more than a crawl. As we neared the centre we passed one or two people in delapidated wheelchairs attempting the hazardous journey to the main road. Most of the 120 people that lived at the centre were war veterans or war victims. Considering the condition of the patients, the medical resources available to the staff were woeful. Pressure sores and infections were a recurring problem. Most of the patients/residents needed daily medical care and it seemed clear that many were not in a position to travel far from the centre. Few, if any, seemed likely to be able to take part in the kind of training we were planning. In the meantime, though, there was nothing by way of either occupational or recreational pursuits for these once active people, isolated and cut off from their communities.

The centre itself was in desperate need of resources of all kinds. Although I felt that dance was way down on the list of priorities, I hoped that if our project succeeded, at some point the Adugna dancers might be able to use their performance skills as a way of raising awareness and of drawing attention to the centre's needs for medical support, an employment programme, and a decent level pathway for wheelchairs users and their families to the main road, for example. Then perhaps our students might return to introduce dance as a social, artistic and remedial activity. Every environment requires a different dance.

For more information on the Adugna Dance Initiative, see Appendix 1.

Notes

72 The real battle in Japan is convincing a top-down bureaucracy that it is not enough to pour money into buildings, but that they must begin to fund the messy, muddy, grass-roots practice that will generate real arts involvement, and that this, in turn, will not only nurture Japanese artists of the future, it will also generate audiences.
73 The Adugna Dance Initiative was founded by Royston Maldoon initially in an attempt to train street children in Addis Ababa through dance. I was later asked to bring disabled youngsters into the project.

21 Graceful ways, or searching for clews

We were all nomads once, and crossed the deserts and the seas on tracks that could not be detected, but were clear to those who knew the way.

(Jeanette Winterson, 1990)

Some of us need to get lost more often.

(David Zambrano, 2000)

INTRODUCTION

In a good improvisation the dancers always appear to know when and where to move. Far from 'making it up', it is as if they are skilfully acquiescing and responding to a world that constructs itself as they move through it, following pathways visible only to themselves.

In reality, most improvisations are a bit like moving through a labyrinth or maze that is occasionally illuminated and occasionally thrown into darkness. Sometimes the way ahead seems clear and at other times uncertain and fraught with danger.

In Greek mythology, Theseus has to find his way through the Minotaur's labyrinth. This frightening and unpredictable journey is made possible thanks to a ball of thread given to him by Ariadne.[74] In other words Theseus's journey in the dark was made possible because Ariadne presented him with a clew (clew – meaning a ball of thread – the origin of our word 'clue').

In the medieval Christian adaption of this myth, the Minotaur was airbrushed out and Ariadne's gift to Theseus came to represent the idea of God's grace guiding the seeker through the many twists and turns of life. This new perception of grace offered an alternative perspective to the Greek (Platonic) concept whereby grace and goodness were considered the unique attribute of those possessed of classical form and feature. Christianity would in time become responsible for a host of disablist institutions and persecutions, but this original Christian reinterpretation was radical in making grace accessible to all. It not only challenged the philosophical and aesthetic hierarchies of the Greeks and Romans, who had considered those lacking grace to be inferior, it also opened the possibility for a new kind of beauty which was dependent not on God-given outward appearances but on inner virtues, individual choices and actions.

Whether we prefer the idea of Ariadne's gift or the later Christian concept, both would suggest that when we become confused or blocked in an improvisation, the answers we seek may not be in our own hands. Confronted with our own limitations we need the 'grace' to accept solutions or clues offered by those with whom we dance.

IMPROV 29: TRAVERSE – TRAVELLING IN A GROUP

Listening skills
Ingenuity
Beginnings and endings
Stagecraft

Introduction

It is a good idea to start this with small groups (3 to 7) crossing the space. **Flock** is a good warm-up for this improvisation and will be particularly helpful in developing the listening necessary to achieve a collective stillness. One of the specific areas of focus here is how the group deals with beginnings and endings (see Improv 32 **the far side**, below).

Interloper and **cascade** can be used to great effect when led as a **traverse**.

Directions

a. The group starts at one side of the studio with the objective of crossing to the other side. Dancers still need to find their own pathway while acknowledging that they are part of a group improvisation. Again this means really searching for your own beginning (revisit **crossing the line** – see Improv 16, Chapter 19). Don't just go when the group goes.

b. The principle movement of **traverse** is from one side of the studio to the other, but don't forget there is still ample scope for movement upstage and downstage. The journey between two points doesn't have to be linear.

Visually impaired dancers

Unsighted or visually impaired dancers may need help locating the starting point and direction of the traverse but should be encouraged to position themselves and then be joined by a self-selected team of 2, 3 or more other dancers.

Option 1

The entire group must become still at least once (or twice, depending on the size of the studio) on its journey across the studio, not including the start or the end of the journey.

Option 2

Cross with different numbers of dancers in contact (2, 3, 4 or 5 depending on the size of the group).

Option 3

Every member must be supported off the ground for a minimum of three seconds.

Option 4

Try a linear traverse in which the dancers cross the space in a line like a slowly advancing wave.

Option 5

Have two different groups cross simultaneously from opposing sides of the studio.

Option 6

Have two groups each with a blind or unsighted dancer cross from opposite sides. The 'blind' dancers change group midway returning to their point of origin with the opposite group.
See Improv 21 **vocal scores** in Chapter 19.

Discuss each crossing, drawing on the experience both of the dancers and those watching. Did anyone get left behind? How did that feel? Was it an addition or a distraction? What solutions were the group able to see in hindsight or receive from the watchers? What moments stood out as particularly interesting – dramatic – funny – sad.

Less experienced students trying **traverse** sometimes find this a daunting exercise and may try to hatch a plan before starting. 'Pre-match talks' should be politely banned. Thus robbed of the opportunity to agree a strategy, it is not uncommon to see a sudden shifting of the group's focus particularly towards any disabled dancer/s (or to the unsighted dancer). The result is that the journey can take on the appearance of an ill-planned social services outing at which too many carers have been allotted and only one client has turned up. Visually impaired or blind dancers often fall prey to this kind of unecessary shepherding.

Example

In Matsuyama, Japan, a blind dancer was repeatedly guided and 'man handled' across the space by two physiotherapists in his group. When I encouraged them to concentrate on their own journey, the blind dancer began to dance the most astonishing, brittle, insect-like dance which included an amazing low-level knee walk. It was something that we were not able to see until the other dancers allowed him to move on his own. Feedback should help to sort this out (revisit Improv 10 **interloper** in Chapter 18).

Teaching notes

- **Traverse** is an excellent improvisation to enable you to begin to consider the performance aspects of improvisation. Because it is a group improvisation that progresses from one side of the stage to the other there will frequently be dancers who are unseen, and potentially interesting interactions may take place hidden (upstage) of the group. This raises important issues about improvisation and stagecraft. To be a successful improviser it is not just necessary to be able to generate interesting movement but also to develop a choreographer's sense of timing and position so that material produced can be shared with the audience.
- Someone using a large electric wheelchair[75] for example, who constantly faces upstage will not only hide their own actions with the back of their chair, but will mask most of what takes place upstage. A dancer who monopolises the downstage position will also mask dancers. No matter how talented he or she may be, eventually all we see is a certain selfishness or at best a lack of awareness of others who share the stage. These are important issues but feedback as ever needs to be leavened with humour and tact.

IMPROV 30: NARRATIVE TRAVERSE –
ALLOWING DANCE TO SPEAK[76]

Spoken word
Timing
Framing
Group understanding
From 2 to 7 dancers per crossing

Preparation

To begin, take a partner and tell each other your story. Now tell
your partner again, but try to reduce what you say to a shortened
version. Now tell it a third time reducing it to the essential bare
bones. This simple material is the best kind of text to begin
working with. It may only be two or three short sentences.

Improvisation

- Initially try and find the optimal moments to deliver lines.
  Keep the amount said succinct, and use moments of rest or
  tranquillity in which to speak. The aim is that the **words
  should be clearly heard by those watching**. Try again and
  avoid obscuring the narrator when he or she is speaking.
- The dancer/storyteller begins at the edge of the studio with
  eyes closed and is joined by a self-selected group from those
  watching.
- Either movement or text can begin the improv.
- The blind dancer tells the story, while being guided across the
  space (using all the skills already explored in **traverse**).
- The travelling group is focused on its task of traversing and
  guiding and is not attempting to 'describe' or act the story.
- Allow the audience to make their own connections between
  text and movement. The task for the dancers and the narrator
  or storyteller includes finding a satisfying ending or conclusion
  to both the movement and the text (see Improv 32 **the far side**,
  below).
- More advanced groups can explore more personal stories.
  The more meaning the story has for the narrator, the greater
  the chance the improvisation has of taking off.

Option 1

Once the improv is understood, try two stories being told by
storytellers in two groups traversing the space from opposite sides.
Again, they must find ways not to 'talk over' each other but allow
space for each to deliver their lines.

Teaching notes

- Encourage students to speak in their native language. It is remarkable how much meaning can be conveyed even when the words themselves are not understood.
- Beware of those who want to describe every detail and act out the stories as they are travelling. Remind students that the movement task is abstract, and not related specifically to the text, though ideas and responses may arise from it.

IMPROV 31: NARRATIVE, MUSICAL, TRAVERSE

For musicians and dancers plus text
2 to 7 dancers
See Chapter 28

Directions

a. A development of **narrative traverse** (see above) in which a musician also plays or accompanies the journey.
b. The musician's focus can be either on the movement of the dancers or on the text but must allow space and time for the storyteller to deliver lines. The aim is for movement, music and spoken word to coexist on stage.
c. Musician(s) can remain at the edge of the studio when this improv is first explored, those interested may want to try travelling with the group.

IMPROV 32: THE FAR SIDE

> Every journey conceals another journey within its lines; the paths not taken and the forgotten angle.
>
> (Jeanette Winterson, 1989)

Endings
Problem-solving
3 to 9 dancers

Introduction

The ending of **traverse** provides an opportunity to explore and consider conclusions. It is not unusual to see a kind of traffic jam occurring towards the end of **traverse** and this may be heightened when the group includes wheelchair users. It is as if those dancers who arrive first effectively close a door on the remaining dancers still in the space. This may either be because those arriving last are physically obstructed from leaving the space, or because those arriving first have disassociated themselves from the improvisation, and have become onlookers. Reaching the far side does not necessarily mean you have finished. There may be numerous physical and psychological negotiations to explore before the group finally settles. There is an unmistakable sense of completion to a well-ended traverse which may have many different qualities but invariably says to those watching 'This particular journey is now ended.'

Option 1

Run many small improvisations one after another and have the watching dancers call 'End!' at any convincing place in the journey. This can also be a score for **crossing the line**.

Option 2

In addition to using **traverse** as a structure for **freewheeling**, i.e. in which one of the travelling group travels with eyes closed, other themes or tasks can be set by the watching group to add a particular edge to this improvisation (and many others). This might take the form of:

- A physical task.
- A theme that has been discussed or a work of art that has recently been studied.
- Advanced groups might want to try doing their improvisations 'in the style of':

  - Siobhan Davies;
  - Merce Cunningham;
  - Nigel Charnock;
  - Shobana Jeysingh;
  - classical, folk or ballroom.

Teaching notes

Tension can be used here as a way to think about and offer feedback. For example, were there moments on the journey when the group lost its way, when it seemed to be going nowhere (tension falling) or conversely when there seemed to be too much happening? Were the dancers or watchers able to sense possible endings or pauses en route?

IMPROV 33: AMOEBA, AND THE SINGLE-CELL SOLO

Soloist in relation to the group
Up to 15 dancers

Introduction

Understanding the relationship between the individual and the group, between cooperation and individuality, is an ancient human concern. In modern times, it was a theme explored by Doris Humphrey in a piece called *New Dance* (1935), at a time when a generation of young American artists were looking towards socialism for answers to problems they saw around them. Humphrey's work envisaged a world 'Where each human being has a clear and harmonious relationship to his fellow being.'[77] It was a good thirty-five years before new dance as a movement became established in the UK, seeking to understand the individual's voice in relationship to the collective, and a good thirty-five millennia after the first attempt by an amoeba to solve the same problem.

Directions

a. The group task is to create an improvisation which maintains an amoeba-like quality; constantly changing shape it meanders around the space, the group's direction and speed being determined by its slowest members. Essentially, there is no hurry, no goal, you have no deadlines to meet, you are going nowhere in particular, you have a tiny brain.

b. Occasionally the odd, single cell breaks off into space to boldly go where no single cell has gone before. It is an evolutionary jumping-off point – the single-cell solo. This may attract at most one other dancer to break away so that a duet may occur, but no more than two dancers can be away from the group at a time. (Remember, there's safety in numbers.)

c. The solos or duets end by being absorbed back into the group. The amoeba may respond to those returning in different ways, or it may just carry on doing what amoebas do . . .

Teaching notes

The aim of the improv is to encourage individuals to take the opportunity to break away from the group when the time is right and otherwise to gel and harmonise. These two activities are complementary. If successful, the amoeba doesn't compete with the solos, but may on occasion heave itself into moments of activity. The aim is never to have more than two extended points of focus on stage, the group and the soloist. If this improvisation is understood, it can be an effective device to use in improvised group performances.

Notes

74 In another version the gift is an illuminated crown – originally a gift of Dionysus.
75 The considerable and often nerve-wracking demands of controlling a large powered wheelchair among potentially vulnerable dancers on the floor can often make us unaware of the positions we take in an improvisation. If you've never steered one of these machines, ask to have a go. It will make you far more understanding of the problems involved.
76 This improvisation came from the research carried out by The Stare Cases Project at the Place Choreodrome, London, 1998. Special thanks to Danny Scheinmann.
77 *New Dance* was part of a trilogy. The second part *Theatre Piece* dealt with the struggle for survival in a competitive world and the third part *With My Red Fires* dealt with relationships.

22 Individual considerations

The onlooker is a partner who must be forgotten and still constantly kept in mind: a gesture is statement, expression, communication and a private manifestation of loneliness.

(Peter Brook, 1990)

Accept me for what I am and I'll accept you for what you're accepted as.

(Christopher Nolan, 1987)

IMPROV 34: SOLOING – AN EXERCISE IN CONFRONTING DRAGONS[78]

Focus
Timing
Dealing with creative blocks

Introduction

Soloing explores the dancer's ability to engage our attention with the minimum of technique and instead to work solely with the play of tension through time and space. Dancers take turns in traversing the studio, unaccompanied by sound, music or props. The rest of the class watch to see and feel when and where the dancer is sustaining, raising or losing tension. (See also Chapter 10.)

Option 1

The soloist is required to stop (once or twice) on their journey.

Option 2

Have two dancers cross at the same time from opposite sides of the studio.

Option 3

Two dancers cross from the same side but positioned wide apart, both blindfolded.

Teaching notes

Feedback needs to be supportive and should be designed to help your students to recognise the moments when they move away from or towards tension. Such work requires courage, integrity and a preparedness to get it wrong, so feedback needs to be tempered through your own experience as an improviser, giving and receiving feed-back with others.

Exposed to the scrutiny of those watching, dancers may feel under pressure 'to perform' and resort to tricks, showy technique or acting. In one class, a disabled dancer trying **soloing** repeatedly tried to entertain those watching, doing comic steps and striking poses. Time and again the tension waned and the interest in the watching group dissipated, to be replaced by a polite though rather uncomfortable silence. When I asked her just to walk without trying to entertain us there was a quiet dignity about her presence. The tension on the stage rose and remained even after she had disappeared into the wings. Remember increased action does not necessarily raise tension. Here we are looking for something far rarer and less manufactured, something that cannot have been 'prepared earlier' – a presence that acknowledges and moves with the ever present risk of 'failure', or of losing face, of **vulnerability** – revealing what we would normally hide in the everyday world for fear of being wounded.

This sense of vulnerability is perhaps the most essential of qualities for the improviser, for it provides an opening for the understanding between the dancer and his or her inner world, and between the dancer and audience. In order to be 'sense abled' we have to allow ourselves to be touched.

IMPROV 35: CONTRADICTION – CREATING COUNTER-MOVEMENTS

> Seriousness seeks to exclude play, whereas play can very well include seriousness.
>
> (J. Huizinga, 1970)

> You can laugh but you must be sincere.
>
> (Baaba Maal, 1997)

2 dancers (or groups of up to six)

Introduction

Before exploring the improvisations of contrasting and conflicting impulses in this section, it is a good idea to re-establish a baseline of mutual listening and agreement by revisiting **leading and following** (Improv 9, Chapter 18) or **flock** (Improv 2, Chapter 17). Remember it is not possible to disagree with any great skill or ingenuity until you understand what you're disagreeing with.

Directions

a. 'Create a shape! Any shape!' 'Don't think about it, just do it!' Students often get horribly stuck when asked to do this. Remember, the human body takes up space – so it is impossible for us not to make shapes! A dancer not knowing what to do may pull a face and touch their head with their hand or fractionally move their head backwards as if to get a better look at your suggestion.

b. Encourage those watching to call 'Freeze!' in order to capture shapes and expressions that 'stuck' dancers are unconsciously creating. Dancers may need to be congratulated on the shapes they are making, especially when they think they aren't!

c. Once everyone has got used to the idea of being full-time shape-makers, one person at a time makes a shape and the rest of the group respond with forms that they feel contrast, disagree or oppose. Below are a few simple examples of obvious disagreements:

> i   First dancer looks up, the others look down.
> ii First dancer brings her hands together, others spread their hands wide apart.
> iii First dancer looks happy, others look sad.

Teaching notes

*   If dancers can't think of how to respond, encourage them to make any response, rather than offering nothing at all; what is important is that they loosen up and don't become too intellectual about the exercise. Once the principle is broadly understood, you can begin to respond more creatively to the first dancer. The aim now is to avoid offering an obvious response. For example, it would in most circumstances be obvious to take the hand of someone who offers it.

*   Here are some examples of less obvious responses.

    *   The first dancer looks at the others and points angrily at the door.

Simultaneously:

- The second dancer appears to collapse in fright.
- The third points at the floor and seems to listen intently.
- The fourth dances a waltz.

All these 'disagree' in that none of the dancers takes one of the more obvious directions (of leaving via the door). Instead each dancer responds with a unique reaction based on his/her personal interpretation and idiosyncrasies. Don't censor your imagination. Celebrate any responses you come up with!

Option 1

The responding dancers can disagree on different levels:

- On the level of form, i.e. creating an abstract shape that works in opposition.
- On the level of intention, i.e. creating a gesture that disagrees.
- On the level of dynamics, i.e. by creating a form whose dynamic energy is different.
- On the level of location, i.e. by positioning yourself somewhere that contrasts spatially.

Option 2

Split dancers into groups, or have some dancers sit out to watch and provide feedback. When a level of harmony or agreement has been achieved among the dancing group, begin to allow moments of disagreement to enter the improvisation.

Questions for watching group

- What happens when too many people all start disagreeing at the same time?
- Which contradictions stood out clearly? Why?
- What are the hallmarks of a successful disagreement?
- What different levels of disagreement can you detect?

Try to remember who did what so that you can provide accurate feedback.

Example

Watching improvisation I sometimes find myself thinking 'Oh no, please, please don't do that!' as I watch events unfold with all the predictability of a B-movie. It is a gut response to watching dancers fulfil expectations or scenarios that have been set up and are rolling relentlessly to a foregone conclusion. During **traverse**, M, who uses a wheelchair, was involved in a personal and theatrical enactment in which he seemed to be wheeling up a tremendous slope, apparently cut off from the other dancers who had mostly crossed the space and were waiting uneasily for him to finish. At this point, Mark Glover, who was just on the point of reaching the far side of the studio, picked up one of the onlooking dancers, carried her to M and placed her like a child on his lap.

This action was not in response to the acted story (it would be counter-intuitive to place a person on the lap of someone wheeling up a mountain) but came from Mark's actual feelings about M's separateness from the group. He was responding from a different frame of reference. The piece ended with M accepting the dancer, giving up his story and his 'uphill struggle' and finding a new connection with the other people in the improvisation (see Chapter 8).

As a teacher of improvisation, you have to be able to juggle the differing needs of your group. Beginners may need guidance and direction to help them overcome destructive, annoying or dangerous traits, and to understand the rules of an improvisation, while experienced students need help to think about the options and possibilities that these difficult moments give rise to (see Chapter 7). Witnessing dancers generate unique and unexpected solutions to the problems they encounter while dancing, remains for me one of the greatest pleasures in teaching, watching and performing improvisation.

Note

78 This is perhaps one of the most difficult of improvisations, called soloing because as in solo rock climbing there are no supports (no safety) and because the risks though injurious only to the ego, still feel life threatening.

23 Lightly balanced on the edge of centre: weight-sharing in an unequal world

INTRODUCTION

In any dance workshop, the strength, age and size of bodies may vary dramatically, so weight-sharing needs to be approached gently with common sense and awareness. As dancers in an unequal world, our aim is to understand our own centre of gravity and be able to play with and use weight in appropriate measure (Figure 23.1).

Giving and taking weight should first be explored with experienced teachers before being taught or used in workshop or class settings. Having said this, there is a great deal of simple work that can be explored safely if relevant information is shared before starting. The general rule, however, is, if you are not confident and comfortable with material, then don't teach it.

There are many different ways to give weight successfully; they vary from the giving of the smallest part of one's weight with pinpoint precision (i.e. at the highest point of a balance) to the surrender of the entire weight of the body. Although it is important to know how to release and surrender our weight, when muscles are entirely relaxed the body becomes like a dead weight, unable to sustain balance and difficult (if not impossible) to lift.

When giving weight in the following exercises try, wherever possible, to be sensitive to the strength of the supports offered and relaxed enough to make subtle adjustments to your balance. Think of the upward direction of supports moving up and through your own body. You may find that if you extend or create forms that have a sense of length to them, you will be more easily supported. This principle becomes particularly important as giving weight shifts into lifting. If you think 'up' you will make better use of supports than if you are thinking 'down'.

23.1 Gladys Agulhas, Malcolm Black and Tiro Motlhatlhedi in
      The Querist's Quire, Tshwaragano Dance Company, 2001.
      Choreography by Benjamin. (Photographer John Hogg)

IMPROV 36: REACHING – A WARM-UP OR PREPARATION FOR LIGHT WEIGHT-SHARING

Directions

a. Explore the space around you without travelling, but by reaching through the body and involving as much of yourself as possible in each extension.
b. Try not to make the body hard or rigid as you reach, but allow the movement to come from inside so that you have the feeling of growing and lengthening. Imagine that the extended limb is passing through a waterfall into an unknown space. (This is also a way of approaching **making an entrance**: see Improv 18, Chapter 19.)
c. Keep your face relaxed and continue to breathe naturally as you extend through different parts of the body. For example try extending through:

   i   Your elbow.
   ii   Through the crown of the head.
   iii Through your toes.
   iv   Shoulder.
   v   Wrist.
   vi   Knee.

d. Once you have lengthened and eased the body in different directions, begin to take each 'reach' to the point at which you risk losing your balance, and then return to a central position before growing and reaching with another part of your body in a different direction.

e. Don't strain in these positions, but try to remain relaxed enough to feel at that point the outer limit of your stretch takes you off balance.

With a partner

• When you have explored the different directions and levels that are available to you, take a partner and position your-selves close enough to be able to touch . . . but don't.

• Your partner begins a 'reach' but before they have completed the movement, you too begin to reach so that your movements closely intersect without touching or obstructing. The final shape created together should have the appearance of two strong diagonal lines of energy angling past each other.

• If you are the first to move, start slowly so that your partner has time to interpret the direction of your movement and intersect it. This can be speeded up as you become more confi-dent. Remember to breathe as you cut through each other's space.

• When both of you arrive at a full stretch, slowly return to a balanced, centred position, drawing apart as though drawing a sword from each other's body! Now swap over or try alternating.

• Explore this exercise using different levels and different speeds. Remember the idea is not to touch but to extend your energy through your partner's space while remaining relaxed and aware of each other. If you are too far apart, this will feel 'empty'. You need to be close to get the full effect of this exercise.

IMPROV 37: SUSPENDED WEIGHT –
A DEVELOPMENT OF REACHING

Understanding weight and support
Timing
Positioning
2 dancers

Introduction

Imagine a tall pine tree that has been cut through at its base yet has remained perfectly balanced. A small bird flutters down out of the sky and perches on a branch near the top. The tree begins imperceptibly to move off centre. However, before it has gone more than a centimetre, an eagle settles on a branch on the far side of the tree. The tree balances temporarily, but now, due to the larger bird's weight, begins to lean in the opposite direction. If the eagle had arrived two seconds later, the tree would already have been falling and, gaining momentum, the bird's weight would not have prevented the fall.

In the following exercise you can think about the weight of the body like the weight of the tree. We are trying to control large amounts of weight with the minimum of effort. The aim of the exercise is to understand falling weights – not stand under them.

Directions

a.   In the warm-up exercise **reaching** (Improv 36, above) we looked at the point when the body goes off balance. Remind yourself of this.

b.   This time your partner reaches out a little further – to the point where they are in danger of going 'off balance'. As your partner extends, position yourself as a support.

c.   If you move too soon, you will prevent the off-balance moment, and no weight will be shared. If you arrive too late, then you will have to deal with a lot of weight that is already falling. Very little weight is actually involved at this stage which means that weight-sharing can be accomplished by dancers with very different physicalities.

d.   Moving into each extension slowly gives your partner time to understand the direction of the fall so that he/she can position themselves accordingly to prevent it.

Option 1

Blind dancers can adapt this exercise by standing close to their partners and having a light contact around the partner's waist, thereby feeling the direction of the partner's reach and either suspending him/her by counter-balancing or by moving round to offer support.

Option 2

Try this contact version with both dancers blindfolded.

Option 3

Dancers using chairs can utilise surfaces of the chair itself or use their bodies to take the weight of their partner.

See **tilts and balances** to look at taking chairs into off-balance positions (Chapter 24).

Teaching notes

- Allow time to rest and breathe in each supporting moment.
- Explore improvisation as a group.
- Supporting dancers can give a small impulse to return the leaning dancer to centre, alternatively, try and find a natural pathway out of the support, or introduce **placement replacement** (see Exercise 49, Chapter 25).

IMPROV 38: TESTING STRUCTURES

An exploration of the properties of physical forms that take weight
2 dancers

Introduction

Discuss the properties of structures that are designed to take weight (tables, cars, beds). What can we learn from looking at these structures?

Directions

a.   The first dancer creates a weight-bearing form.
b.   By leaning or placing partial weight on the different surfaces, the second dancer begins to discover gently his/her strengths and weaknesses.

Teaching notes

Note: whenever there is doubt about whether your partner can or can't take weight, ask, never assume. At the same time, don't accept that someone is unable to take weight simply because they tend not to favour the use of a particular limb. An arm that doesn't have great range isn't necessarily weak or unusable, and even a weak limb or immobile limb may still be able to support some weight. Go gently, ask questions, find out. From this period of questioning and testing see if you can progress into a non-verbal exploration moving from one support into the next. Punctuate each support with a moment of rest. See if you can be aware of each other's breathing. The rise and fall of the rib cage and the subtle bodily shifts that occur as a result can be used to generate a shared sense of timing, and can become the impulse that moves you into your next support. Giving and taking weight still imply an adherence to all the 'listening' skills explored in **leading and following** (Improv 9, Chapter 18).

Option 1

Try a version of 'paper, scissors, stone'. Both of you think of a body part but don't say it. Count '1, 2, 3!' and call out the name of the body part you've thought of. Now try to support each other using these two parts. Though very simple, this device can lead to some extraordinary supports and balances.

Option 2

2 groups or more

A group of dancers make an interwoven mesh structure, another group travels through and around the sculpture, taking whatever supports or lifts/rests are available. Have the first group left sufficient openings for dancers using wheelchairs to pass through? What spatial and structural considerations do wheelchair users introduce to the shapes made? Try the same but with your eyes closed.

Option 3

Groups of 5 to 10

Combine **sculptural form** and **traverse**: twigs float down a stream occasionally snagging then drifting free. Small gatherings of twigs congregate and eventually liberate themselves to float on again. Repeat randomly.

IMPROV 39: TILTING SCULPTURAL FORMS

Understanding weight-supporting structures
2 to 3 dancers

Directions

a.   Look at your partner moving in space. Call 'Freeze!' so that your partner holds whatever position they are in like a statue.

b.   Can you see or feel a place where you think your partner can be easily tilted?

c.   Position yourself close by, creating a sense of security and support, and then gently, using your own body, tilt your partner fractionally off balance. You'll need to be close enough to your partner so that they don't panic and relinquish his/her position. If you have accurately identified their centre of gravity, your partner should tilt easily. If you have to try to force or heave your partner over, then you probably need to look again. You only need to move your partner a couple of inches off centre and then return them to their original position.

d.   When being tilted, try to maintain the integrity of your original shape. Some students may need greater support – if so, two people can do the tilting and supporting. Now see **placement replacement** (Exercise 49, Chapter 25).

IMPROV 40: DYNAMIC STRETCH

Still forms with dynamic energy
Approached gently – can be used as a warm-up
A choreographic device for developing duets
Linear understanding and weight for blind dancers
Learning about a partner's strengths
2 dancers

Introduction

In a dynamic stretch you are creating potential energy. This energy would be released (at least one of you would fall) if you let go. Where safe, you can test this by letting go! The felt sense of tension within a dynamic stretch is also a valuable tool in helping blind students to understand linear forms. Indeed it makes far more sense to approach linearity through stretching than through placement, which, for example, in ballet is achieved through endless mirror work and correction. This is primarily a visual asthetic, and one which makes little sense to impose on those without sight, unless it comes from a felt sense (see also Improv 48 **impressions** in Chapter 25).

Directions

a.   Start facing your partner or side by side, holding hands or interlocking elbows, and then explore different ways that you can lean away from each other, either simultaneously in a counter-balance or in turns, with one of you offering an anchorage while the other leans away.

b.   Start with small amounts of weight and gradually increase. Don't be afraid to ask each other for information at this stage.

c.   Continue to breathe as you stretch and use your breath to enter more fully into each movement.

d.   Try to keep the stretch alive so that there is always a feeling of elasticity between you and your partner and avoid going so far that you feel overstretched or trapped in a position from which you can't recover.

e.   The aim is to maintain a manoeuvrability and flexibility so that you can feel the limits of one stretch yet still be able to return and find a new connection.

f.   After an initial period of exploration and familiarisation, try moving from one stretch into another without discussion. Continue into a duet of continually expanding and contracting energy, seeing if you can coordinate your movement with the rhythm of your breath. Rest when you need to.

g.   Ask dancers to look at each other's work to see if couples are achieving a dynamic stretch.

Wheelchair users

•   This is an ideal way to learn about the stability and the degree of friction you command on the surface you're working on. Remember every surface offers different traction to your tyres and what may work very easily in a studio may have to be adapted for different performance settings. You will find this exercise easier with your brakes on. Once mastered, explore what happens with one on, one off.

•   Notice how the angle and placement of your partner affects the stability of your chair. In which directions are you able to take weight and which feel more 'tilty' or precarious? Discuss these discoveries with your partner.

Now try **ropes and mountains** as a sustained improvisation (Improv 41, below).

Example

Using **dynamic stretch**, two dancers, one disabled and one non-disabled with cerebral palsy, developed a beautiful duet in which they moved through a variety of different supports and counter-balances. The sequence involved precise attention to the releasing of muscles and sudden changes in tempo as the point of balance changed and counter-balance gave way to supported falls. I then asked the pair to teach their duet to a group of non-disabled dancers. It was suprising how difficult it was for the other dancers to see and appreciate the subtleties of the disabled dancer's movement and timing, and instead they produced an 'able-bodied' version of the duet. Is it OK to imitate the movement of a disabled dancer? There is no simple answer to this question; rather, it depends for what purpose and in what context the movement is used, but within the studio, students should feel able to investigate and learn about all sorts of movement regardless of their origin.

IMPROV 41: ROPES AND MOUNTAINS

Group exercise to follow individual warm-up or partnered weight-sharing

Directions

a. Create a circle with everyone facing in. Everyone moves gradually towards the centre reaching out to someone on the far side (or nearer at hand if your reach is limited).

b. Take hold of anyone that you can until everyone in the group is holding or being held by at least one other person (if you can't use your hand, use something else). When everyone is in contact you are all 'on the mountain'.

c. Without releasing your first hold, reach for someone else with your free hand or foot. Anyone who is at any time without someone to hold onto would have fallen off the mountain! So it is only when you have got hold of someone else that you can release your first contact. When everyone is comfortable with this, begin to make each contact into a small stretch (as if testing a rope).

d. Now begin to add a little weight to these stretches (as if satisfied that the rope will hold more of your weight) so that you are really beginning to support each other, i.e. if you let go at least one of you would fall (see Improv 40 **dynamic stretch**, above).

e. As you lean away from your partner, you may find yourself inadvertently supported by someone behind you. This constitutes a 'ledge', a place where you can rest without holding on. You are now free to let go and make use of the support, but you cannot move on until someone offers a hand (or arm or foot to pull you gently off again).

f. Allow the improvisation to progress with dancers offering supports and providing ledges.

g. Explore 'falling' or travelling away from the centre to watch and 'climbing' back towards centre to rejoin the improvisation.

Notes on lifting

Lifting constitutes one of the more physically spectacular elements within improvisation. Good lifts grow from the principles of giving and taking weight, combined with an understanding of how to translate horizontal momentum into vertical lift.

Lifting, however, is not something that should be learned from a book. It is best to study and practise these skills with an experienced teacher of contact improvisation. These notes are meant only as preparation and as reminders and pointers for those needing to refresh or go over basics.

23.2 David Toole and Helen Baggett, CandoCo, 1997. (Photographer Anthony Crickmay)

IMPROV 42: THE GENTLE CIRCLE

Introduction

Tracing an unbroken pathway around the surface of the body while in contact with a partner is sometimes called 'mapping'. It is a technique that comes from contact improvisation and release work, and has its origins in soft martial arts such as Aikido and Tai Chi, where this same physical skill is used to connect to and then redirect an assailant's attack without using force. In our dance work, two dancers make a light contact with each other; they may be seated, standing or in any position of their choosing. The body is relaxed but alert and the rolling pathways are used to travel around the surface of the body while remaining in contact.

Preparation

- Before looking at how we roll up and onto a partner we will explore the opposite: how to roll around, down and away from a partner.
- Allow a small amount of weight to be shared so that there is a recognisable, single, clear point of contact.This might be:

  - head to head;
  - through the back;

- shoulder to shoulder;
- hip to hip.

- Now just rest in that position, giving weight to each other, and find your own natural breathing. Notice the breathing of your partner and after a while see if you can fall into the same cycle of inhalation and exhalation.
- Don't try to 'make' something happen, but give your attention to the shared point of contact. Is the point suggesting a direction to move in? Which way? Can you allow this point of contact to roll (like two balls rotating around one another), tracing an unbroken pathway around the surface of your body so that both you and your partner take up a new position without separating? Don't force it. If the movement stops, stop with it, breathe, relax and listen for a new shift.
- After exploring in this way, you come into contact with another part of your partner's body, so that there are now two points of contact. Release the first point and focus your attention and your weight into this new connection, and allow yourself to follow this new circular rolling pathway. Try always to work with only one clear point of contact.

Option 1

You may find when working on the exercise above that there are moments when your momentum takes you away from your partner. When this occurs, continue to move naturally into space and allow the idea of circling to bring you back together.

Option 2

Try not to pre-plan any new connection, but just see how you end up. Although you should remain relaxed in this exercise, try to keep a little energy in the body and a little space between yourself and the ground otherwise the exercise can repeatedly collapse into a shapeless heap with nothing happening.

Option 3

The pathway away from your partner might be either a turning circle or have the feeling of a wave moving away, suspending and then gently returning. If you breathe naturally, you will have an additional source of cohesion and rhythm, which will inform the return phase of your dance.

Option 4

As the centred dancer, you can now begin to assist your partner
by offering supporting surfaces as your partner approaches and
encourages a little upward energy as they make contact with you.
Remember: don't try to grab or hoist your partner; just be aware,
if the opportunity arises, to assist them in their upward rolling
pathway. Try to do this without exerting yourself but by following
the momentum of your partner's journey. Any small, partial
assistance is preferable to a manufactured 'hoist' using force.

Option 5

If you find yourself being momentarily lifted use your in-breath
to sustain the moment and then roll gently out and away again as
you breathe out. Ideally, this should happen naturally and spontaneously without being forced or coerced. A good lift feels almost
weightless; when this happens there is a heightened sense not only
of balance but of momentum (the flow of weight), of timing and
rhythm. A good lift has a musicality to it.

See the work of Doris Humphrey and José Limon for a full
account of the use of breath, fall, recovery and suspension.

DISABLED STUDENTS AND LIFTING

Due to government legislation in England, disabled students in
schools are no longer supposed to be lifted from their chairs except
by 'trained' care assistants. Although this move may help to
prevent back injury in over-pressed carers, it leaves us in a patently
ridiculous position in the dance class when non-disabled students
are permitted by law to lift each other, but not their disabled
colleagues. Only a government department could have come up
with this one!

Unfortunately, as England has increasingly adopted the
American propensity to sue on sight, this issue has made schools
increasingly jittery. The medical model of disability will usually
be invoked to justify the no-lifting policy and tends to casts a long
shadow over teachers often working in isolation and having
to make their own decisions. Because of this regulation some
schools will not allow disabled students out of their wheelchairs
even during dance, thus not only lifting but, more importantly,
movement on the floor becomes outlawed. Thus bound to the
wheelchair the stereotype of immobility is reinforced and something that is perfectly natural for disabled students outside school
(to get out of their chair) becomes taboo within it.

In most other dance settings lifting is an accord between
the disabled and non-disabled person and the group leader, and

23.3 Lucy Moelwyn-Hughes, Katie Marsh and Tom St-Louis, Tardis Dance Company, *Wallpaper Dancing*, 1998. Choreography by Janet Smith. (Photographer Adam Benjamin)

should only be attempted when all those concerned feel comfortable and confident with each other. For most disabled people it is not a big deal, though there may be some people who need to share more specific and detailed information before being lifted.[79]

I have sometimes resisted lifting during sessions when I am carrying an injury myself or when there have been insufficient people available to make the exploration of lifting a sensible option. When making work in student groups I have never avoided a lift when it felt the right thing for the student and the group. Within restrictive legislation, especially that which impinges on personal freedom, we all have to make personal choices guided by our own convictions.

Note

79 A student may for example have a urinary bag attached to their leg and fear of embarrassment could prevent them from leaving the chair to work on the floor. As a teacher, a quiet word about making sure the bag is emptied before class may help, and with time the student may be able to explain how the bag works and thus the kind of movements that will cause difficulties.

24 Counter-balances and chair tilts: dicing with Newtonian physics

> The characteristic most common to actors and dancers from different cultures and times is the abandonment of daily balance in favour of a 'precarious' or extra-daily 'balance'. Extra-daily balance demands a greater physical effort – it is this extra effort which dilates the body's tensions in such a way that the performer seems to be alive even before he begins to express.
>
> (Eugenio Barba, 1991)

One of the elements that companies such as CandoCo and Light Motion exploited in the early 1990s was the idea of balances performed by wheelchair users. It was a technique that took the dancing partnership into a new realm of shared risk, and shattered the 'sedentary' appearance of dancers in wheelchairs. This idea was further explored by the Stare Cases Project who transposed chair tilts and balances onto public staircases and by Touch Compass who hoisted chairs and their occupants skyward.

Although some people become very anxious about wheelchairs being used for tilts and balances, wheelchairs are in fact designed to fulfil this function. Without forward and backward tilting you would never be able to mount a kerb or descend a step. In addition, many modern chairs have exceptional balancing qualities.

Executing safe balances requires a thorough understanding of, and familiarity with, the physics of the wheelchair. As part of his warm-ups for the Stare Cases Project, Andrew Maclay would join the company sitting on the floor and pass round his wheelchair for each dancer to improvise with while the rest of the company watched. This led to an increased, shared knowledge of the dynamics of his chair (vital to this group who perform in the most precarious of situations) and allowed dancers to make discoveries that were then used creatively in performance.

Preparation for working with tilts and balances should include checking that tyres are well pumped and that brakes are properly fitted and working. Carefully positioned mats may also be advisable for less experienced dancers, though these should always

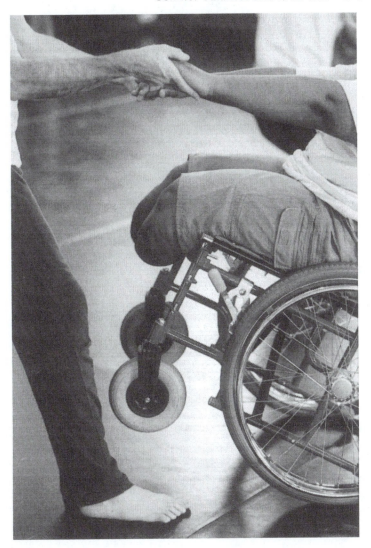

24.1 Makhotso Sompane and author. Back tilt. (Photographer John
 Hogg)

be placed alongside or behind the chair so that the wheels remain
in contact with the floor. Remember that different surfaces offer
different friction. A tilt achieved on a dance floor may come out
very differently on a shiny wooden surface.

If you are not a wheelchair user, do not attempt to teach tilting
or balancing until you have tried out all the following exercises
yourself from a chair. Spend as much time in a wheelchair as
you can to understand the movement dynamics, areas of stability
and instability, and finally remember that no two chairs are alike
– each has its unique characteristics, which will be affected by the
weight and posture of any new occupant.

Dancers new to tilting will often want lots of people around before they try, although it is good to have an additional dancer for safety. Tilting is essentially a negotiation of weight between two people (one dancer in the chair, one out).[80]

A wheelchair in a forward/backward tilt when both brakes are on acts like a pivot. It is not uncommon to see inexperienced groups with one dancer at the front of the chair and one at the back, unintentionally fighting against each other in an effort to maintain a balance while the person in the chair sits bemused doing nothing. Remember, once the initial inertia is overcome to get the chair out of its normal resting position, most modern manual chairs balance easily. Being in a balance requires the same effort needed to stay on a bike; if your knuckles are turning white, or you are cutting off the circulation in your partner's hand, you may need to relax a bit!

EXERCISE 43: BACK TILTING FROM THE FRONT

3 dancers
Wheelchair user and partner plus one for safety

Introduction

This is the most common tilt for a wheelchair and is a good place to start. Whenever you mount a kerb in a wheelchair whether aided or solo you are effectively doing a back tilt. (A 'wheelie' is an example of a sustained back tilt or balance.) For most people new to wheelchairs the motion of the chair tipping backwards is quite alarming, so go gently into these exercises. Though essentially a partner exercise, it is advisable to have a third dancer placed behind the chair, ready to offer support if needed when you first begin. (If you are a chair user, remember to get out and have a go at supporting as well as tilting.)

Directions

a.   Put your brakes on and sit in your chair facing your partner. Your partner stands facing you, though slightly to one side. (a third dancer is behind you for safety).
b.   If your chair has good brakes, and is fairly light, you can push against each other by extending your right arms (or left arms). Otherwise, both of you hold both arms out in front of you, place your hands palm to palm or in a way that you can offer resistance to each other and begin calmly but firmly to push towards each other until you feel the front wheels of the chair begin to lift off the ground (Figure 24.1).

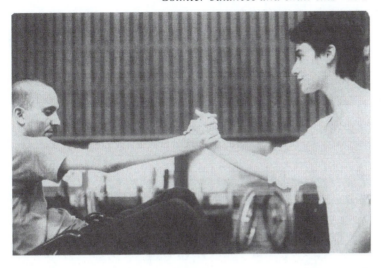

24.2 Vertigo Dance Company. Noa Wertheim and Hai Cohen, Israel.
(Photographer Michal Chitayat)

c. Keep going very gradually until you begin to feel the pressure (the loading) in your hands decrease; this means that you are approaching the point where the person in the chair is beginning to balance (Figure 24.2).

d. A common error when first doing this exercise is to grip your partner's hand instead of maintaining a relaxed, more open contact. Remind yourself that there is someone behind the wheelchair to catch if the chair goes too far (Figure 24.3).

e. This is a good time to notice how breathing changes in moments of stress! Avoid sudden movements and try to maintain the open contact in your hands as you push against each other. Now see if you can detect the balance point.

f. Try to move into and out of the balance point noticing how the pressure in your hands changes. If you want to you can try this with your eyes closed.

g. When the wheelchair is balanced on its back wheels it feels virtually weightless, so now you can shift forwards and back so that your entire weight can be controlled through your thumb which is 'bracketed' between the thumb and first finger of your partner's hand.

h. When you are completely familiar with the balance point, begin an exploration of the counter-balance that is now available as you pass beyond the point of balance and into the back tilt. The position of the standing or supporting dancer will determine the stability of the chair in the tilt. Some readjustment of foot positions for the standing dancer may be necessary as the chair tilts and the footplates rise.

i. Always try to ensure that the dancer in the chair initiates and controls the direction and speed of the movement.

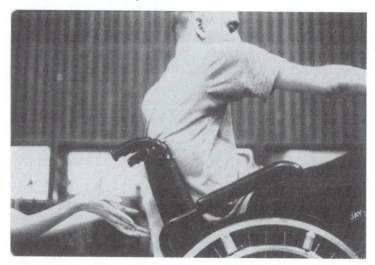

24.3 Vertigo Dance Company, Israel. (Photographer Michal Chitayat)

j.   A dancer in a wheelchair can also push a partner seated in an ordinary chair up onto its back legs and support them in a back or side tilt.

Teaching notes

Some wheelchairs are fitted with spoilers that prevent back tilting; these can usually be removed, but remember to replace them after class.

EXERCISE 44: BACK TILTING FROM BEHIND

Wheelchair user and partner

Directions

Caution: make sure that you have sufficient head support if you have any history of neck problems before attempting back tilting.

a.   Have additional dancers available to help and provide safety. But remember, this is essentially a two-person exercise (see Exercise 43, above).
b.   There are a variety of methods of tilting from behind. Some can be achieved through dancer-to-dancer contact, others, which are more passive, though still great fun, through the dancer on the floor manipulating the chair itself.
c.   Put the brakes on. One dancer sits in the wheelchair, the second sits on the floor immediately behind the seated dancer

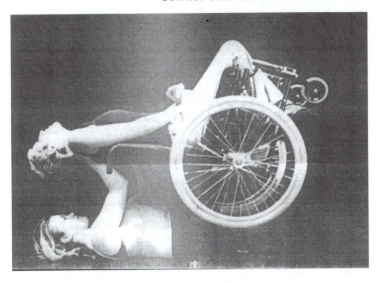

24.4 Back tilt progressed into a lift. Vicky Day Fox (below) and Karen Langley. CandoCo Summer School, 2000. (Photographer Kalpesh Lathigra)

with his/her feet slightly under the chair. When both are ready, the dancer on the floor places both hands on the chair handles or back frame and gently pulls (by leaning backwards), thereby raising the front wheels of the chair off the ground. (This part can also be achieved by working in groups of three, with a partner pushing from the front as described in Exercise 43 **back tilting from the front,** above).

d. When you are familiar with where your balance point is (see Exercise 43, direction h), ask your partner to take you gently beyond this point into a more off-balance backward tilt (Figure 24.5.

e. If you are the dancer on the floor, you may want to try out different positions, sitting, lying on your back or using your shins against the chairback to support your partner. Find out what works for you.

Option 1: advanced

- With confidence and a high level of cooperation and trust the wheelchair user can control more of the elements of this move, including going up into a wheelie and dropping back onto a supporting dancer. This is an advanced move and needs to be approached with caution as the brakes are not used. Be aware that the chair will tend to roll away from the supporter as it tilts all the way back. This can be easily controlled by the chair user holding and therefore 'braking' the wheels during the last part of the tilt.

24.5 Tom St-Louis and Katie MacCabe rehearse *Limited Choices*. (Photographer Debra Hudson)

EXERCISE 45: PARTNERED SIDE TILT USING A MANUAL CHAIR

Introduction

Manual wheelchairs are designed to tilt backwards but they are not, however, designed to tilt sideways and some, particularly sports models, are designed to specifically counter any such tendency through having cambered wheels. As well as being difficult to accomplish, the side tilt puts additional strain on the structure of, and therefore the longevity of, the chair. It also demands some strength in the upper body (though a partnered side tilt is well within the reach of most tetraplegic dancers). Having said all this, the side tilt is an unusual and spectacular manoeuvre and fairly irresistible for those interested in taking their dance (and their chairs) that little bit further.

Initially, this tilt can put a lot of strain on your arms and sides. With practice and improved timing, you'll find the tilt becomes faster and involves far less effort. The following notes are reminders. **It is advisable only to explore side tilts with an experienced teacher.**

Directions

a. Sit in your chair, brakes on, with your partner sitting on the floor to the right of you, facing you at right angles, i.e. in line with the wheel axles. You are going to attempt a balance on the right wheel (for left-wheel balance, just do everything on the other side).

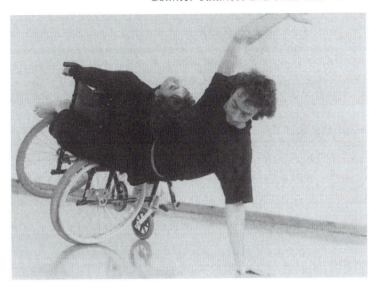

24.6 Adam Benjamin and Celeste Dandeker rehearsing *For Starters*, 1990, Middlesex University. (Photographer Mary Morrison)

b. You partner places one foot alongside the small front wheels of the chair, this will prevent the chair swinging round as you pull. Their other foot braces the bottom of the large wheel, though make sure it is not pressing on the spokes.

c. Now offer your hand or the crook of your right elbow to your partner, depending on your respective proportions. Hold the far (left) wheel rim with your other hand. Before you attempt to lift the wheel, explore a shared rocking action, towards and away from the left wheel, and allow this to develop so that the momentum begins to help raise the wheel of the chair. You may need to experiment with different holds and grips until you find a way that works for you.

d. Get other students to watch and to be on hand for the odd spill! Eventually you should be able to lift the wheel and establish your balance point. Remember, the balance point is often further than you might think.

Development for advanced students

•   When you are comfortable in a side balance, and you and your partner are able to relax, breathe and take time to feel and control the chair in balance, you can then look at replacing/ changing supports.

•   If you have gone into the balance using a hand-to-hand grip, you should now be able to relax a little and hold the balance. Decide where you intend to support next. For example, can you now support the balance with your hand on your partner's shoulder, or release your hand and gently fall to replace it on your partner's knee? This is a tricky manoeuvre but with practice you may also be able to drop a hand to the floor, thereby allowing your partner to move away altogether, or explore as in **placement replacement** (Exercise 49, Chapter 25).

Option 4

Some wheelchair users will be able to accomplish a solo side tilt. To the right side this involves gripping the left-wheel rim with the left hand and rocking first left and then hard right using the left hand to pull up the left wheel while the right hand descends to the floor to stabilise the tilt.

Notes

80 Tilting can also be done by two dancers in chairs.

25 Art and theatre

I don't believe in barriers or caged beauty. There is no way in
these fast times that we can define what dance is. We cannot even
define what art is.

(Javier de Frutos, 2001)

The visual and plastic arts offer dancers a wealth of insight into
the process of creation, of 'mark making' and of design. They
provide a rich ground for exploration and inspiration both for the
would-be choreographer and the improviser. Below are just a few
ideas that have arisen from the integration of visual art and dance.

IMPROV 46: FREEZE-FRAME

a hopeless technology for what
can only be developed in the heart

(William Oxley, 1987)

Seeing movement
Remembering movement
For 2 to 5 dancers

Introduction

The ability to grasp the essence or flavour of a movement phrase
is a valuable skill, both for choreographers and improvisers. These
exercises aim to sharpen awareness of these 'essential' movement
moments.

   The exercise known as mirroring is probably one of the first
games many of us played. Although students may not always be
able to mirror one another exactly, the aim here is to identify some
essential feature of our partner's movement and find a way of
reflecting it back. It is as though the mirror reflects back an instant
artist's sketch or impression rather than the whole picture.

25.1 Yoachim Bracher in *Brooding Angels*, 1997, HandiCapace Tanz
Kompanie. Choreography by Benjamin. (Photographer Claus
Langer)

Directions

a.   One dancer completes a single swift and uncomplicated movement, using one part of the body or the whole of the body.
For example, a fall from sitting to slumped forwards/sideways,
a movement of the arm or a leap.

b.   The other dancer(s) observe the movement and immediately reflect back any moment that captures a particular instant of the pathway they have just witnessed. The first dancer continues to work to generate simple movements, taking a pause between each to look at what the other dancers are presenting.

c.   When each student has tried this, begin to alternate the first, second and third student with the others reflecting.

Option 1

Bring in paper and pencil and actually try doing 5-second sketches of each other moving. Do lots of these. Pin up your favourites around the studio.

Option 2

Take any you are really embarrassed about. Look again closely. Find three single tiny marks or parts of your drawing that interest you. Tear them out. Lick them and stick them to different parts of your body. Dance the marks.

Option 3

Develop this idea choreographically.

IMPROV 47: LINE DANCE

Fast impressions
For groups of 5 to 24

Directions

a.   All but one of the dancers form a line facing into the dance space with about an arm's length between each.
b.   The one remaining dancer travels along the line in front of the other dancers. To begin with, this should be a simple, plain journey.
c.   Each person in the line reflects and holds an impression of the movement in the instant the dancer passes directly in front of them.
d.   The whole group holds the positions created in response to the travelling dancer.
e.   The traveller then goes back to see the impression of their journey held in the bodies of the dancers in the line and then joins the line and another dancer travels.
f.   Once all of the group have tried this, the solo sequences can be developed and made more complex. Try to keep things simple and 'readable'.

Teaching note

It is helpful if the journey starts a little before the first dancer in line and continues a little beyond the last. Remind dancers to observe the image their journey creates.

IMPROV 48: IMPRESSIONS

> A man sitting in the quiet of his study, holding the photograph of a woman, a pained look on his face. An osprey framed in the sky, its wings out-stretched, the sun rays piercing between feathers. A young boy sitting in an empty auditorium, his heart racing as if he were on stage. Footprints in snow on a winter island.
>
> (Alan Lightman, 1993: 76)

Partner work
Problem-solving and setting
Articulation of body parts
Particularly suited to blind dancers
Impressions can be used both as a beautiful choreographic device and as a starting point for improvisation. They bring awareness of form and structure; awareness of skin surface v. skeleton structure; exterior v. interior (Figure 25.2).

Introduction

Every time we meet someone we are left with an impression, sometimes this is 'fleeting', sometimes strong, deep, lasting. People: 'leave their mark on us'; 'touch us deeply'; 'disappear without trace'; 'impress us'; 'scar us' or 'dent our egos'.

Ask students to bring in different objects or images that have resulted from impressions. Send them out to photograph impressions in the local environment.

Arrange an art session, creating impressions out of clay, potato cuts, tinfoil, cardboard. Put down strips of wallpaper on the studio floor and create track paintings, with feet and wheels.[81] Alternatively, wait until winter and go and play in the snow.

Directions

a.   Dancer A puts an arm around B, or makes contact with B in any natural, spontaneous way. Make sure that this first contact is comfortable and confident. It should feel reassuring and bring awareness to the skin and muscles of the body.

b.   Once this contact has been made, A freezes in space as though becoming a statue. This doesn't mean squeezing or changing the pressure of contact; rather, it entails a change of attention from the surface of the body where contact is being made

25.2 Bird print in snow. (Photographer Yoshinao Nakazawa)

to include an awareness of the skeleton so that the position becomes frozen.

c. Partner B stays still until able to feel the physical change in partner A. When this change from relaxed to rigid is complete, B moves away carefully, without using any force and without disturbing the structure created by A, leaving an impression like the print left in a rock when a fossil is removed.

d. Look at this 'negative space'. If you want you can try repositioning yourself to see if the fit is still exact.

e. It is now B's turn. The exercise is repeated as B makes contact and then 'freezes'. Partner A now softens and moves away.

f. You can make the exercise more challenging by creating more complex, or interwoven, shapes with each other and also by trying to find rapid escapes. Be careful, the aim is always to get out without disturbing your partner. Remember, you can't use force to escape so every 'embrace', even the most complex, **must** leave a way out.

Teaching notes

Some students don't like the feeling of restricting their partner's escape and feel that they are somehow going against first principles (not to use force). However, in this improvisation you are using your strength to maintain your own position, not to manipulate someone; your intention is that your partner should begin to use his/her felt sense rather than his/her thought/intellectual sense. If possible, even your fingertips should be frozen and hard. If you soften or relax (say, because you feel sorry for your partner), then you effectively deprive them of the opportunity to learn.

Choreographic uses

The physical adjustments dancers make as they escape the confines of their partner's frozen embrace generate the most complex and original movements. The beauty of **impressions** for blind students is that the forms created come from a felt sense and not from an externally imposed linear or 'sighted aesthetic'.

Although there are undoubted benefits to be had from elongated linear forms, these can best be taught and felt through exercises like **dynamic stretch** (see Improv 40, Chapter 23).

Option 1

The group forms a circle of paired dancers. The escaping member of **impressions** moves on to the next pair and embraces the 'empty' statue, who in turn escapes, and so on around the circle. This is an improv structure that can be used with a variety of different exercises.

The timing of the changes can be called initially. Later, try dancing it randomly so dancers have to negotiate joining and leaving their partners in their own time. This means sometimes there will be three dancers together (see Option 2, below).

Dancers who find themselves alone can work on mirroring the movement of an adjacent dancer or simply hold their statue position.

Option 2

Develop **impressions** as an improvisation by adding more dancers. Try with three and then four dancers working together. Play with the different possibilities that arise.

Option 3

Capture the emotional content of the initial embrace and try to maintain the feeling, sense or presence of the dancer for a time after the dancer has left, as though you are still holding onto the feeling. The sculpture you create has emotional as well as structural qualities.

Option 4

Continue to improvise with the movements you find as you escape from the statue. The statue then comes to life and recaptures the dancer in motion, arresting the phrase and creating a new statue.

EXERCISE 49: PLACEMENT REPLACEMENT – A DEVELOPMENT OF IMPRESSIONS AND TILTING SCULPTURAL FORMS INVOLVING WEIGHT-SHARING

> Look at an Egyptian statue: it looks rigid to us, yet we sense in it the image of a body capable of movement and which, despite its rigidity, is animated.
>
> (Matisse, 1908)

Controlling weight
Supports
Blind and sighted students
3 or 4 dancers

Introduction

When we first worked with this exercise in a school for blind students the teachers simply couldn't understand how their students were managing to work with such clarity and complexity, while supporting and being supported by each other. It was an exercise that convinced the school of the value of dance as part of their programme.

Directions

a. Dancer A offers a support. Dancer B gently rests or leans a small amount of weight, a bit like a statue propped up against a table. Dancer A is now unable to move away (as in **impressions**, without disturbing the partner's position in space). This problem is solved by the introduction of a third dancer.

b. As you settle into the support, think of lengthening so that your body, though now off centre, is not slumped or collapsed but extended. Make sure that only B is leaning, i.e. this is a one-person support not a counter-balance.

c. Now both A and B close their eyes and a third dancer with eyes open comes in and seeks to take the weight of B away from A by introducing a new support. The aim of the exercise is that the actual position of dancer B in space remains exactly the same. It is only the weight (the loading) that changes.

d. The new support is introduced gradually so that the original supporting dancer can feel the weight they were carrying decreasing to the point where there is only contact but no weight. Remember, the weight is taken without the body moving in space. It is like lifting a piano so that you can move a carpet – the piano is still very lightly touching the carpet but there is no longer any weight, so the carpet can be removed.

e. When the dancer who provided the first support feels the weight has been taken, that dancer will be able to move away, still with eyes closed. The communication here is all about recognising weight transfer through changes in pressure. The cue to move is tactile, not visual.

f. This principle can build into a complex and wonderful improvisation for large and small groups of students dancing together, or be used in choreography, particularly for blind dancers.

Teaching notes

Ensure that students do not to give weight to someone who is already taking the weight of another dancer. Advanced students will have the sensitivity to be able to deal with this but inexperienced students may need guidance.

Option 1

Vocal score
7 to 12 dancers

Each dancer is given a number. Dancers move at will into the centre of the studio, either offering or making use of stable structures until the group has created an interlinked and interdependent sculpture, which includes weight-sharing.

Those watching then call out a number (or name) to remove a dancer. If a dancer who is called is supporting someone that dancer must call 'Replace!' so that the dancer's supporting role is taken on by one of those watching. Or, 'Replace from within' in which case one of the dancers in the group takes over the supporting role.

Start slowly and build in speed.

See also **aerial pathways** for a development for advanced groups (Improv 15, Chapter 18).

Note

81 See CandoCo's film *OutSide In*.

26 Speed and timing

And as we are liberated from our own fear, our presence auto-
matically liberates others.

(Nelson Mandela, 1994)

These exercises involve a degree of risk. However, if rules and
safety precautions are fully understood **gateway** can, like skiing
or rock climbing, be made accessible to everyone. Remember,
make sure you fully understand and have mastered any exercise
before attempting to teach it.

Having created a safe dance space in which to work, and
generated an ethos of careful and patient exploration, it may
seem something of a contradiction to entertain the idea of metal
chairs flying past barefooted dancers at speed. To realign any
lingering visions of fragility that you may have, take a trip to watch
your local wheelchair basketball team in action. Although not
everyone who uses a wheelchair will necessarily have this kind of
constitution or physicality, it was the reluctance of those leading
community/disability groups to deal with this kind of energy that
kept (and continues to keep) some of the most athletic disabled
people out of dance. This said, there will be some people for whom
a fall from a chair would constitute a serious and dangerous
occurrence; our aim is to find ways of accommodating the entire
range of physicality within a challenging and exciting dance
experience (Figure 26.1).

All too often so-called integrated work fails to integrate speed
with fragility. In theatre, film and literature it is very often the
juxtaposition of frailty and threat that creates excitement (the
pram scene in *The Untouchables*, or the children on the track in
The Railway Children). If we understand these elements then very
slow movement can be used to create high tension.

NB: Safety check, see Chapter 16.

26.1 Judith Bayha falling backward. As Sandra Seiz runs past, Georg Jung
      catches. HandiCapace rehearsals, 1997. (Photographer Claus Langer)

EXERCISE 50: GATEWAY – WITHOUT DEVIATION
OR HESITATION

Speed/timing
Precision
Trust
Risk
Needs a large studio and demands a high level of concentration.

Introduction

Gateway and **gauntlet** were inspired by practices in Japanese martial arts, particularly by the clear linear energy used in sword work, notably the practice of Eiko conceived by Hiroyuki Aoki, the founder of Shintaido. Central to this practice is the idea that the powerful, cutting energy of the sword can be channelled into a life-enhancing encounter. An advanced exercise to be approached in a calm and careful manner (swords not necessary).

In this exercise dancers move directly into and through each other's space without deviating or hesitating. The aim is to develop a clear linear 'cutting' energy which heightens and develops centredness, breath and confidence in oneself and one's partner. When done well, you will hear onlookers catch their breath. Not for the faint-hearted!

Although an 'advanced exercise', **gateway** can, like all the exercises in this section, be modified for different dancers and levels of experience. I have used it successfully, as a means of teaching dance discipline and timing, with school groups and professionals.

Directions

a. Dancer A is positioned in the centre of the studio facing dancer B who is at the edge of the studio.

b. Directions for dancer A:

i Imagine that you are an open gateway in a wall that stretches away on either side of you. Dancer B moves towards the gateway (initially at walking pace) with the intention of passing directly through your space.

ii Wait until the very last second before moving out of the way. This should be achieved without causing B to slow down or deviate from the linear pathway they are travelling.

c. Take turns watching other couples working. Students will often slow down or veer to one side as they approach. Onlooking students can give feedback concerning deviation or hesitation.

d. Start slowly and as you gain confidence gradually build up speed. If using a power chair, be particularly careful to go slowly at first.

Notes for ambulant dancers

*   When standing in the gateway position, keep your centre low, and your knees slightly bent. To move out of the way effectively, try not to move backwards, away from the oncoming dancer, instead stay low and move slightly forward on the diagonal as the dancer approaches, opening your body so that you are effectively moving alongside the dancer as they pass.

- If your partner is using a wheelchair, this means stepping diagonally forward into a lunge – the trailing leg lifts out of the way at the last moment. The final feeling should be like a piece of cork being brushed aside by the bow wave of a fast boat.

Notes for dancers using wheelchairs

- If you're using a wheelchair (particularly a power chair), you may find that it isn't possible to move out of the way quickly enough without causing your partner to slow down. If this is the case, try setting yourself at right angles to your partner's pathway and imagine yourself to be a sliding door that will open in front of your partner. You must now agree a crossing point as your partner will no longer be facing you directly when you start.
- Make sure you both travel on straight pathways crossing at 90° angles. You should feel a bit like a car crossing a railway line fractionally in front of an oncoming locomotive. You will probably have to start moving slightly sooner but aim to cut across closely and at speed. Notice what happens to your breathing as you pass each other. If you don't feel a 'rush' when you're doing the exercise, then you are moving too soon. Remember, if you don't feel excited by your actions, an audience is unlikely to!

Teaching notes

- Start your first attempt at a walking pace so that you can build a rapport with your partner before you try at higher speed.
- When travelling, dancer B should not look directly at the gateway dancer but beyond that dancer. This avoids subtle non-verbal signs being passed or communicated. B should try and maintain a constant speed as this will help A time their evasion to the very last second.
- When you begin travelling at speed, stay relaxed and keep breathing. Going faster does not mean dashing or panicking. If you're not breathing as you travel, then you're no longer relaxed and this means you will not be able to respond intelligently if your partner fails to move out of the way.

Development

- Take the gateway idea and explore using a pair of dancers, or more, to create a variety of gateways. The emphasis is still on the uninterrupted energy of the travelling dancer.
- Two dancers creating a counter-balance: make sure you understand how the counter-balance will break open, and

where your fall or movement takes you, i.e. it should take you out of the line of the travelling dancer. Make counter-balances and supports dependent on a single grip or point of contact so that only one decision is needed to prompt the release. Now try slowly with a third dancer travelling. Release the counter-balance at the moment the travelling dancer arrives, thereby creating a space for that dancer to pass through. Try different counter-balances. Remember to delay the moment of release until the very last instant.

- Now see if the group can create a variety of gateways and send a series of travelling dancers through. Each gateway reforms into a new position before the arrival of the next travelling dancer. This may be used as a choreographic device.
- Using additional tactile and sound cues **gateway** is a challenging and exciting exercise for blind and visually impaired dancers, though it should only be introduced by teachers with considerable experience.

Option 1

Set up a group improvisation in which dancers can only move at right angles through the space, cutting across each other, stopping or jumping out of each other's way. This can be made more challenging by reducing the space in which they are allowed to move. Keep a eye open for overexcited or reckless students: this is an improvisation only to be tried with an aware and cooperative group. See the rule below: – if you're late, wait.

EXERCISE 51: GAUNTLET

For large groups of up to 30

The principles of **gateway** should be fully understood and confidently demonstrated before attempting this exercise.

Directions

a. Divide the group into two. Now make two lines along opposing sides of the studio. Each dancer in the line is separated by at least an arm's length. Stagger the two lines so that every dancer is facing one of the spaces in the opposite line, i.e. every dancer now has a clear pathway across the studio to the far side.

b. Practise this simple cross-over manoeuvre with the two groups changing sides. Make sure that all the dancers understand that they cannot deviate from their 'track' across the studio.

c.   A solitary dancer takes up a position at the end of the studio
     facing down the centre line between the two groups. The
     solitary dancer now begins to travel slowly down the centre
     of the studio while the dancers on either side begin their cross-
     over pattern, each one trying to pass just in front without
     touching, or disrupting, the dancer's journey.

Teaching notes

*   The teacher should always demonstrate this exercise and
    ensure that everyone in the group understands what they are
    doing before asking students to try.
*   The most essential rule for the dancers crossing is: **if you're
    late – wait!** The single dancer travelling the centre line **always**
    has right of way. This means if a crossing dancer is late and
    fails to cut in front of the dancer walking the gauntlet they
    must stop and cross behind. If they deviate in an attempt to
    get round they may well obstruct or, worse still, be mown
    down by a dancer crossing in the opposite direction!

Option 1

Those crossing from side to side can begin to explore different
ways of travelling. Creativity should not replace care and attention
to the rules and the central task of the exercise!

*   Start early but travel slowly.
*   Start late and travel fast.
*   Crawl.
*   Jump.
*   Dive.

Option 2

Advanced gauntlet

Much good integrated work is marked by the willingness of disabled students to take risks, often placing themselves in the hands
of their non-disabled colleagues. Here the boot (or wheel) can be
placed on the other foot.

With a group that has mastered and fully understood the
exercise, the teacher may wish to go further by demonstrating
the most challenging versions of gauntlet.

*   Travelling backwards down the centre line.
*   Travelling blindfolded down the centre line (see below).
*   Two dancers facing each other but separated by about four
    paces travel down the centre line, the crossing dancers cross

twice cutting in front of each dancer – be careful, or make the gap bigger if there are dancers in wheelchairs crossing.

Gateway and gauntlet with visually impaired students

Gauntlet can be tried by blind students – maintaining a straight pathway can be ensured by having another student tap, clap or play an instrument at the opposite side of the studio (see Improv 35 **calling** in Chapter 28). If you intend to teach this, and you are not visually impaired then make sure that you try the blindfolded version yourself first.

27 A little more time: Exercises to develop an understanding of rhythm and the duration of a simple gesture or action

'What are you doing here?' growled the watchdog.
'Just killing time,' replied Milo apologetically.
'You see – '
'KILLING TIME!' roared the dog – so furious that his alarm went off. 'It's bad enough wasting time without killing it.' And he shuddered at the thought.

(Norton Juster, 1962)

Introduction

The exercises in this section are intended to develop an understanding of the rhythmicity and musicality of movement through appreciating the duration of a simple gesture or action. I am indebted to Juleyn Hamilton for these (and many other) inspiring ideas! He describes here how the exercise first came about.

> It was born one afternoon when teaching a workshop; having been shopping in the pause returned to class with a bag of lemons – feeling wondrous as exactly what next to do in the project we somehow began throwing these lemons among each other and soon this had produced not only a messy studio floor but a new exercise.[82]

I came very close to discovering the exercise myself when a group of HandiCapace dancers became involved in a similar activity with a bowl of tangerines; sadly, however, we only came up with a new way of making fruit salad.

EXERCISE 52: A SIMPLE EXERCISE IN TIMING

Requires: beanbag or rolled-up sweatshirt, socks, lemons, etc.
2 dancers

Introduction

In this and the following series it is important that no attempt is made to play with or fool your partner. All actions need to be clear and simple in order to encourage the ability to read and understand the rhythmicity of movement. With a little thought, this exercise can be used with blind and with deaf students.

Directions

a. Throw the beanbag in the air and stamp, tap or clap as it lands. When this is mastered, the sound is made simultaneously as the object lands.

b. Now try responding just before and then try just after the object lands. Note: if you are too early or too late the events will seem disconnected. The aim is to establish a rhythmicity between the two sounds: 'bu–bum' rather than

   thud... thud.

c. Now try the same exercise but throw the beanbag over your head so that it lands behind you. Again, try stamping or shouting:

   i   As it lands.
   ii Just before it lands.
   iii Just after it lands.

With a partner

- Position yourself facing your partner about 8 ft. apart.
- When you are both ready, your partner throws the beanbag over your head so that it lands behind you.
- Without looking behind, stamp (or clap or shout) at the moment you think the beanbag lands.
- Adapt the exercise to meet your needs.

With a blind or visually impaired partner

Begin with thowing and catching a bag as a solo exercise so the connection can be made between the effort and trajectory of an object and the time it takes to land. When this has been clearly understood, the throw and trajectory and landing can be vocalised by a partner. For example: 'I'll swing the bag on "and" and will accompany the upward flight with the word "uuuuuuup". The fall is in silence – stamp or clap when you think the beanbag will hit the floor.'

Stay relaxed and open. Breathe! Remember, a tense body is slow to react. If this is difficult to master, then take the principle and explore it through the body. Falling and catching, swinging or dropping, with the dancer calling his or her own rythms. Then try again with objects.

EXERCISE 53: A NOT SO SIMPLE EXERCISE IN TIMING

Timing
Phrasing
2 dancers

Directions

a. Create a simple action that has a clearly defined beginning and ending. Your partner watches and clicks her fingers, claps, taps or calls 'now' immediately the action ends. For example, if your action is a jump, your partner claps as you hit the floor.
b. Actions, for example like swinging, jumping, flicking or falling are most suited to this exercise, though for profoundly disabled students, the movement may be a simple turn of the head or a small gesture with the hand. Just be clear that the sound comes at the very end of the movement.

Option 1

Have a student or group of students improvise watched by a second group with percussion instruments. The second group tap or bang their instruments each time they consider a movement is completed.

Option 2

Now have those watching make a noise just before a movement is completed.

Option 3

Now, just after.
Discuss afterwards. Were dancers able to tell when they were being accompanied? Were any dancers easier to accompany than others? If so why?

EXERCISE 54: A NOT AT ALL SIMPLE EXERCISE IN TIMING

It is important to ask questions to which there are no answers
(Krishnamurti, attributed)

Introduction

This is on the surface a thoroughly impossible exercise. But if you've mastered the other exercises in this section, have a go. The results are often hilarious and at times astonishing!

Directions

a. Face your partner, close your eyes.
b. Your partner, keeping their eyes open, throws the beanbag over your head so that it lands behind you.
c. Stamp (or call out) simultaneously as it lands.
d. Try with two or three dancers side by side all with eyes closed. A single beanbag is thrown over to land behind them. Each tries to clap as the bag lands.

Teaching notes

If you are finding this completely impossible the throwing dancer should try and instruct the dancers to close their eyes and then throw the bag. For example 'Ready? . . . Eyes closed!'

And then throw the bag/orange/rolled up sock.

Note

82 From correspondence with the author.

28 Live music

Musical innovation is full of danger to the State, for when modes of music change, the laws of the State always change with them.

(Plato, the *Republic*)

I am not a chair

(Itzak Perlman, 1999)

A great deal of my teaching in the studio takes place without music and it is not uncommon for students who have danced intensely for several hours to notice afterwards, with surprise, that they have done so entirely without accompaniment of any kind.

Music can relax, lift or inspire us to move. It can lead us to shared experience and celebration, even trance. But it can also distract us from some of the most demanding and rewarding areas of our work as improvisers. Given a rhythm to follow and sufficient encouragement people will dance. The advent of rave culture means that thousands of people in Britain can and regularly do dance together *en masse*[83]. People seem to share the experience and appear to be dancing together but elements of individual choice are sacrificed within such dance events for the anonymity of mass experience. The music, and often the pharmaceutical industry, call the tune.

When improvising we are also interested in going beyond our everyday experiences and music can certainly help us to do that, but it is of little value if we are not able to recognise the pathways and turnings that we take and which make up the journey. It is for this reason that I will often leave introducing music to the later stages of a workshop or class, until the principles of 'listening' internally, and to each other, have had a chance to be absorbed. If musicians share in the process of listening, then the eventual integration of music and dance can be one of the most satisfying and joyful of experiences.

Some of the most ancient musical traditions used music as a language which involved elaborate messages conveyed through sound. A call or rhythm from one player would be responded to

28.1 Yidnekachew Essatu, Morka Geremew and Andualem Kebede. Adugna Dance Initiative, Addis Ababa, 2001. (Photographer Adam Benjamin)

by affirmations and elaborations from others. Call and response still play a central part in many drumming traditions. **Calling** is a contemporary journey into this time-honoured relationship between musicians and dancers.

IMPROV 55: CALLING[83]

> My favorite piece of music is the one we hear all the time if we are quiet
>
> (John Cage)

An advanced exercise for both dancers and musicians
Requires an acute sensitivity and honesty of response
Listening and responding
1 dancer and 1 musician (more can be added later)

Directions

a. One musician and one dancer are positioned at opposite ends of the studio. The dancer starts facing away from the musician (can be done with eyes open or closed). The musician's task is to 'call' the dancer across the studio solely through the use of sound.

b. The dancer only travels when genuinely 'moved' to do so and otherwise remains still or even moves away if the music or sound is displeasing or irritating. The musician remains on the same spot throughout the exercise.

- Calling can be attempted with any instrument including the voice.

Option 1

Once the exercise has been clearly demonstrated and understood it can be tried with more than one musician. Here it is vital that the musicians listen not only to the dancer but to the effect of their music and that of their colleagues.

Option 2

Now try with two dancers moving independently. The same sound can have very different effects on different dancers or may draw parallel reactions. See how the musicians solve this problem.

Option 3

Deaf dancers working blindfolded. With a floor that has a good acoustic, try calling using drums; the exercise can be ended when the dancer places a hand on the drum skin itself.

In some instances, the drummer may need to work closer and move across the floor with the dancer. Experiment and find out what works.

- Alternatively try in a theatre space using a lighting rig, using different colours.
- Or try working visually, calling through offering shapes instead of sounds.

Option 4

A further development is to introduce elements of **leading and following** (Improv 9, Chapter 18). Groups that have explored and fully understand **cascade** (Improv 14, Chapter 18) can guide a dancer who is responding to a musician calling.

Option 5

With a group that has clearly understood the improv, the musicians can begin to play with attracting and repelling a dancer through the use of sound, playing with them a bit like a fish on a line.

In the beginning of *Scrunch*[84] the musician's sound held a dancer on the far wall of the theatre, an effect heightened by the voices of the other performers chatting offstage. The sound isolated and pushed the soloist away, only gradually relinquishing her and allowing her to enter the dance floor.

Teaching notes

- It is important that the musician closely observes the effects of what is being played and begins to pinpoint the melodies, notes or even silences which create a pathway or opening for the dancer.
- The dancer need not 'dance'. What is important is to respond honestly to what attracts (and repels), so providing an accurate 'barometer' for the musician.
- Be wary of the dancer who 'makes it easy' for the musician, who simply hears the music and begins to dance across the studio. (For such students, try working with broken notes and silences.)
- Ensure there is room for the dancers to reach the musician, i.e. that the floor is not obstructed with unused instruments or watching dancers.

Examples

Calling can on occasion be a very challenging exercise for musicians. A very wonderful and talented pianist I was working with was reduced to tears through her inability to call a dancer. The longer the dancer remained still, the more desperately she played, calling on an astonishing range of jazz and classical pieces. What she hadn't noticed was that each time she paused in silence and looked down at the keyboard to think of a new piece, the dancer began to inch forward. As soon as she began to play she looked up to see the dancer once again frozen to the spot. The dancer's movement had not been recognised, he had not been 'heard' and his movement was once again arrested by the torrent of 'beautiful' music.

On another occasion a very talented drummer from the Pan African company Adzido played so engagingly that the dancer he was calling was held in the space dancing to his drumming. In this instance the music gave the dancer such a desire to dance that the task was completely forgotten and she simply never 'arrived'. Remember, the task is for the dancer to reach the musician physically.

In the improvised performance of *An Egg is Enough*,[85] the audience were given little eggs containing beads. A label on the egg read 'You can start and end the show with this egg.' At the beginning of each performance the dancers waited in silence for members of the audience to shake their eggs. The more the dancers listened and responded, the more clearly the audience understood the connection and their contribution to the performance. It was always a tense, risky and invigorating start to the evening.

28.2 Tamara Foos balances on Georg Jung while playing piano. Rehearsals for *Table Stories*, HandiCapace Tanz Kompanie, 2000. Choreography by Benjamin and T.C. Howard. (Photographer Claus Langer)

MUSICIANS AND DANCERS

If the group are familiar with **leading and following** and **freewheeling** (Improvs 9 and 12, Chapter 18), wonderful improvisations can be built that integrate live music – and live musicians (see Figure 28.2). Try to include musicians in any physical warm-ups and early preparatory work. Musicians who are willing to move and play can begin to explore entering the dance space, moving around the 'unsighted' and seeing dancers like soloists in **freewheeling**. Delightful and unexpected connections can be made as the 'unsighted' dancers link either with each other or with the musicians, or as musicians become drawn to play to certain events or individuals. Again what is important is that sufficient work has been put in so that individuals are able to recognise the phrasing of the improvisations and understand how to co-exist and complement rather than compete. This does not mean that contradictions can't be explored, but establishing a baseline of understanding will need to precede any such departures.

IMPROV 56: IN OPPOSITION

An advanced improvisation for musicians and dancers
Contradicting
Demands a wide range of musical and dance experience. (Can be adapted for less experienced groups)

28.3 Tamara Foos in *Table Stories*. Choreography by Benjamin and
T.C. Howard. (Photographer Claus Langer)

Introduction

The starting point for this exercise, which can also be used as a
group warm-up, is a straightforward music visualisation. It is the
kind of improvisational work pioneered by the early modern
dancers, allowing for free association of movement and dance.
Each dancer allows the music to draw forth a journey or story that
they portray spontaneously through their movement. This may
feel horribly literal for dancers more used to abstract non-narrative
improvisations but is well worth exploring. In this exercise the
musicians should play pieces that have clear emotional flavours
and thematic developments.

Further preparation

Have dancers introduce and teach different dance styles and
rythms, i.e. waltz, tango, salsa or experiment with different counts.

Directions

a. In silence the dancer begins to improvise to a particular
    rhythm, or dance style that she alone 'hears'.
b. The musicians watch and then begin an appropriate accom-
    paniment, picking up on the dancer's rhythm, mood or style.
c. When the dancer and musicians have established an accord,
    i.e. the musicians have recognised the dancer's rhythm and
    have joined with an accompaniment, the dancer then shifts to
    a different tempo to dance in opposition to the musicians.

d. The music now seems inappropriate. Without stopping, the musicians keep watching the dancer and begin to shift tempo to come into a new accord.

e. Once again, the dancer experiences the music catching up, indulges the musicians for a short while and then perversely shifts ground into a completely new mood or style.

Teaching notes

*   The dancer can use dance styles or radically different improvisations, but what is important is that the dancer can identify and contradict each new accompaniment, and that the musicians are able to read and follow each new movement theme. This can also be done in reverse, with the musicians leading and changing and the dancers following. This is a good example of needing to understand a rule in order to break it with dexterity.

*   **In opposition** can be modified for less experienced groups using dramatic themes rather than dance styles. For example, the dancer improvises around a dramatic situation (the death of a child); the musicians begin a sorrowful accompaniment. When the dancer feels that the mood has been accurately matched, they break the accord by skipping about gaily chasing butterflies; the musicians now shift to accommodate the new scene. Once again the dancer allows the musicians a few bars of harmonious accompaniment and then veers off into a new situation (the poisoning of a spouse or the receipt of a parking ticket).

*   Always allow a period of accord, where the dancers and musicians are combining to the same effect before the dancer or dancers begin to shift to new ground, otherwise the changes will lose their distinctiveness.

*   The length of each improvisation will depend to some extent on the experience of the dancers and musicians. This ability to move against music is another important skill in moving improvisations forward when they become predictable or stuck.

Example

Towards the end of a remarkably powerful **calling** improvisation in which dancers were responding to live music led by the musician Chris Benstead, a single disabled dancer remained in the space. All the other dancers had now joined the musicians and were drawing the dancer from the space with the most wonderful soundscape. Somewhere out of the abstract music emerged the melody of *Amazing Grace* and the whole group picked this up in an improvised and very beautiful rendition.

The dancer still had half the studio to cross before he could rejoin the group, but somehow, the end seemed to be determined. Despite the beauty of the harmonies, the original sentiment was surreptitiously transforming itself into a sugary, sentimental and predictable ending (disabled man crosses vast space alone to return to welcoming arms of loving friends).

It was some time before the group realised that the dancer had stopped in his tracks, the music that had begun so spontaneously had become 'prescriptive'. The dancer had smelled a rat and was steadfastly refusing to play the game. Instead, he contradicted the music, and beating the dance floor with his palms, established a new and original rhythm that the musicians amplified, leading the improvisation to a finale unexpectedly accompanied by thunderous drumming.

Notes

83 I am indebted to the Besht Tellers, Danny Scheinmann and, more recently the musicians of the Stare Cases Project, particularly Neiyre Ashworth and Ashley Drees, and to the inspirational drumming of Landing Mane.
84 Adam Benjamin and Dancers, Holland, December 2000.
85 Performed in de Warande theatre in Belgium by Adam Benjamin and Dancers 1999.

Appendix 1
Contacts

The following list includes those companies, groups and organisations mentioned in the book (plus a few significant others), some, but not all of whom, have a specifically inclusive policy (IP) and work with disabled and non-disabled performers and/or students.

This list is not exhaustive and inevitably many excellent groups, individuals and organisations have been omitted. Such lists also become outdated very quickly. To locate companies and teachers involved in integrated practice in your own area, approach your local dance agency, browse the Web or approach one of the contacts mentioned below – most of whom will be able to point you in the right direction. In the UK your first port of call should be:

Foundation for Community Dance

Director
Ken Bartlett
Cathedral Chambers
2 Peacock lane
Leicester LE1 5PX, UK
T +44 (0)116 251 0516
F +44 (0)116 251 0517
email: info@communitydance.org.ok
web: www.communitydance.org.uk

Or contact CandoCo Dance Company for their education schedule.

Another very useful point of connection, particularly for Europe, is the quarterly Newsletter for DanceAbility and related projects, produced by Beate Schmitt. This contains details of inclusive projects, performances and workshops.

Newsletter

Beate Schmitt
Hohe Str.26
63069 Offenbach

Germany
T 00 49 (0) 69 835857
email: KurtWiessner@compuserve.com

In the USA two excellent Websites exist; see AXIS website for many of the companies currently active in the States and beyond – http://axisdance.org (full address see below) and DanceAbility's website for its extensive workshop and teacher training programme around the world – www.streamcommunication.com/danceability.

Contact Quarterly is a wide reaching journal about contact improvisation that also publicises inclusive workshops, projects and teachers, particularly in the USA but also elsewhere. Most companies today have a web site or mailing list and will happily give details of their activities.

Contact Quarterly

PO BOX 603
Northampton
MA, 01061
USA
contactq@crocker.com

ARGENTINA

Danza sin Límites (IP)
Andrea Fernández, Marina Gubbay,
Gabriela Guebel
Dr Penna 1024
Vicente López (1638)
Provincia de Buenos Aires
Argentina
T (54 11) 4791-9624
T/F (54 11) 4791-6005 / (54 11)
4521-9931
email: danzasinlimites@fibertel.com.ar

AUSTRIA

Bilderwerfer (IP)
Daniel Aschwanden
Jacquingasse 4/12
1030 Vienna
Austria
email: office@bilderwerfer.com
      da@bilderwerfer.com
website: http://bilderwerfer.com

Brigitte Jagg (IP)
freelance
teacher/choreographer/performer
email: brigitte.jagg@gmx.at

AUSTRALIA

Arts in Action (IP)
Disability arts organisation
Invites companies from all over the
world for perform/workshop.
Tony Doyle
Adelaide
email: artsinaction@senet.com.au
www.artsinaction.asn.au/highbeamfestival

Australian Dance Council
Jeff Meiners
Outreach development Officer
T 02 9241 4022
F 02 9241 1331
email: ausdanceNSW@dance.net.au

Janice Florence (IP)
Weave Movement Theatre
State of Flux
Dancer and educator, researching a
combination of improvisation and
choreography.
Melbourne, Australia
T 613 9416 9673
email: jflorence@vtown.com.au

Igneous (IP)
James Cunningham
59 Beech Street
Evans Head
NSW 2473
Australia
T 61-2-6682 4015
F 61-2-6682 5691
igneous@lis.net.au
www.lis.net.au/~igneous/hands
www.lis.net.au/~igneous/bodyinquestion.
htm

ISTHMUS (IP)
Inclusive contact improvisation
Nerida Wyatt Spratt
Accessible Arts
email: aarts@ozemail.com.au
ned_pam@hotmail.com

Weave Movement Theatre (IP)
see Janice Florence

Kat Worth (IP)
Freelance teacher/choreographer
mobile phone: 0412 992 513
email: dancingkat@iprimus.com.au
dancingkat99@yahoo.co.uk

State of Flux (IP)
see Janice Florence

BELGIUM

de Warande, integrated dance project,
Bieke Suykerbuyk – dance programmer
teacher
Johan D'haese & Goele Van Dijck (IP)

Culturel Centre de Warande
Turnhout
Belgium
T +32.14.47.21.53
Bieke.Suykerbuyk@Turnhout.be
email: info@warande.be
www.warande.be

Suzan Fuks
Suzon@finart.be
T +32 474 75 39 78.
(also see Igneous/Australia)

Les Ballets C de la B.
Citadellaan 40, 9000 Ghent
Belgium
T+32 (0)9 221 75 01
F+32 (0)9 221 8172

CANADA

KICKSTART (festival **IP**)
Geoff McMurchy
Executive Director
c/o Society for Disability Arts and
Culture
204–456 West Broadway Vancouver
BC V5Y 1R3.
F 604 875 9227
email: geoffmcm@istar.ca OR
s4dac@istar.ca

EIRE

Arts and Disability Ireland (IP)
and Counterbalance Dance Project
Vici Wredford-Sinnott
23/25 Moss Street
Dublin 2
T/F + 353 (1) 6716518
email: info@vsarts.ie

ENGLAND

ASPIRE National Training Centre (IP)
(fully acccessible recreation centre and
studio/theatre)
Wood Lane

Stanmore
Middlesex HA7 4AP
T +44 (0)208 954 5759
F +44 (0)208 420 6352
www.aspire.org.uk

Anjali Dance Company (IP)
Nicole Thomson-Stuart
The Mills Arts Centre
Mill Cottage
Spiceball Park
Banbury
Oxfordshire OX16 8QE
T/F +44 (0)1295 251 909
email: info@anjali.co.uk

AMICI (IP)
Wolfgang Stange
68 Barons Court Rd
London W14 9DU
T/F +44 (0)207 385 1327

Adam Benjamin and dancers (IP)
http://www.adambenjamin.co.uk

Blue Eyed Soul Dance Company (IP)
Rachel Freeman
Belmont Arts Centre
5 Belmont
Shrewsbury SY1 1TE
T +44 (0)1743 245998
email:
admin@blueyedsoul.freeserve.co.uk
www.blueyedsoul.freeserve.co.uk

Bretton Hall, University of Leeds
Has promoted the inclusion of disabled
students on its performing arts course
Jo Butterworth
Centre For Dance Studies
Power House 1. Smythe St.
Wakefield
WF4 4LG
UK
T +44 (0)1924 832071
F +44 (0)1924 832070

CandoCo Dance Company (IP)
Touring company – performing and
teaching worldwide
Artistic Director: Celeste Dandeker
2L Leroy House
436 Essex Rd
London N1 3QP
England
T +44 (0)20 7704 6845
F +44 (0)20 7704 1645
email: info@candoco.co.uk
www.candoco.co.uk

**DAIL Magazine (Disability Arts in
London)**
c/o Artsline
5 Crowndale Road
London NW1 1TU
T +44 (0)20 7387 5911 (voice and
minicom)
F +44 (0)7383 2653

Dance United (IP)
International community dance
programme
171 Glenarm Road
Hackney
London E5 0NB
T +44 (0)20 8533 0001
F +44 (0)20 8985 4424
email: Mags.Byrne@btinternet.com
or DanceUnited@aol.com

DV8 Physical Theatre
T +44 (0)207 247 5102

Eye Contact (IP)
Workshop programme with and for
visually impaired
See Salamader Tandem

Freedom in Dance (IP)
Diane Amans
25 Hawk Green Road
Marple Stockport
Cheshire SK6 7HU
T/F +44 (0)161 427 5093
email: freedom@amans.fsnet.co.uk

Foundation for Community Dance (see above)

Graeae Theatre Company
A touring theatre company of people
with physical and sensory impairments
Hampstead Town Hall
213 Haverstock Hill
London
NW3 4PQ
UK
T +44 (0) 207 6814755
F +44 (0) 207 681 4756
email: info @ graeae.org
www.graeae.org

Green Candle Dance Company (IP)
Fergus Early
20.6 Aberdeen Studios
The Aberdeen Centre
22 Highbury Grove
London N5 2DQ
UK
T +44 (0)20 7359 8776
F +44 (0)20 7359 5840
email: info@greencandledance.com
www.greencandledance.com

Hereward College (IP)
Residential college – offers places to
disabled and non-disabled students in
the arts
Margaret Taylor
Hereward College
Branston Cres
Tile Hill
Coventry CV4 9SW
T +44 (0)1203 461 231
F +44 (0)1203 694305

Louise Katerega (IP)
Freelance Dance Artist & Educator
(Simpson Board teacher)
Flat b
8 Conifer Close
Leicester LE2 1GB
T/F +44 (0)116 254 1974

The Laban Centre London
Alysoun Tomkins
Community Dance Course (1 year) –
offers places to disabled students
Laurie Grove
London SE14 6NH
T +44 (0)208 692 4070
F +44 (0)208 694 8749
email: a.tomkins@laban.co.uk
web www.laban.co.uk

The Language of Dance Centre
To order the Simpson Board
17 Holland Park
London W11 3TD
T +44 (0)207 229 3780
email: info@lodc.org
www.lodc.org

Motion House (IP)
13 Spencer St
Leamington Spa
Warwickshire CV31 3NE
T +44 (0)1926 887 052
F +44 (0)1926 316 734
email: admin@motionhouse.demon.co.uk
website:www motionhouse.co.uk

National Disability Arts Forum
Mea House
Ellison Place
Newcastle NE1 8XS
T +44 (0)191 261 1628
F +44 (0)191 222 0573
email: ndaf@ndaf.org
website: www.ndaf.org

New Vic (IP)
Offers a fully accessible course:
HND Performing Arts in the
Community (IP)
Newham Sixth Form College
Prince Regent Lane
London E13 8SG
T +44 (0)207 473 4110
http://www.newham-vic.ac.uk

The Orpheus Centre (IP)
Inclusive residential performing arts
centre
North Park Lane
Godstone
Surrey RH9 8ND
T +44 (0)1883 744664
F +44 (0)1883 744994
enquiries@orpheus.org.uk
web www.orpheus.org.uk

The Place Dance Services
(An invaluable source of all things dance
in the UK and beyond)
T +44 (0)207 383 3524
F +44 (0)207 388 5407
email: danceservices@theplace.org.uk

**Salamander Tandem (and Eye Contact)
(IP)**
workshops/performance/publications
Isabel Jones
38 Laurie Ave
Nottingham
NG7 6PN
T/F +44 (0)115 942 0706
email: info@salamanda-tandem.org

Shape
LVS Resource Centre
356 Holloway Road
London N7 6PA
T +44 (0)207 700 8139
F +44 (0)207 700 8143
email: info@shape-uk.co.uk

Simpson Board
See Language of Dance Centre
and Louise Katerega

Solid Foundations (IP)
Offers a Certificate in Higher Education.
The course has been designed with and
for disabled people.
Course Leader: Mandy Redvers-Rowe
Liverpool Institute for Performing Arts
Mount Street
Liverpool L1 9HF

T +44 (0)151 330 3000
F +44 (0)151 330 3131
email: admissions@lipa.ac.uk
www.lipa.ac.uk

Stopgap (IP)
Vicki Balaam
PO BOX 2
Woking
Surrey
email: vicki@stopgap.uk.com

Tardis Dance Company (IP)
c/o East London Dance
Stratford Circus
Theatre Square
Stratford
London E15 1BX
T +44 (0)208 279 1050
F +44 (0)208 279 1054
email: eastlondondance.org

Touchdown Dance (IP)
Katy Dymoke
42 Edge St
Manchester M4 IHN
T +44 (0)161 278 1499
email: touchdd@aol.com

Velcro Integrated Dance Company (IP)
Jacky Poole
Gloucester Dance
Colwell Centre For Arts
Derby Road
Gloucester GL1 4AD
UK
T +44 (0)1452 550 431
F +44 (0)1452 541 303
email: admin@glosdance.u-net.com

ETHIOPIA

Adugna Community Dance Initiative
Adugna Potentials (IP)
Royston Maldoon and Mags Byrne
c/o Ethiopian Gemini Trust
Addis Ababa, Ethiopia
E Africa

T Adis Ababa 531986
(also see **Dance United** England)

FRANCE

Handicap International (IP)
ERAC
14, avenue Bertelot
F - 69361 Lyon cdex 07
France
T +33 (0)4 78 69 79 79
F +33 (0)4 78 69 79 94
Email : handicap-international@infonie.fr
www.handicap-international.org

Programme France
contact: Jean-Marc Boivin
17 Boulevard Chambaud de la Bruyère,
Bâtiment Jacquard
69007 Lyon
France
T +33(0) 4 72 76 88 44
F + 33(0)4 72 76 88 48
email :progfra@handicap-icom.asso.fr

Groupe Signe (IP)
Christine Molina
Claude Chalaguier
4 Rue de la Concierge
69009 Lyon
France
T +(0) 4 78 23 78 21
T +(0) 4 78 47 27 89
email: agroupesignes@free.fr

Oiseau Mouche (IP)
136–138 rue Pierre-de-Roubaix
59100 Roubaix
France
T +33 (0)3 20 65 96 50
F +33 (0)3 20 73 61 72
email: oiseau-mouche@nordnet.fr

GERMANY

Contact 17 (IP)
Stina K Bollman
Oelkersallee 65, D - 22769
Hamburg
Germany

Beate Schmitt (IP)
freelance dance teacher
email: beate.schmitt22@gmx.de
(see above: Newsletter)

DIN A 13 Tanzcompany (IP)
Artistic director
Gerda König
Gereonshof 4
D - 50670 Köln
Germany
T/F: 221 136 153
email: gerda.koenig@din-a13.de
http://www.din-a13.de

HandiCapace Tanz Kompanie (IP)
Kunstzentrum Karlskaserne
Rainer Kittel
Hindenburgstr. 29/1
D-71638 Ludwigsburg
Deutschland/Germany
T +49 7141 9103241
F +49 7141 904764
email: kunstschule@ludwigsburg-
karlskaserne.de

HOLLAND

Petra Zingel (IP)
FIDODA
inclusive dance workshops.
email: p.zingel@tip.nl

ISRAEL

Vertigo Dance Company (IP)
Mail Box: 6403
Jerusalem
Israel
email: vertigo@netvision.net.il
http://www.ndtechnology.com/vertigo

Tamar Borer (IP)
10 Hoshea St
Ramat Chen
Ramat Gan 52245
Israel
T: 03 6749733

ITALY

Vi-Kap (IP)
contacts: Roberto Penzo and Anna
Bertarelli.
Bologna
Italy
email: wallyone@libero.it

JAPAN

MUSE Company (IP)
Organises community dance workshops
and performances
Yuko Ijichi
4-6-10-101 minami-aoyama
Minatoku
Tokyo 107-0062
Japan
T +81 (0)3 3479 8535
F +81 (0)3 3402 5438
email: MuseKK@aol.com
http://www.musekk.co.jp

Taihan (IP)
Manri Kim
Taihen
5-1-11 Awaji
Osaka 533-0032
Japan
F +81 6 320 0344
email: taihen@japan.ne.jp
www.asahi-net.or.jp

LITHUANIA

Find out more via
New Baltic Dance Festival
Lithuania
email: dancelt@takas.

NEW MEXICO

The Buen Viaje Dancers (IP)
PO Box 7784 Albuquerque, NM 87194

NEW ZEALAND

Touch Compass Dance Trust (IP)
PO Box 90136
Auckland Mail Centre
New Zealand.
email: cchappell@clear.net.nz
http://www.url.co.nz/arts/Touch/
Compass/

Danz
for all things dance in NZ
email: danz@danz.org.nz

NORTHERN IRELAND

Dance Northern Ireland
Source of all things dance in N Ireland
Vicky Maguire
15 Church St
Belfast BT1 1PG
email: vjm.dcni@ukonline.co.uk
T 02 89024 9930

POLAND

Vicky Day Fox (IP)
`Slaski Theatr Tànca
UL zeromskiego 27
Bytom
Woj. `Slaskie
Poland
email: foxyday@hotmail.com

PORTUGAL

LPDM.CRS (IP)
Contacts Cristina Passos and Rafael
Alvarez
email: lj.lpdm.crs@mail.telepac.pt
Lisbon
Portugal

ROMANIA

Contact Sally Wood (IP)
Lamont Centre
Cluj
via the British Council in Bucharest,
Romania

RUSSIA

Centre for Contemporary Choreography
Contact Margarita Moyzhes **(IP)**
email: volgodans@interdacom.ru
Volgograd,
Russia

SCOTLAND

Jenna Agate (IP)
Dance Artist
Studio on the Green
19 The green
Selkirk TD7 5AA
T 01750 21997
thestudioonthegreen@talk21.com
email: info@scottishyouthdance.org

Scottish Dance Theatre
Dundee Rep Theatre
Tay Square
Dundee DD1 1PB
T 01382 342 600
F 01382 228 609

SENEGAL

Oumar Diop (IP)
Président de HANDICAP FormEduC
Formation Education Communication et
Culture
Specialising in new information
technology and communication
Rue Belfort angle Avenue Malick
B.P. 7520 Médina - Dakar
Senegal
T (221) 687 64 11/821 31 14
email: oumardiophfe@hotmail.com

Papa Oumar Faye (IP)
Président de l'Association Nationale des
Sourds du Sénégal
(ANASSEN)
Rue Marsat - Reines
à Reubess
Senegal
B.P. 7052 Dakar

Directeur du Centre Privé d'Education
Intégrée pour les
Déficients Auditifs - C E P E I D A
BP: 7486 - Dakar
T 822 99 50
Cell 657 50 92 (Message)
email: pofaye@caramail.com

SINGAPORE

Very Special Arts Singapore. (IP)
contacts: Kok Wai and Lim Lin Da
email: general@vsa.org.sg

SOUTH AFRICA

Tshwaragano Dance Company (IP)
South Africa
Johannesburg
Jill Waterman and Gladys Agulhas
email: waterman.arts@pixie.coza

Remix Dance Company (IP)
Nicola Visser
7 Edward Mansions
Main Road, Kalk Bay
Cape Town 7975
S Africa
T 021-788-5380
email: mwnicnic@mweb.co.za

SPAIN

Julyen Hamilton
email: julyen@julyenhamilton.com
http:/www.julyenhamilton.com

SWEDEN

Moomstheatre (IP)
Kjell Stjernholm
T +46 40 21 4790
F +46 40 212 193
email: office@moomsteatern.com
http:/www.moomsteatern.com

SWITZERLAND

BewegGrund (IP)
Susanne Schneider
Roschistrasse 7, 3007 Bern,
Switzerland
T 00 41 31 371 26 30
email: schneider-saner@bluewin.ch

USA

Alito Alessi (IP)
(See Dance Ability)

**aTa The Association for Theatre and
Accessibility (IP)**
c/o the National Arts and Disability
Center
300 UCLA Medical Plaza, Ste 3330
Los Angeles, CA 90095-6967
Voice phone (310) 794 1141
Text phone (310) 825 8863
F (310) 794 1143

AXIS Dance Company (IP)
1428 Alice Street. 201
Oakland, CA 94612
USA
T (510) 625 0110
T (415) 641 1656
F (510) 625 0321
email: info@axisdance.org
http://axisdance.org

Bruce Curtis (IP)
Paradox Dance
2100 8th Street
Berkeley
California, CA 94710
http://www.geocities.com/paradoxdance/

Dancing Wheels (IP)
Provides career opportunities in the arts
for people with disabilities
Mary Verdi-Fletcher and Sabatino
Verlezza
Professional Flair/ Dancing Wheels
3615 Euclid Ave
3rd Floor
Cleveland, Ohio 44115
email: proflair1@aol.com
www.gggreg.com/dancingwheels.htm
T 216 432 0306
F 216 432 0308

**DanceAbility/ Joint Forces Dance Co
(IP)**
DanceAbility is a project of the Joint
Forces Dance Co, under the direction of
Alito Alessi
Provides extensive workshop and
teacher training for disabled and non-
disabled dancers
P.O. Box 3686
Eugene, OR,
U.S.A. 97403
T 541-342-3273
email: alito22@yahoo.com
www.streamcommunication.com/
danceability

Diverse Dance (IP)
Diverse Dance Research Retreat
Karen Nelson
email: knchu@aol.com

Infinity Dance Theatre (IP)
Artistic Director
Kitty Lunn
220 West 93rd Street #6C
New York, NY 10025
T 212 877 3490
F 212 799 1922
www.infinitydance.com
Joint Forces (see DanceAbility)

Light Motion (IP)
Charlene Curtiss
1520 32nd Avenue South
Seattle, WA 98144
T 001 206 328 0818

Los Angeles Performers With Disabilities
(L.A PWD)
http://www.syncweb.com/1405.htm

National Arts and Disability Center (IP)
Beth Stoffmacher
Technical Assistance Coordinator
National Arts and Disability Center
300 UCLA Medical Plaza, Ste. 3310
Los Angeles, CA 90095-6967
T (310) 825-5054
F (310) 794-1143
email: bstoffmacher@mednet.ucla.edu
http://nadc.ucla.edu

Paradox arts
Riccardo Morrison
PO BOX 42503
Santa Barbara, cal 93140
USA
email: riccomoves@aol.com

Petra Kuppers (IP)
Investigates connections between
identity politics, community arts and
new media
Bryants College
1150 Douglas Pike
Smithfield
Rhode island 02917
email: petrakuppers@olimpias.net
www.olimpias.net

WALES

Rubicon Dance
Nora Street
Adamsdown
Cardiff CF24 1ND
T +44 (029) 2049 1477
F +44 (029) 2047 2240
email: info@rubicondance.co.uk
www.rubicondance.co.uk

Use this space for your own contacts:

Appendix 2
Excerpts from an African diary

In 1997 as director of education for CandoCo Dance Company I was invited to lead a project in Senegal. It was the first of many visits to Africa, and the first workshop of its kind on that continent. The project was supported by the British Council and Handicap International (France). I was accompanied by Thomas St. Louis, Lucy Moelywn-Hughes, Katie Marsh and Debbie Thomas.

Friday. Arrival in Dakar

The poverty hits you like a punch in the face. Hassle takes on a whole new dimension as boys and young men constantly pick up our bags and walk off with them towards waiting taxis (driven by 'a friend' or 'my uncle'), try and sell trinkets 'I make you good price!' or exchange a fistful of CFAs. The taxis themselves have the appearance of stock-car racers, which makes sense the moment you take a ride in one. The journey from the airport to the hotel could be described as a near-death experience . There was some debate as to whether our own driver had in fact ever driven before: it transpired he had just been given the job. Did anyone ask to see his driving licence? Selecting gears seemed a random exercise, the handbrake was often only taken off at our prompting and reverse seemed an entirely unexplored universe to be entered into only in extreme circumstances and with utmost caution.

In the darkness we walk past the mosque next to the hotel. During the festival that has just passed, the pavement outside has become the temporary encampment for some of the most wretched people I have ever seen. Dreadful poverty and disability that we walk past as if in shock. There seems nothing to do or say. I think Tom's big heart will break.

We are told that we will be working each day on the Isle de Gorée; for us an amazing and exciting discovery rendered somewhat daunting on our first recce visit on Sunday after manhandling Tom in his wheelchair from dock-side to boat across 3 ft. of open water (no gangway). On Monday we will do the same but with five wheelchair users, two blind and four deaf students!

Meetings and planning ramble on through the morning and into the hot afternoon, interspersed with jokes, stories and cups of obscenely sweet 'cha'.

First cup . . . friendship, second cup . . . health, third cup . . . love! The Museé Historique has no wooden floors, they are all stone or concrete of varying degrees of unflatness. I check out the nearby school, but this also has a cement floor.

We agree to do a site-specific piece in the Museé, a beautiful, circular building of interconnected rooms, each opening via a white wooden door onto the central courtyard. Above turquoise sky and drifting eagles. The building speaks dance. I am eager to get started.

Goreé is a small island paradise a stone's throw from the madness of Dakar. Bright painted houses, old Portuguese architecture, wandering goats, fish being cooked on open grills and everywhere people and children eager to talk.

Monday

I arrange for all the students to meet on the quayside so that getting on and off the chaloupe becomes a shared part of our daily schedule; an exercise that will teach more about trust than anything I can possibly organise in a studio!

Despite a few scary moments, we all make it safely onto the chaloupe along with the daily shipment of vegetables, bread and assorted hardware needed by the islanders, all of which is passed manually over the side of the boat. Thus laden, we head out on the first of our many crossings to Goreé. Looking across the crowded deck to Lu, Katie, Tom and Deb, I wonder what the week holds in store for us.

When we arrive our rag-tag band limp, roll, hobble and guide each other over the beach, around the jetty and up to the Museé Historique. There is not a single smooth path or ramp on the entire island. There then follows a hysterical half-hour of organising in an attempt to discover who wants 'poisson' or 'viande' for lunch. It is an opportunity to see the difficulties that lie ahead as people try to communicate in French, English, Wolof, French sign, English sign . . . and, what do you mean, 'vegetarian?!'

'Hands up if you want meat!' shouts our coordinator in French, by the time this has been translated and signed, half the group are voting for fish; we have arrived in Africa and I begin to understand why the first dates of the project simply passed by and that we were indeed lucky to have made it before autumn.

I resist the proposal that everyone wears name labels, preferring instead the effort needed to learn names.

It was a great first day despite the difficulties of working in four interconnected spaces (no single space was big enough for the whole group), but with Tom, Lu, Katie and Deb all participating we managed to carry everyone with us. Lu in particular managed great work with Martar, one of the blind students. The basics of leading and following were eagerly absorbed, and the afternoon saw the first duets arising from support and counter-balance work.

Tuesday

Miraculously our driver has not yet killed anyone with the Land Rover; however he came close to wiping out a fruit stall and several pedestrians and managed to crash into the other Handicap International vehicle. It transpired that he was previously: a bus driver. Such information has ceased to surprise us.

The work is progressing well. Though wonderful individual performers, the students have very little experience of contact work of any kind and we have to watch like hawks to make sure everything is safe. The blind students in particular have never been stretched and it is in this area that we have most to offer.

M. Martin, the ever youthful Director of Dance and Choreography at the Ecole National des Arts, says to me the work is about making links; I agree, but add that it is also about breaking unnecessary ones. The blind students Martar and Mar Sow continue to make huge progress.

Today's session ends with groups showing choreographed traverses over the bumpy courtyard – only one spill! The challenge now is to bring the students' own dance style into the performance. How do we channel this boundless energy into a framework which serves us all? Three days left and it seems we have all known each other forever. We have learned so much from the group, Papa Oumar Faye and Eugène Diatta teach us new signs every day and Katie is picking it up quickly and signs with clarity and confidence.

Samba's crutch, lost overboard while boarding the ferry last night, is returned by boys from the island who dived in to retrieve it after the chaloupe left.

Leaving the museum, we walk under a huge banner and it is only later we turn to look to see it announces the CandoCo workshop and the show on Friday evening; another is hanging proudly over the port building at Dakar as we descend from the ferry. No turning back now!

We decide that we will integrate our own quartet into the performance rather than presenting it as a separate item, joining the students in one continuous event that we present together.

Tomorrow I must work with Eugène and Aida to call on their signing, which is both eloquent and beautiful, and also set up the sound system so that we can run a quartet rehearsal. We'll need all the help we can get to dance it on the uneven ground of the courtyard.

Wednesday

On the ferry I sit with Eugène, Aida and Oumar and they teach me to sign the words I have written.

'Seulement si je ne te tiens pas trop fort, tu peux retourner vers moi' (Only if I do not hold you too strongly, can you return to me).

The words reflect a 'movement principle' that we have been working on but that also speaks about our lives, about the fact that we will be leaving soon, about Tom and his extraordinary journey into dance, and through dance back to Africa, and the place of his family's exodus as slaves from Saint-Louis, the old capital of Senegal most likely via Goreé on the slave route to the West Indies.

That day, Eugene, Oumar and Aida taught everyone the sign phrase. This takes time as the phrase must first be translated into Wolof and the signs shaped in the hands of Matar and Mar Sow who cannot see.

The full structure of the piece is beginning to take shape. The building itself suggests so many images. In the afternoon we begin working with the idea of 'leading and following' but using our hands to cover each other's eyes. Thus linked, couples emerge from the doorways into the courtyard; they appear to be charged with meaning and significance. Two whole new sections emerged today and Eugène came through as a striking and powerful performer – he will lead the signing section.

Today we discovered that both Martar and Mar Sow are able to locate the doorways independently of guidance. Increasingly they are able to command the space. This is, I'm sure, partly to do with familiarity but also is a result of the high expectations we have of them. I find myself instructing the other students to leave them alone on stage, to give them the time and space to make their own decisions about where and how they travel. They are both responding with a determination and resolution that is inspiring and full of dignity.

Thursday

Meeting everyone at the dock each morning has become a ritual that we all look forward to. The openness of our greetings in French, in Sign and Wolof, spreads like a warm glow seeming to encompass the entire ferry. How on earth are we going to leave these people?

A young girl disabled with polio is helped onto the ferry. With no wheelchair she gets around on hands and knees. Arriving on the island I remember my elbow pads and dig them out. They fit her knees perfectly. She becomes our companion for the remainder of our stay. Watching, fascinated by the work, though reluctant to join in, she accepts a lift from the students and is carried back and forwards to the Museé and the café each day.

We get Tom in his wheelchair up on the flat roof of the building for the first time. I am aware that this is hard for him and that being up there is going to bring back thoughts of the day of his accident. We walk the edge together until Tom gains confidence and makes his first solo traverse. It is an extraordinary image as he passes high above the courtyard framed by the intense blue sky. What a role model he has been for these students. His strength, humour, confidence and visible to all . . . his heart.

We work hard through the morning, taking a late lunch until the first four sections of the performance are up and running. At lunchtime, I return to the museum to try and make some headway with the sound system. The cassette player is out of the last century . . . its eccentricities in some way explained by the host of tiny creatures that seem to be living inside it and who wander across the dials and panels like citizens of a miniature electronic metropolis. I point out as politely as I can that the machine is not going to be usable. Half an hour later I am presented with something equally ancient but that can at least manage rewind and plays to speed.

By late afternoon the piece looks near completion. Everyone is very tired but content. Sandwiches and cha are brought out and a few minutes later out come the djembes . . . within minutes the courtyard is alive with drumming and dancing. There is simply no barrier between the Senegalese and dance, no inhibitions to overcome, no false modesty, simply an uncontainable delight in life that erupts spontaneously at the slightest invitation. The disabled dancers are spinning on their hands or balancing on sticks and crutches. Each of us is called up in turn to dance solo in front of Landing Mane's thunderous drumming. Martar dances with white eyes open to the sky, skin glistening with sweat, arms raised, palms down, turning and stamping to the drums, dancing like an eagle.

As Lu and I wait on the chaloupe to depart that evening we see Oumar Diop, our coordinator and by now dear friend, on the far side of the bay racing to catch the ferry, carrying his huge frame on his two crutches. Diop at once so strong and powerful rendered vulnerable by his lack of speed. Simple joy as he makes it across the beach, up the pier and into our company for the homeward trip. The bonds of affection that have grown in the short time we have been together are tangible. We could not have wished for more.

Back at the hotel we talk about the day that's passed and the day to come. We decide to rename our quartet 'Seulement si je ne te tiens pas trop fort', and to keep the signing that we had introduced for the performance in Africa when we return to England.

Friday

Last day. Hurrying into the changing room where we meet each morning, a student strides out purposefully in the opposite direction. It is not until several minutes later that I stop, shocked by the realisation that it was Mar Sow whom I had just passed. The student who at the beginning of the week seemed almost crushed by his blindness.

After the warm-up we perform the quartet for the students. The uneven ground seems no longer to matter . . . How we have learned to adapt! We perform on the hot stones of the courtyard under the bright African sun. When I lie on the ground ready to catch Katie I look up to see eagles hovering above us on the ocean breeze. Lu becomes adept at standing on her heels to stop the soles of her feet burning.

After lunch we return from the café in procession with Landing, Mar Sow and Joseph drumming and everyone singing. What a way to approach work!

A final run through and time to rest before the performance. The courtyard fills to overflowing with an estimated 150 spectators. Though in true African style people are still arriving to see the show in the evening when we leave to catch the ferry for the last time!

The show goes wonderfully. African crowds clap whenever and wherever the mood takes them. The audience was enthralled and enthusiastic, and the performance on the hot stones of the courtyard was showered with bursts of applause from beginning to end.

The finale sees the courtyard filled with people as the audience join the dancers for a last celebration.

Our farewells are heartfelt. Oumar Diop tells me to shake hands left-handed as this means that we will see each other again in the future. Landing finally hands over his djembe and I feel as if he is handing me his heart . . . Saying goodbye to Eugène and Papa Oumar Faye without words is too much for any of us and our eyes sign to them unprompted, tearful farewells.

Our departure is delayed by three days due to the eccentricities of Air Afrique known locally as Air Peut-être (Air Maybe). In our spare time we schedule a visit to Ecole des Arts in Dakar to rehearse for our rapidly approaching performance in England, and visit M. Martin the director who along with his students had contributed so much to the week. Ecole des Arts had by this time taken on almost mythological proportions in my imagination; home to the extraordinary dancers and musicians with whom we had worked all week.

The school in reality boasted one tiny studio with a concrete floor. In the corner of the studio sat a single battered cassette player. I recognised it as the one I had rejected on the island, now back in full-time use at the school. In our high-tech multi-media world it is a timely reminder of how much we take for granted and how far we sometimes stray from the true heart of dance. A heart that without doubt was shown to us in Senegal, West Africa.

Appendix 3
Glossary

Aesthetics The branch of philosophy concerned with the appreciation of beauty.

Aikido A Japanese form of self-defence that evolved from Judo, it employs circular movements combined with an understanding of the use and action of the joints of the body in order to deflect an attack, control and throw an opponent. Close bodywork and an emphasis on falling and rolling made it a rich learning ground for the Judson Church Group. (See below)

ASPIRE The Association for Spinal Injury Research Rehabilitation and Reintegration. The national spinal injuries charity is based at the Mike Heaffey Centre in North London and is where CandoCo's first workshops were held.

Authentic Movement An authentic movement is one that is unpremeditated, that comes from a very direct, natural, inner response rather than from a thought or technique, connecting the individual to hidden parts of themselves. Authentic Movement was established as a field of study by the dance movement pioneers Janet Alder, Mary Starks Whitehouse and Joan Chodorow in the 1950s and 1960s.

Ballet for All An offshoot of the Royal Ballet, founded in 1964 to bring ballet to new audiences in Britain. Its first director was Peter Brinson, who created special ballet-plays that combined dance with narration in an effort to educate its audience. The company was disbanded in 1979.

Ballet-Makers An open-door dance forum founded by Teresa Early in London 1963 as an alternative to ballet schools, a place where dancers could create, experiment and choreograph regardless of their body type.

Bliss board A selection of signs and symbols used for communication particularly among people with cerebral palsy who have minimal movement and who are unable to spell. Developed by Charles K Bliss (1971). The book or board is usually held by an aid or assistant while the user selects symbols by indicating them with his or her eyes. A computer-graphic version has been developed in Canada by Rachel Zimmerman. For more information on Bliss go to: http://home.istas.ca/~bci/blin2.htm

Butoh Japanese contemporary dance form, concerned with being rather than moving. Butoh has its roots in the 1940s, pioneered by dancers like Kazuo Ohno. Later Ankoku Butoh's 'The dance of utter darkness' responded to the effects of the atomic bombs dropped on Japan at the end of the Second World War.

Cerebral palsy Physical and sensory impairment usually arising from lack of oxygen at birth; symptoms when mild may be minor mobility problems, but in more severe instances can lead to severely impaired movement and speech. Usually referred to as CP, cerebral palsy is a non-progressive condition.

Chaos Theory Branch of physics that deals with the rules governing the unpredictable behaviour of the natural world. one premise for example, is that "A butterfly flapping its wings in South America can create a thunderstorm on the other side of the world."

CND Campaign for Nuclear Disarmament.

Contact improvisation Primarily an improvised dance, a duet in which movements arise through a sensitive sharing and readjusting of a partner's body weight while in physical contact. The resulting dance can be delicate and balanced, or dynamic, energetic and off balance. Originating in 1972, it is widely associated with the pioneering work of Steve Paxton and grew from experimentations of the Judson Church Group in the USA.

Contemporary dance The name given in the UK to loosely describe what in America was termed modern dance. (First developed in the 1930s, it was pioneered by Martha Graham and Doris Humphrey.) Though in Britain the term contemporary dance embraces much of what in America is considered post modern, i.e. from Merce Cunningham onwards, it generally refers to those modern and post modern forms that have a recognised and formal technique such as Graham, Cunningham and Limon, as opposed to the more improvisational styles which are generally considered a part of new dance.

Cunningham, Merce (1919–) He originally danced with Martha Graham, and left to explore non-narrative (dance that does not attempt to tell a story) and chance choreographic structures. Generally regarded as the father of post modernism, he was a long-time collaborator with the musician John Cage.

Dance Animateur Term used in the UK to describe a professional dance artist/teacher who works in the community, taking dance into schools and community centres, promoting and developing dance in a region. Often attached to a regional dance agency (RDA). See Brinson, P. (1991).

Deutsche Tanzbühne The Tanzbühne was a system of dance clubs and activities which people attended or subscribed to in pre-war Germany. The system was then taken up by the National Socialists to promote Nazi ideology.

Duncan, Isadora (1878–1927) Widely acknowledged as the founder of modern dance at the beginning of the twentieth century. She took as her influences the natural movement of dancers portrayed in Greek art and believed in dancing bare foot and in loose, flowing clothing.

Graham Martha (1894–1991) American pioneer of modern dance, first performed in London to bemused audiences in 1954. Her dance technique later provided the principle training for modern/contemporary dance throughout the 1970s and is still highly influential today.

Human potential movement The movement concerned with the growth and fulfilment of the individual. It was a radical departure from large-scale political movements of the pre- and post-war periods where individuality had been subsumed within mass action. The Human Potential Movement considered the body and mind to be equally important and drew on the work of teachers such as Carl Jung, Wilhelm Reich and Alfred Adler.

Improvisation (improv) Improvisation in dance refers to the practice of dancing without choreographed steps. Improvisation often takes the form of creative exploration through movement. The dancers themselves may be highly trained or beginners. It may involve partner work as in Contact Improvisation or be individual or group orientated. Often used as a means of deriving material for choreographed work, it is also on occasion used in performance by more experienced practitioners.

Judson Church Group   Took their name from the Judson Memorial Church in New York where they met. A collective of predominantly women dancers and choreographers who radically challenged what dance stood for in the 1960s. The work was highly experimental, introducing everyday (or found) movement, old and young dancers, nudity and the politics of feminism and pacifism.

Keller, Helen (1880–1968)   Author, teacher, women's and disability rights campaigner. Lost hearing and vision aged 9 months. (Learned finger-spelled words as her first language.) Worked, toured and taught extensively with her teacher and companion Annie Sullivan.

Laban Rudolph (1879–1958)   Artist, teacher, theorist, dance pioneer. Born in Austria/Hungary, Laban's life spanned the most dramatic period in modern history. He sought to create a foundation for the development of modern dance that would be based on an understanding of *choric* dance, dance that was not centred around virtuoso performance but that involved a community of dancers.

Lawrence, D.H. (1885–1930)   Radical author who championed a new, robust and sensual language of the body in books like *Lady Chatterley's Lover*. A contemporary of Laban, his wife Frieda van Richthofen, was a visitor weekly at Ascona, Laban's dance school, where improvisation, nudity and alternative life styles were explored a good fifty years before 'Flower Power' and the post modern dance movement got under way in the USA.

Medical model of disability   The Medical Model of Disability: focuses attention on physical impairment as the cause of disablement placing the problem in the person rather than in the educational, economic or architectural obstacles that exist in society.

New dance   New Dance is an English term which is equivalent, and as all encompassing as the American term post modern dance. This means that disabled dancers, dance with video, dance in situ, physical theatre and improvisation might all be termed new dance. Contact improvisation and Release-based dance are associated with new dance but new dance can also embrace ballet and physical theatre depending on how these movements are framed or presented to the public. New dance is characterised by its open-endedness and by a frequent mixing of styles and approaches.

Platonic Solids   The five possible regular polyhedra (many-sided objects). Cube, tetrahedron, octahedron, icosahedron and dodecahedron. Plato was the first to list them. Laban used them as a means to understand and describe movement in 3-dimensional space.

Physical theatre   A loose term describing the combination of theatre, mime, and partnering dance technique derived from CI, particularly lifting, catching and falling. There is a far greater expectation to see some kind of 'story' being explored in Physical Theatre than within contemporary or new dance works. It suggests in particular a dynamic corporeal presence. DV8 is a good example of British physical theatre company. CandoCo has also been described as such when presenting works such as Emilyn Claid's *Back to Front with Side Shows* or Guilherme Bethelo's *Trades and Trusts*.

Release technique   Pioneered by Joan Skinner in the 1960s. A dance style based on the natural movement of the body when tension is released and the joints are allowed to move freely and spontaneously. Although often associated with improvisation it is a style of movement that has been drawn on extensively by choreographers such as Siobhan Davies and Trisha Brown.

Sensory impairment The loss, partial or total of speech, vision or hearing.

Simpson Board An eye-indicator board (like the Bliss board) on which movement, space and time directions are laid out, allowing profoundly disabled students to select information by eye direction and thus choreograph without using words. (See Bliss board.)

The Social Model of Disability. The Social Model regards difficulties that arise from physical and or sensory impairment as being a result of environmental, attitudinal or architectural features of society. So it is society's over-reliance on the motor car that disables asthmatics, and our inaccessible public transport systems which disable the elderly and those in wheelchairs. (The raised uneven tracks on the pavements (sidewalks) designed to help blind people find their way around Tokyo also, therefore, disable people in wheelchairs, and the elderly who tend to stumble on them.)

Strange Attractor A term used in Chaos Theory and Theories of Turbulence. It is the ordering principle that pulls pattern from apparently chaotic events. The initial event that marks the site of a strange attractor seems random, as do the accumulation of further events until an ordered picture begins to emerge. (See Ruelle. Strange Attractors, Mathematical Intelligencer 2 (1980). p. 126–37 or Gleick.)

Tai Chi Chuan A form of self-defence originating in China in the 12th Century, believed to have evolved from the needs of travelling monks to defend themselves without violence. One of the 'internal' schools of martial arts it uses soft circular and spiral movements around a dynamic interior energy. In learning Tai Chi a relaxed and soft body allows the mind to determine the movement, and this slow but flowing movement in turn maintains the body in a natural, healthy condition. Tai Chi is more commonly taught today in the West as a health and/or meditation practice. Its emphasis on 'listening' to the movements of a partner or opponent made it (like Aikido) a valuable field of study for many new dance practitioners.

Tension – stem of tendere stretch
1   The condition in any part of the body, of being stretched or strained, a sensation indicating or suggestion this; a feeling of tightness . . .
2   The balance created by the interplay of conflicting or contrasting elements in a work of art, especially a poem.

Tetrarapegic or **quadraplegic** Degree of paralysis affecting all four limbs.

Wim Vandezeybus Flemish and Belgian choreographer associated with 'Euro Crash' in the 1980s; a highly physical style of dance theatre, involving jumping, catching and falling.

Bibliography

Alsop, J. (1982) *The Life and Times of Franklin D. Roosevelt*, London: Thames & Hudson.

Albright, A.C. (1997) *Choreographing Difference: The Body and Identity in Contemporary Dance*, Hanover, USA: Wesleyan University Press/University Press of New England.

Banes, S. (1987) *Terpsichore in Sneakers: Post Modern Dance*, Connecticut, Wesleyan University Press.

Barba. E. and Savarese, N. (1991) *The Dictionary of Theatre Anthropology: The Secret Art of the Performer*, London: Routledge.

Bauby, J.D. (1997) *The Diving Bell and the Butterfly*, New York: Alfred A. Knopf.

Benjamin, A. (1993) 'Unfound movement' *Dance Theatre Journal*, 10(4).

—— (1995) 'In search of integrity' *Dance Theatre Journal*, 12(1).

—— 'The problem with steps', *Animated*, 1999, autumn issue.

Bernières, L. de (1995) *Captain Corelli's Mandolin*, London: Vintage.

—— (1998) *The Troublesome Offspring of Cardinal Guzman*, London: Vintage.

Blom, L.A. and Chaplin, L.T. (1988) *The Moment of Movement: Dance Improvisation*, London: Dance Books.

Brinson, P. (1991) *Dance As Education: Towards a National Dance Culture*, Great Britain: Falmer Press.

Brisenden, S. (1998) *The Disability Reader, Independent Living and the Medical Model of Disability*, edited by Shakespeare, T., London and New York: Cassell.

Brook, P. (1990) *The Empty Space*, England: Penguin.

Butterworth, J. and Clarke, G. (1998) *Dance Maker's Portfolio: Conversations with Choreographers*, Bretton Hall, England, Centre for Dance Studies. ISBN 1900–85-7200

Carey, J. (1992) *The Intellectuals and the Masses*, London: Faber.

Chodorow, J. (1991) *Dance Therapy and Depth Psychology*, London: Routledge.

Critchlow, K. (1979) *Time Stands Still*, London: Gordon Fraser.

Cunningham, M. with Lesschaeve, J. (1991) *The Dancer and the Dance*, London and New York: Marion Boyars Publishers Ltd.

Davies, N. (1997) *Europe: A History*, London: Pimlico.

Deane, S. (1996) *Reading in the Dark*, London: Vintage.

Duberman, M. (1974) *Black Mountain. An exploration in community*, Great Britain: Wildwood House.

Duncan, I. (1928) *The Dance of the Future*, New York: Theatre Arts Books, cited in *Dance as a Theatre Art* (1992), Princeton NJ, Dance Horizons Books edited by S.J. Cohen, pub 1992.

Foucault, M. (1980) (ed. C. Gordon) *Power/Knowledge: Selected Interviews and other Writings 1972–1977*, Hemel Hempstead: Harvester Wheatsheaf.

Garner, A. (1996) *Strandloper*, London: Harvill Press.

Glieck, J. (1987) *Chaos: The Amazing Science of the Unpredictable*, London: Vintage.

Graham, M. (1992) *Blood Memory: An Autobiography*, London: Macmillan.

Graves, R. (1955) *The Greek Myths*, London: Penguin.

Hopkins, G.M. (1963) *Gerard Manley Hopkins: Poems and Prose*, edited by W.H. Gardner, London: Penguin.

Humphrey, D. (1959) *The Art of Making Dances*, Holt: New York: Grove Press.

Huizinga, J. (1970) *Homo Ludens: A Study of the Play Elements in Culture*, London: MauriceTemple Smith.

Johnstone, K. (1981) *Improv*, London: Methuen.

Jones, I. (1998) *Connection through movement*, pub: Surrey University.

Jordan, S. (1992) *Striding Out: Aspects of Contemporary and New Dance in Britain*, London: Dance Books.

Juster, N. (1962) *The Phantom Tollbooth*, London: Collins.

Keenan, B. (1993) *An Evil Cradling*, London: Hutchinson.

Kesey, K. (1962) *One Flew Over the Cuckoo's Nest*, London: Methuen & Co.

Kuppers, P. (2000) *Accessible Education: Aesthetics and disability*, Research in Dance Education, Vol. 1, No. 2.

Kuusisto, S. (1998) *Planet of the Blind*, USA and UK: Faber & Faber.

Lash, J.P. (1980) *Helen and Teacher*, London: Allen Lane.

Levete, G. (1982) *No Handicap to Dance*, London: Souvenir Press.

Lightman, A. (1993) *Einstein's Dreams* London: Sceptre.

—— (1996) *Good Benito*, London: Sceptre.

Mackrell, J. (1992) *Out of Line: The Story of British New Dance*, London: Dance Books.

McEwan, I. (1997) *Enduring Love*, London, Jonathan Cape.

Morris, W. (1993) *'News From Nowhere' & Other Writings*, London: Penguin Classics, Penguin.

Neill A.S. (1968) *Summerhill*, Middlesex, England: Pelican Books.

Ness, S. A. (1996) *Corporealities*, edited by S.L. Foster, London: Routledge.

Novack, C. J. (1979) *Sharing The Dance: Contact Improvisation and American Culture*, Wisconsin: University of Wisconsin Press.

Nolan, C. (1987) *Under the Eye of the Clock*, Great Britain: Picador.

Nunez, S. (1995) *A Feather on the Breath of God*, New York: Harper and Collins.

Pallaro, P. (1999) *Authentic Movement*. Essays by Mary Starks Whitehouse, Janet Adler and Joan Chodrorow, London: Jessica Kingsley.

Parker, T. (1993) *May the Lord in His mercy be kind to Belfast*, London: Jonathan Cape.

Paxton, S. and Kilcoyne, A. (1993) 'On the Braille in the Body', *Dance Research* XI(1), spring.

Preston-Dunlop, V. (1998) *Rudolf Laban: An Extraordinary Life*, London, Dance Books.

Proctor, R. N. (1988) *Racial Hygiene: Medicine Under the Nazis*, Cambridge, Massachusetts and London, England: Harvard University Press.

Reed Doob, P. (1990) *The Idea of the Labyrinth from Classical Antiquity through the Middle Ages*, New York: Cornell.

Robinson, M. (1991) *Housekeeping*, London: Faber & Faber.

Rowe, N. (2000) 'Dance in Palestine', *Dance Europe*, July.

Sakurai, K. (1999) 'The body as Dance. An introduction to the study of Butoh-ology' http://www.t3.rim.or.jp/~sakura/butoh.html

Toolan, D. 'Dance for the Disabled', *Dance News* Ireland 7/3 autumn 1994.

Tufnell, M. and Crickmay, C. (1990) *Body, Space, Image: Notes Towards Improvisation and Performance*, London: Virago Press.

Wisehart, C. (1996) *Storms and Illuminations: 18 Years of Access Theatre*, Emily Publications.

Winterson, J. (1990) *Sexing the Cherry*, London: Vintage.

Index